THE STORY OF THE NATIONS

THE
PAPAL MONARCHY

FROM ST. GREGORY THE GREAT TO BONIFACE VIII.

(590–1303)

BY

WILLIAM BARRY, D.D.

FORMERLY SCHOLAR OF THE ENGLISH COLLEGE, ROME; AND PROFESSOR OF
ECCLESIASTICAL HISTORY IN ST. MARY'S COLLEGE, OSCOTT; AUTHOR
OF "THE NEW ANTIGONE," "ARDEN MASSITER," ETC.

" Roman, forget not thou to sway the world;
These be thy arts ;—bring in the reign of Peace;
Spare subject nations ; put the haughty down."
ÆNEID, vi. 851-4

NEW YORK
G. P. PUTNAM'S SONS
LONDON: T. FISHER UNWIN
1911

Kessinger Publishing's Rare Reprints
Thousands of Scarce and Hard-to-Find Books!

Heroes of the Nations

A Series of Biographical Studies presenting the lives and work of certain representative historical characters, about whom have gathered the traditions of the nations to which they belong, and who have, in the majority of instances, been accepted as types of the several national ideals.

———

FOR FULL LIST SEE END OF THIS VOLUME

ST. PETER IN CATHEDRA.

(Ancient bronze figure in the Vatican Basilica, uncertain date.)

PREFACE

——

IN the first two chapters of this book I have endeavoured to explain its drift and purpose. As a contribution to the Story of the Nations it aims at brevity, clearness, and accuracy in outline; but it makes no pretension to do more than open a large subject and serve the purpose of a sketch-map or general introduction to the volumes of Baronius, Muratori, and other classic historians. The course followed, it will be seen, is neither that of a theologian writing on dogma, nor that of an apologist who desires to exhibit conclusions in favour of a religious system. I am concerned with the facts of history, not with inferences and deductions from them, which belong to another department and are foreign to the present series. Not the Pope as a teacher, but the Pope as a ruler of men, in affairs which may be viewed under a secular as well as a religious aspect, will furnish the matter of my volume.

To attempt a bibliography commensurate with the

subject would be no less difficult than superfluous, on occasion of a sketch like the following. Students will know what sources to consult better than I can tell them. But the general reader may be put in mind of some late or early works, accessible to him without much effort. Milman's " Latin Christianity " has long enjoyed popular favour ; it is in some sort a comment upon Gibbon, to be supplemented or corrected by more recent publications. Gregorovius, in his voluminous " History of the City of Rome during the Middle Ages," is learned, eloquent, picturesque, and Ghibelline. Cardinal Hergen- röther has given us the Guelf counter-pleading with equal erudition and hardly less vehemence in his " Catholic Church and Christian State,"—a work of accurate scholarship, abundant in original citations. The late Professor of Church History at Kiel, Dr. William Moeller, a Lutheran, has dealt with the Church in the Middle Ages at great length in the second volume of his well-known course, which contains an exhaustive and minute catalogue of the sources in every language. And Professor H. Grisar, S.J., has begun to publish a most interesting as well as authentic survey of the same period, historical and antiquarian, which it is hoped will appear in English ; but only the introduction, coming down to Gregory the Great, is thus far in print.

To these must be added, as indispensable to students, Mgr. L. Duchesne's standard edition of the " Liber Pontificalis." And Hauck's " History of the Church in Germany," which travels over the same ground but in another direction, may be compared with the French author's "Origin of the Temporal Power." These works are not translated.

On special subjects and particular persons the following will be found useful: Lightfoot, "St. Clement of Rome," and "St. Ignatius of Antioch"; the volumes of Harnack's "History of Dogma" which bear on the Roman Church at its beginning; Newman, "Development of Christian Doctrine"; Allies, "Formation of Christendom"; Bryce, "The Holy Roman Empire"; Hergenröther, "Photius"; Voigt and Bowden on Pope Gregory VII.; Cotter Morrison, "St. Bernard of Clairvaux"; Hurter, "Innocent III."; L. Tocco (in Italian), "Heresy in the Middle Age"; P. Sabatier, "St. Francis of Assisi," and other works; E. A. Abbott, "St. Thomas of Canterbury, his Death and Miracles"; Professor Maitland, "Roman Canon Law in the English Church"; Montalembert, "Monks of the West," with introduction by Abbot F. A. Gasquet; W. S. Lilly, "Chapters in European History"; L. Eckenstein, "Women under Monasticism"; Gosselin, "Power of the Popes in the Middle Ages"; Tosti, "Boniface VIII. and His Times"; Rodocanachi, "Communal Institutions of Rome under the Papacy"; and "Workmen's Corporations from the Fall of the Empire."

There is no end to this or any other list of authorities. Let me remark that I have, in my narrative, touched as briefly as possible on the relations of England with Rome during the medieval period, feeling that they were treated at length in many text-books.   I conclude with the words which Pope Leo XIII. has quoted from Cicero : " Above all things let writers bear in mind that the first law of history is never to dare to say that which is not true ; and the second never to fear to say that which is true ; lest the suspicion of hate or favour fall upon their statements."

WILLIAM BARRY.

DORCHESTER, OXFORD,
November 9, 1001.

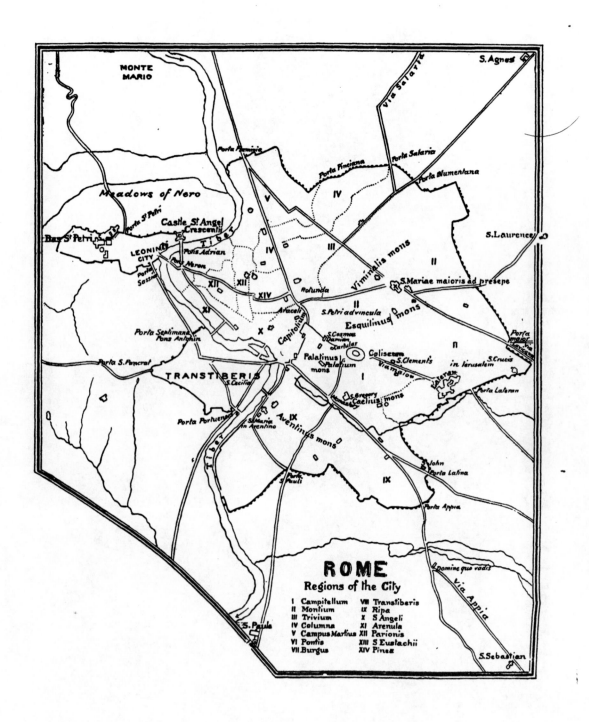

MONTE MARIO

Meadows of Nero

S. Agnes

Via Salaria

Porta Flaminia

Porta Pinciana

Porta Salaria

Porta Nomentana

IV

V

Castle St Angel
Crescentii

Porta St Petri

Bas St Petri

LEONINE CITY

Pons Adrian

Porta Maron

Porta Sassia

Tiber

IV

III

S. Laurence

II

XII

XII

XIV

Rotunda

S. Mariae maioris ad presepe

XI

Araceli

S. Petri ad vincula

Esquilinus mons

Viminalis mons

Porta maior

Porta Septimana
Pons Antehin

X

Capitolium

II

S. Cosmas
& Damian
Cattular

Coliseum
S. Clements

S. Crucis
in Ierusalem

Porta S. Pancrat

Palatinus
Palatium
mons

Via maior

Laferan

TRANSTIBERIS

S. Cecilia

I

S. Gregory
Caelius mons

Porta Lateran

Porta Portuenes

S. Maria
in Aventino

IX

Aventinus mons

S. John
Porta Latina

Tiber

Porta
S. Pauli

IX

Porta Appia

Domine quo vadis

S. Paula

Via Appia

S. Sebastian

ROME
Regions of the City

I Campitellum	VIII Transtiberis
II Montium	IX Ripa
III Trivium	X S Angeli
IV Columna	XI Arenula
V Campus Martius	XII Parionis
VI Pontis	XIII S Eustachii
VII Burgus	XIV Pinea

CONTENTS

vii

X.

XI.

XII.

of Henry VI. to Constance of Sicily—A man of blood and iron—His frightful executions at Palermo—Frederick II. born—Death of Henry ; election of Innocent III.—Great reign begins—Takes Frederick under his protection ; subdues Central Italy—Philip and Otho candidates for Empire— Long war, was it due to Innocent ?—He sides with Otho, then with Philip, then with Otho again—The latter cruel and rapacious—Germans offer Frederick the crown—Innocent confirms it—Brilliant adventure of the young king— Otho deposed, dies in monastery.

Fulk of Neuilly—Fourth Crusade starts from Venice—Takes Zara ; is condemned by Pope ; but seizes and plunders Constantinople—Fatal Latin Empire—First example of crusade against Christians—Followed by war of Albi— Interests at stake—Languedoc, Manichean Judea—Raymund VI. of Toulouse—Preaching Cistercians—Legate murdered—Burgundy marches on Provence—Simon de Montfort—Horrors of Béziers, &c.—Pedro of Arragon killed at Muret—Total ruin of the Count and his people—Louis VIII. renews crusade—Provence falls to French crown— Retrospect and prospect from the garden of Gibbon at Lausanne over these religious wars and their consequences.

Italian tyrants—Luxury and leprosy— Francis of Assisi saves the Church in Italy, adds a page to the New Testament— Unique among Saints—Appeals to the Gospel and the people —Policy towards him of Cardinal Ugolino—Moderates and Spirituals—The Friars a Papal Militia—St. Dominic ; not founder of Inquisition—What these new Orders accom-

LIST OF ILLUSTRATIONS.

MAPS.

THE PAPAL MONARCHY

PAPAL MONARCHY

I

ORIGINS

(B.C. 753–A.D. 67)

In the night of the 24th of August, 410, Alaric, King of the Western Goths, entered Rome with his army, by the Salarian Gate — outside of which Hannibal had encamped long ago — and took the Imperial City. Eleven hundred and sixty-four years had passed since its legendary foundation under Romulus; four hundred and forty-one since the battle of Actium, which made Augustus Lord in deed, if not in name, of the Roman world. When the Gothic trump sounded at midnight, it announced that ancient history had come to an end, and that our modern time was born. St. Jerome, who in his cell at Bethlehem saw the Capitol given over to fire and flame, was justified from an historical point of view when he wrote to the noble virgin Demetrias, "Thy city, once the head of the universe, is the sepulchre of the Roman people." Even in that age

2

of immense and growing confusion, the nations held
their breath when these tidings broke upon them.
Adherents of the classic religion who still survived
felt in them a judgment of the gods ; they charged
on Christians the long sequel of calamities which

HEAD OF THE REDEEMER.
(*Fresco in Catacomb of San Callisto—Third Century.*)

had come down upon the once invincible Empire.
Christians retorted that its fall was the chastisement
of idolatry. And their supreme philosopher, the
African Father St. Augustine, wrote his monumental
work, " Of the City of God," by way of proving that

there was a Divine kingdom which heathen Rome could persecute in the martyrs, but the final triumph of which it could never prevent. This magnificent conception, wrought out in a vein of prophecy, and with an eloquence which has not lost its power, furnished to succeeding times an Apocalypse no less than a justification of the Gospel. Instead of heathen Rome, it set up an ideal Christendom. But the centre, the meeting-place, of old and new, was the City on the Seven Hills.

To the Roman Empire succeeded the Papal Monarchy. The Pope called himself Pontifex Maximus; and if this hieratic name—the oldest in Europe —signifies "the priest that offered sacrifice on the Sublician bridge," it denotes, in a curious symbolic fashion, what the Papacy was destined to achieve, as well as the inward strength on which it relied, during the thousand years that stretch between the invasion of the Barbarians and the Renaissance. When we speak of the Middle Ages we mean this second, spiritual and Christian Rome, in conflict with the Northern tribes and then their teacher; the mother of civilisation, the source to Western peoples of religion, law, and order, of learning, art, and civic institutions. It became to them what Delphi had been to the Greeks, and especially to the Dorians, an oracle which decided the issues of peace and war, which held them in a common brotherhood, and which never ceased to be a rallying point amid their fiercest dissensions. Thus it gave to the multitude of tribes which wandered or settled down within the boundaries of the West, from Lithuania to Ireland, from Illyria to Portugal, and from Sicily to the North Cape, a brain, a conscience, and an imagination, which at length transformed them into the Christendom that Augustine had foreseen.

If the Papacy were blotted out from the world's chronicle, the Middle Ages would vanish along with it. But modern Europe cannot be deduced, as was thought in the last century by writers like Voltaire and Montesquieu, from Augustan Rome, with no regard for the long transition which connects them together. It is in this way that the medieval Popes take their place in the Story of the Nations; they continue the Roman history; they account in no small degree for the institutions under which we are living; and their fortunes, so exalted, so unhappy, and not seldom so tragical, shape themselves into a drama, the scenes and vicissitudes of which are as highly romantic as they are expressive of one great ruling idea.

The stage on which this mighty miracle-play was enacted, though spacious, was well defined. Our direct concern will not be with any dogmatic or strictly religious claims put forth by the Popes— these belong to the theologian—but with the sovereignty which they exercised, the nations affected by their decretals, the Holy Roman Empire which their word called into being, and the kingdoms which gladly or reluctantly acknowledged in them a feudal lordship. Thus their dominion never, if we except passing interludes, went beyond the old Patriarchate of the West, as recognised at the Council of Nicæa. Not even the haughtiest Pontiffs pretended to make

or unmake the Byzantine Emperors. They dealt
otherwise with the Frankish or Suabian chiefs, whom
they anointed, crowned, excommunicated, and deposed at the tomb of the Apostles. But until
Gregory II. in 731 cast off his allegiance, they had
been subjects, not suzerains, of Constantinople.
With Latin Emperors they felt themselves able to
cope; but the majesty of that earlier Rome lingered
yet on the shores of the Bosporus; and the Papal
Monarchy vails its crest before it, unless when the
Franks have usurped a precarious and hateful power
in Byzance after the Fourth Crusade, or the Normans
and Venetians divide between them the strong places
of Attica and the Morea. Always the Pope is
Western, not Eastern, though he may become a slave
of the palace during the two hundred years which
follow on the conquest of Italy by Belisarius. Yet
even in that period of depression he was slowly
winning ground outside the Empire, and every tribe
made Christian was bringing a fresh stone to build
up the arch of the Papal power, fated for so long
to stride visibly across the kingdoms of Europe.

Had the Emperors of the East known how to
withstand the onset of those hordes which streamed
down over the Alps; could they have overthrown or
subdued the Lombards, and so kept the Pepins and
Charlemagnes at home, it may be questioned whether
any Pope would have dreamt of playing the great
part in politics which was found inviting or inevitable
as time went on. But the old Empire shrank to the
Exarchate of Ravenna; it could barely maintain
itself on the edge of the Ionian Sea. The Pontiff,

looking round for help against the now converted
but always detestable Longbeards of Pavia, signalled
to the most daring of the new Christian nations.
Pepin answered his call; overcame Astolphus;
bestowed on St. Peter a patrimony in lands, serfs,
and cities; and paved the way for his son's coronation in 800 as Emperor of the West. He certainly
did not foresee that the " Sacerdotium " and the
" Imperium " — those divided members which in
heathen Rome had been united in the same person—
would struggle during the next seven hundred years
in a doubtful contest, until both sank exhausted and
the Reformation broke Christendom in twain. As
there is a unity of place, determined by the bounds
of the Lower Greek Empire, which includes this vast
and exceedingly human series of transactions, so
there is a unity of time, but as might be expected,
not marked by such definite limits. St. Gregory
the Great is its herald and anticipation; Boniface
VIII. brings it to a close. But as several centuries
take us slowly on to the culminating point, so the
fourteenth and fifteenth lead us downwards again
until the idea of an Imperial Papal Christendom has
spent its force. The Lateran Monarchy stood at its
height during some two hundred years — from
Gregory VII. to Innocent III., or perhaps to
Gregory X. (1073–1274). Its creative influence, if
we regard European civilisation as a whole, had
begun sooner and lasted longer; it was often visible
at the extremities when Rome itself had sunk into a
strange barbarism. Its spiritual energy neither rose
nor fell in exact proportion to the outward splendour

of the Holy See, as many instances will prove in the pages that follow.

But another condition of this second rise to greatness on the part of Rome has been often overlooked. If St. Peter was considered to be the spiritual

HEADS OF SS. PETER AND PAUL.
(*From a very Ancient Glass Patera.*)

founder of the Papacy, and if the Emperor Constantine, by removing the seat of government to the Golden Horn, had left it room in which to expand, yet the marvellous apparition of Mohammed, and the conquests of his lieutenants or successors, broke the power of the Christian East, and in so doing allowed the West time to develop without hindrance on its own lines. The Caliphate bears, indeed, more than one point of resemblance, external at least, to the dynasty of the Vicars of Christ established in Rome. But it is the long series of invasions, stripping off province after province from the weak Emperors of Byzantium, laying waste the churches of Syria and Egypt, reducing the Patriarchates of Antioch, Alexandria, and Jerusalem to barren names, and thus abolishing the older forms of the Christian polity, which we have now in view. Straightway, the fame and consequence of the one remaining Patriarch who dated from Apostolic times must have been indefinitely enhanced. The Pope became, as a great Catholic genius has written, "heir by default" of antiquity. Those Sees, and, above all, the See of Alexandria, which had shared with him in political prestige, and could never be denied a voice when there was question of dogma or discipline, had passed for ever beneath the Moslem yoke. And the Bishop of Constantinople was but the Emperor's chaplain, incapable of pursuing a course for himself—the nominee, the puppet, and sometimes the prisoner of one who claimed in his own person to be most sacred, a Divine delegate, and a god on earth. In Rome the Bishop had no rival or second. He tended more and more to become what Cæsar had been of old, the embodied city, with all its mysterious charm, its predestination to supreme command, its unique and indelible character as a shrine or temple of deity. From the seventh century onwards, Rome appeared in men's eyes to be the Apostolic See *par excellence*. So much, unwittingly, had the Arabian prophet or impostor brought to pass when his armed disciples overran the many thousand bishoprics of Asia and Africa.

An hour there was when Islam appeared likely to conquer not only the Spanish but the Frankish Catholics. Mussulman armies crossed the Pyrenees; they came north as far as Tours; but Charles Martel in a bloody battle drove them south again. Yet could not the unhappy and degenerate Popes of the ninth or tenth century do much to repel their incursions. Under Leo IV. (in 855) they came up to the walls of Rome and sacked St. Peter's—an amazing feat, of which the Leonine City is to this day a monument and witness. But no sooner did the Holy See recover from its low estate than Gregory VII. set his undaunted mind to inaugurate against them a Sacred War—for Hildebrand, as he is the restorer of the Medieval Papacy, is likewise the author of the First Crusade. It was now Pope against Caliph during nearly two hundred years. Yet the conquest of the Holy Land, soon won and in a short episode lost, was by no means the chief gain to Rome of these world-famous expeditions. From them we date the extensive and permanent taxing-powers, enforced all over Christendom, which the Sovereign Pontiffs insisted upon as their rights, the Pope being, so to speak, generalissimo of the armies of the Cross. This war-tribute, levied on such a preamble, but constantly applied to purposes of another, and sometimes an indefensible kind, while it enriched the Holy See, gave rise to murmurings, and at last to rebellions which, like that under John Wyclif, assailed the Papacy itself. It is not untrue to assert that from the Crusades, which in their beginnings heightened so greatly the Roman power, sprang the first attempts at a Reformation.

We can now define, almost in a phrase, the splendid but simple theme which we have undertaken. Let us state it. How, we inquire, did the Pontifex Maximus, heir of old Rome and now its Christian Bishop, deal with the peoples which invaded and occupied the Western Empire? And how did they deal with him? Broadly speaking, we find ourselves in presence of three great world-facts or forces—the Roman, the Christian, the Teutonic. From these three modern civilisation is derived. Their contest fills the Middle Ages; their reconcilement in a purified Church and a Catholic Empire was the dream of Dante; but the poet's own time marks the epoch when Teutons, despairing of Rome as they saw it, turned back to their national aspirations, and when the North was already beginning to be rent from the South, as the Ten Tribes from the Kingdom of Judah. This parallel, which is no less exact than profound, might be carried out into most significant details. It will help us to understand the rise, the decline, and the everlasting attitude towards the German races of a spiritual power which was clad in forms coming down to it from a period long antecedent to Christianity, and from nations like the Etruscan or the Greek no less than the Hebrew.

Until of late years, the immeasurable event known as the "Conversion of the Roman Empire" has been much misunderstood. We ought rather to call it a transformation; elements and institutions already existing were brought under the influence of a few far-reaching ideals, and of a Personality recognised as the Divine Incarnation of these. The old Roman life was not broken up and made over again. While Christians refused to be idolaters, they did not, as so many historians, including Gibbon, have taken for granted, decline to share in the public or private dignities, or to tolerate a multitude of harmless customs, which they found in use. Vehement polemical writers, like the fiery Tertullian, exaggerate a nonconformity which at all times must have been tempered by concessions to the circumstances of every day; while the remains we still possess, from at least the third century, prove that we may not charge upon converted Romans a disdain for the arts, the usages, or the business to which, as subjects of the Empire or citizens of the Capital, they had been accustomed. Their theological system underwent a change; their religion, in the deepest sense of the word, was baptized into a new life; but they took over (and how could it be otherwise?) the language, the ritual, the yearly observances, the festal adornments, and even the artistic symbols, to which they had been brought up. Whatever Puritan dislike to paintings and feastings of the Roman pattern had been nurtured in the Jewish Ghetto on the Janiculum, Christians in no long time must have laid it aside. Not many of them in the third century were Israelite even by descent. And Tertullian himself, who stands for the less accommodating principles, is our witness that the Bishop of Rome (probably Zephyrinus, about 216) was not unwilling to be known as " Episcopus Episcoporum " and " Pontifex Maximus."

The Roman would be a Christian ; but he would not improvise either language or ritual when he found them ready to his hand. What he did was to cleanse them of their idolatrous associations, to combine them more or less skilfully with the teachings of the New Testament and the personages and stories of the Old, until a Catholic Hierarchy and a Christian Liturgy rose into sight, sustaining each other in a majestic and almost overpowering adaptation of outward to inward, of spirit to symbol, and of authority to doctrine. This was no sudden creation, but a slow and imperceptible growth of time, extending over five or six hundred years, so complete at length that as in Pope Leo I. we may contemplate the Romulus, so in Gregory the Great we discern the not unkingly Numa, of a city more sacred than the antique Rome, yet hardly less imperial. Almost every step of this transmuting process can be followed when we pass out from the less lightsome centuries of the Christian origins. The Church in the West was to develop under the style of the Pontifex Maximus, in accordance with old Roman sacred rites, and by the strength of the Roman Law. St. Peter was to inherit all that Numa could bequeath, and to hand it down along the line of his successors.

This word " Pontifex "—meaning the sacrificer on the bridge—was associated from very early times with ceremonies in honour or deprecation of the dead, whom the Romans called Lemures. The feast of the Lemuralia was kept on the Sublician Bridge, which spanned the Tiber between Aventine and Janiculum, during the 9th, 11th, and 13th of May. Customary rites were performed, after which "the pontifices, vestals, prætors, and other citizens," according to the Greek writer, Dionysius, cast into the stream thirty figures, named " Argei," or " Argive men," made of bulrushes and in the human shape. There can be little doubt that these " priscorum simulacra virorum" were a substitute for live men once offered to propitiate the ghosts of the departed; as the legend says, they were invented by Hercules when he did away with human sacrifices formerly made at that spot in honour of Saturn. But a custom with which these Lemuralia seem to bear affinities —of " driving out" or " casting out" Death, at the beginning of summer—has been traced in nearly every part of Europe. Here, then, is the most ancient ritual in which the Pontifex Maximus comes before our view.

Numa, the mythical priest-king of Rome, is said by Livy to have appointed a college of four pontiffs, at the head of which was the Pontifex Maximus. In 81 B.C. the number was raised to fifteen; and Julius Cæsar, who was himself the Sovereign Pontiff, added to it another when he returned from Egypt. Under Augustus, and down to the fall of Paganism, the Emperor always held the title; he was Pope as well as Consul and Imperator. He continued to hold it for some time afterwards; and not only Constantine but his more Christian successors, Valentinian I. and Gratian, are mentioned under this name on inscriptions now extant. Theodosius, however, gave up all pretence to be the High Priest of a heathen worship; and the title passed to the Bishops of Rome, for whose office it must have long seemed a fitting designation.

We learn from Festus, a Latin writer before 400, that the old Roman pontiffs were looked upon as " rerum quæ ad sacra et religiones pertinent, judices et vindices"; they judged and defended the interests of religion at large. They ranked above all other priests, and regulated the general worship of the gods. To them, it was said, Numa had entrusted the sacred " libri pontificales," in which were set down the lawful rites of sacrifice, dedication, and augurship, with their unchanging formulas. They were to guard against the decay of worship and the bringing in of strange gods and mysteries, such as those of Bacchus, Isis, and Serapis, which caused so much trouble at various times in Rome. Another, and, as we have seen, a very primitive department of their duties was concerned with the dead—how funerals were to be carried out; by what expiations the *Manes*, or the souls of the departed were to be given rest. They interpreted the heavenly signs of thunder and lightning. The times of the festivals were in their keeping, and they regulated the Calendar. Julius Cæsar, in his capacity as Pontifex Maximus, reformed it in 46 B.C. And Pope Gregory XIII., under the same title, reformed it again by his Bull of February 24, 1582.

Since the Pontiffs were not subject to any court of

CONFESSION OR TOMB OF ST. PETER IN THE VATICAN BASILICA.

law, neither to the Senate nor the People, we may accurately describe them as exempt from secular jurisdiction. But they had their own courts, to which not only priests but other individuals and even magistrates were bound to submit, in all that related to religion. Over the Vestal virgins they had and exercised criminal jurisdiction. Where existing laws did not suffice to determine the matter, they made fresh rules which were called " Decrees of the Pontiffs." The Supreme Pontiff was present at the most solemn kind of marriage, known as *confarreatio*. He lived in a house which had the sanctity of a temple, on the Via Sacra, not far from that of the Vestals, until the Imperial palace became his home. He received the solemn vows of games and other dedications, whether by the State or private persons ; and it is to be presumed that he used some discernment in allowing them ; he had most probably a dispensing power. Like all pontiffs, he wore the *toga prætextata* and a conical cap, called the *galerus* (which is a name now appropriated to the Cardinal's hat) with a wooden apex fastened to it. He could not, in Republican times, leave Italy. Last of all, the duty was incumbent on him of appointing the six Vestals and the Flamens, or particular priests, of Jupiter, Mars, Quirinus, and other gods.

It was the boast of Cicero, and Virgil's almost hieratic poem of the Æneid bears him out, that the Romans were a deeply religious people. This does not signify that they cultivated a speculative theology, or that their morals were austere and their lives devoted to well-doing ; but that they observed a ritual which left untouched no act of their public or private existence. The gods had no concern with virtue ; that was a man's own acquisition ; but they watched over birth, marriage, death ; over war and peace ; over agriculture and commerce ; they consecrated oaths and treaties, and avenged their violation ; they were pledged to the prosperity of the State. Before every public undertaking they must be consulted. Certain sacred relics, the nature of which could only be guessed at, were tokens of their amity preserved by the Vestals in a secret shrine, before which burned the "everlasting fire." Rome, as it extended its conquests, brought home the vanquished deities ; it became "the temple and the shrine of all gods," but above them towered on his hill Jupiter Capitolinus, and the polytheism of the nations was rapidly merging into a Divine Monarchy, of which Cæsar appeared to be the visible image, the Vicar on Earth, when Christians began to preach their glad tidings in the Jewish Ghetto, over against the Porta Portese, and in the region still known as "across the Tiber."

At what exact period this came to pass we have no means of ascertaining. Was it within ten or twelve years from the death of Christ, or something later ? An early tradition associates it with St. Peter's arrival in Rome and the year 42 A.D., which Eusebius takes for the starting-point of his bishopric ; or, to quote the stronger Latin of St. Jerome, at that date "Peter is sent to Rome, where, preaching the Gospel twenty-five years, he remains Bishop of the same city." But on what primitive testimony

this length of years was stated, it is impossible to
conjecture. In 58 A.D. St. Paul wrote his Epistle to
the Romans, when a Church already existed, some
members of which belonged to Cæsar's household.
Three years later he was living at Rome in his own
hired house, preaching to those who came about him.
The severest critics are willing to allow a journey of
St. Peter to the Capital in 64, when he dated his First
Epistle from Babylon, that is to say, from heathen,
persecuting Rome, as the Sibylline books of Jewish
origin had long ago named it. To the martyrdom
of Peter and Paul under Nero there is abundant
witness, beginning with Clement (95 or 96), who
speaks of the "good Apostles" (which implies that
he knew them personally), and dwells on their sufferings. No explanation of the reference in St. John's
Gospel to Peter's death has ever been suggested, save
that he was crucified in his old age, and, as tradition
affirms, close to the spot where his tomb in the early
third century could be pointed out by Gaius the
Presbyter, who writes (about 220), "I can show thee
the trophies [or relics] of the Apostles. For if thou
wilt go to the Vatican or the Ostian Way, thou wilt
find the trophies of those who founded this Church."
And among his disciples in Rome Peter had "Marcus
my son," his interpreter—whom he sent by and by to
Alexandria—as likewise Silvanus. Paul, we know
for certain, had about him when there Timothy, Titus,
Luke, Apollos. If a doubtful story could be accepted
which Tertullian relates concerning the Apostle
John—he was said to have undergone a trial at Rome
in the reign of Domitian—this Church would have

beheld the chiefest of Christ's followers, and the writers of three out of the four Gospels.

During the second century, Ignatius of Antioch, who was martyred between 100 and 118 A.D.; Papias about 130; Dionysius of Corinth in 170; Irenæus, some twenty years later; and the Muratorian Fragment ascribed to Hippolytus towards 190, confirm these scattered notices, which connect Peter with Rome as founding the Church and dying there in a time of persecution. In like manner, the lists of Roman Bishops carry us back to Peter and Paul, who stand at their head. Five such catalogues are extant, clouded over with errors of transcription, but when duly revised, in agreement as regards the names, years, and order, which last has been preserved in the Latin Canon of the Mass. Hegesippus, a Jewish Christian, writing about the middle of the second century, drew up a list on the spot, now probably accessible in Epiphanius (375). Irenæus of Lyons, who paid a visit to Rome after 177, gives us his own catalogue. A third, due to Hippolytus, may be recovered from the Liberian, edited under the Pope of that name. On these and on Julius Africanus, Eusebius relied in his *Chronicle* and *History*. Irenæus appeals to " the greatest, oldest, and universally known Church, founded and established by the most glorious Apostles Peter and Paul at Rome." And he says that they " delivered the office of the Episcopate to Linus." The order, now recognised by experts, is therefore Linus, Anencletus, Clement, Euarestus, Alexander, Xystus, and so forth. That these names represent historical persons, who were "bishops, in the monarchical sense, of the Roman Church," is admitted by the most competent scholars of our day, and may be safely assumed. Of Clement's "noble remonstrance," addressed to the Corinthian schismatics, Lightfoot has declared that it was "the first step towards Papal domination." He regards the action of Victor, which he disapproves, at the close of the second century, when that Pope excommunicated the Churches of Asia, as a "decided step" forward. When Ignatius looks up to the Roman Church as "presiding in love," this, observes Lightfoot, bears witness to its moral ascendency, which was "the historical foundation of its primacy." Cardinal Newman, as we might expect, takes a loftier view: "It seems to me plain from history," he tells us, "that the Popes from the first considered themselves to have a universal jurisdiction." It is indisputable, to say the least, that before the year 200, the Bishop of Rome was recognised everywhere as the successor of St. Peter, and not only as head of the local Church, but in some degree—to speak with the Clementine *Romance*—as presiding over Christendom.

II

FROM PETER TO LEO THE GREAT

(67–461)

BUT our first glimpses, which are tantalising in their brevity, of the Christians at Rome, show us the Church rather than the Bishop. Clement admonishes the Corinthians in its name, not in his own ; Ignatius of Antioch, if his epistle be authentic, addresses " the Church presiding in charity in the country of the Romans " ; and Pope Soter speaks as representing a community so late as 170 A.D. Thus the Bishop did not stand alone ; like the Pontifex Maximus he was head of a College of clergy ; and the Roman Church, by its central position in the world's Capital ; by its beneficent use of the wealth which it soon acquired ; and by its familiarity with the laws and even the fashions of the Metropolis ;—was marked out for distinction as the Christian system moulded itself on the Imperial, and Bishops fell into their places, according to the importance of the cities over which they ruled. Not even Jerusalem could have resisted a movement so natural and widespread; but the Jewish war had made an end of Jerusalem; and what other city could vie with Rome? By the year 274, Aurelian is found deciding that the Christian Church property at Antioch, which was in dispute, shall be dealt with as the Bishops of Rome and Italy think fit. Cyprian of Carthage, in 256, recognises that Rome is the Chair of Peter, "whence the unity of the priesthood took its rise." These words, and this conception, were to furnish the Magna Charta of the Papacy. For the Popes attribute to themselves all that the " Prince of the Apostles" would claim, were he living on through the centuries. They fuse into one great idea the spiritual prerogatives of their founder and the legal supremacy of Rome over the whole Empire. Rome can be second to none; St. Peter is the first among his brethren. If the Churches of the world ever came into the form of a confederation or a Hierarchy, and they tended to do so from their earliest days, the Roman Church would of necessity be supreme.

As we see in Clement, the old and deeply-ingrained conception of law and order, which is distinctively Roman, had passed over at once into the Christian mind. These converts, whether Jews or Pagans, did not indulge in speculation; they started no new philosophy; and such has been the character of the Church in Rome ever since. It dealt with practice, ritual, discipline; it developed a government, not a school like Alexandria; it held aloof from the wide and remarkable effort of the Gnostics, or " Intellectuals," who attempted during the second century to resolve the tenets of the Gospel into a theosophic

ARCH OF CONSTANTINE THE GREAT.

(Fourth Century.)

23

romance. The Latin mind neither comprehended nor was drawn to these dreams of an Orientalised Greek fancy. In like manner, as it was averse to the speculations of the philosophers, so was the Roman Church unwilling to narrow the bounds of conformity by a regimen too severe for the multitudes, who were now thronging about its doors. It would not permit an esoteric creed to split up the congregation of the faithful into "enlightened" and "ignorant." It refused to shut out sinners from its penance, as the unbending Montanists and Novatians demanded. While conservative in doctrine, it exhibited a sagacious largeness in discipline, and while suffering the strongly forensic mind of Tertullian to model its tradition, it neither approved nor condemned the venturesome thought of Origen and the Alexandrian Clement. None of the early Popes were masters or pupils in philosophy; but this negative wisdom counted for not a little in the respect which was paid to them by the subtle and restless East.

Not individual genius, therefore, but an endemic "custom of the City," acting on a creed not fully developed, and in the strength of what was allowed to be Apostolic tradition, enabled this Church at the centre to grow in pre-eminence. It gave no theologians to Christendom; it produced neither monks nor thinkers; in the list of thirty-two Popes before Constantine, there is only a single illustrious name, that of Clement. But with the fourth century we enter on a new era. The Imperial Government takes the cross and begins by its laws and policy to make the Empire Christian. Constantinople is founded;

Rome ceases to be the capital. And an interminable succession of quarrels on the philosophy of the Creed, associated for ever with the names of Arius, Apollinaris, Macedonius, Nestorius, and Eutyches, rends the East into factions, the Pope looking on from afar, not entangling himself in the nets of metaphysicians, receiving appeals from all sides, sitting umpire in the midst of a theological chaos. Had he played the philosopher, humanly speaking, he might have gone astray. But the Pontifex Maximus was a Roman and a statesman. He left to others the wrangling over terms of Greek art; for him it was enough to insist upon what had been handed down. These gladiatorial displays of logic went on for well-nigh a hundred and seventy years, during which time the only Pope who furnished a statement of any length to the combatants was Leo I.; and his manner is the Roman, sententious and judicial, not argumentative. The Latin language, copious in legal phrase, abounding in the technicalities of ritual, was neither delicate nor flexible enough to express the finer shades of heresy. It was the language of command: strong, plain, and matter of fact. The Eastern Bishops degenerated into sophists; the Roman found himself a ruler in a deserted but always august city.

Though long incorporated with the Empire, Gaul, Spain, and Germany had never exerted the political influence which was a characteristic of the Latin races; nor could they pretend to the charm, or contest the supremacy, of Greek culture. Outlying provinces, on the extreme line of defence, they lay open to attacks from the wandering tribes of the North. At

Treves or Milan the Emperor lived in camp; he was at home only in Central Italy, or in the stately Eastern cities, like Nicomedia, which displayed the riches, the polish, and too often the luxurious softness that were an inheritance from classic Hellas. Taken as a whole, the East was compact in its geography, it had boundless resources of wealth, and could draw upon the mountaineers of the Balkans or the Cilician Taurus to recruit its armies; it could even make good use of Goths and other untamed auxiliaries, without falling a prey to their strong right arm. Considerations such as these weighed with the sagacious but hardly great Emperor Constantine, when he turned the course of the Roman eagles towards the rising sun and left the Eternal City shorn of its crown of dominion. Henceforth, East and West would go their several ways. Europe was to be Latin, Frankish, German, in its political forms; in religion it was to be Papal and Protestant; while the Greeks became more and more Asiatic, and detested their Christian brethren, the Franks, almost as deeply as they feared the armed disciples of Mohammed.

Modern historians have seen in the founding of Constantinople (330 A.D.) a necessary sequel to the Edict of Toleration, published from Milan in 313, by which the Christian Faith was made one of the *religiones licitæ*. The Emperor could not have laid the foundation of his new Church and State on the Palatine, which was still the headquarters of Paganism. Arguments, these, of politicians, plausible enough; but in the Middle Ages legend threw the motives of Constantine into a picturesque and gruesome story, to the glorification of Pope Silvester and the Holy Apostles. Leprosy, that mysterious and almost sacred disease, had laid its taint upon the Emperor; he was tempted to cleanse himself in a bath of children's blood; when Silvester, warned in a dream, stepped between him and this awful experiment; persuaded him to descend into the waters of baptism; and brought him out thence, purified like Naaman in body and soul. Hereupon, Constantine made over to the Pontiff Rome and Italy, with the Islands of the West. He established the Pope where Augustus had reigned, gave him the tokens and state of royalty, and withdrew from the Holy Place. This was the Donation of Constantine, as first told in the eighth century, and believed down to the end of the fifteenth.

It is a prophecy after the event. Paganism, abandoned and soon to be persecuted by its Pontifex Maximus, without the conviction that makes martyrs, and long a hollow formality, was dying. Christians had the State in their hands. What was more, they showed the fiery zeal, the proselytizing spirit, the exuberance in quarrels among themselves, which are signs of a youth rich in hopes, bent upon shaping its own victorious future. Heathen Rome invited them to subdue it. Public policy required that the centre of administration should be at the heart of the Empire. The balance of power was displaced. Neither Pope Silvester nor any Pope for centuries dreamt of disowning the Imperial rule; from the Goths in Italy they suffered grievous things as the first subjects of Constantinople. But Rome left to itself was Rome in the hands of the Papacy, fronting the West and the Barbarians. Constantine had imitated Alexander the Great, who, in setting up his throne at Babylon in 330 B.C.—a curious coincidence—and assuming the tiara, left Europe free to follow its own fortunes. Such was the real Donation, not understood at the time by Pope or Emperor, which never lost its force until the Northern nations grew into a world as rich, as cultivated, and as haughtily self-conscious, as the Greek.

Paganism, it may be briefly said, was to furnish Roman Christianity with many of its holiday or outward shows. And the strange phenomena of heresy were to bring to light its powers of government, which, used at the beginning in disputes of local churches or contending sects, were afterwards applied to provinces and kingdoms. The Pope, we have seen, did not affect a speculative genius; he administered rule—a busy and extensive rule in so frequented a place as Rome—according to the tradition of the first age; he would never hear of innovations on the Creed. "Let there be none such, but only what has been delivered," said Pope Stephen in a quaint phrase to Cyprian (254 A.D.). Now the heretical movement, dating chiefly from Antioch and the Syrian literalists, was an endeavour to lighten the difficulties of the Creed by bringing down its "mysteries" to the capacity of human thought; a process at all times foreign to the spirit of Rome. For Rome, as Döllinger says, "took the world ready-made." It would not vex itself with philosophic inquiries, whether in its former heathen or its present Christian stage. In discipline it was accommodating, in dogma inflexible, and this from of old. When, therefore, conservative Easterns, such as the unconquerable Athanasius, the golden-mouthed Chrysostom, or the violent Cyril, looked round for help in their struggle with the party of Rationalism, it was a matter of course that they should appeal to Rome. And Rome stood by them. The Pope was at a safe distance from Court; he could not easily be taken or sent into banishment; his unswerving attitude, by which he seemed only to be maintaining that which had always been the rule, made him respected in an age when Bishops lost their dignity by engaging in hot and acrimonious disputes. It is significant that the three Popes who have proved embarrassing to Roman apologists—Liberius, Vigilius, and Honorius—were all charged with innovation. There was never any danger in holding to what had been received. Hence the Popes, unlike the Eastern Fathers, do not meet the arguments of heretics with counter-arguments; they decide, but they decline to reason the matter out. They attend no Councils, if they can help it, away from the Lateran. The only creeds which they approve are those of Nicæa in 325 and of Constantinople in 381. Pope Cœlestine imposes on the Council of Ephesus (431) his own judgment by the imperious hands of Cyril; the session begins and ends in a summer's day. Leo the Great sends his "Tome," which is by no means a treatise, to Chalcedon (451), and with the open assistance of Emperor and Empress compels six hundred Bishops to accept it. In a later controversy, Hormisdas (519), relying on the secular arm, makes his creed law throughout the length and breadth of Asia; it is subscribed, or acquiesced in, by perhaps two thousand five hundred Bishops.

But all the writings on divinity of the Roman Pontiffs down to Gregory the Great would not fill a volume of considerable size. Even where they approve, they content themselves with as few words as possible. Contrast the folios of Augustine, to whom they were benignant, with what Innocent, Zosimus, and Cœlestine did not write, on a subject so momentous as that of grace and free will. To others they resigned the task of explaining or defending Christian truth by methods adapted to the intellect. They put down heresy by cutting off the heretic from their communion. In this way, Rome exercised the functions of a Supreme Court of Appeal, and its judgments anticipated those of the General Councils, which were held in the Emperor's presence or that of his lieutenant.

We cannot describe the Popes of the fourth century as men of rare personal qualities. One of them, Damasus (367-384), has some features, in his tumultuous election and his worldly pomp, which forecast the days of Avignon or the Renaissance. Another, Siricius, who followed him immediately, is the first of whom we possess any genuine Decretal, as the letters were styled that the Roman Chancery sent to Bishops on points concerning which its opinion was asked. Yet the Church was steadily mounting towards pre-eminence. The Latin Fathers—this is their golden age—could not but magnify it by their character, their eloquence, and their achievements. Even Cyprian, who a hundred years earlier had quarrelled vehemently with Rome, "did far more," says Milman, "to advance her power by the primacy which he assigned to St. Peter, than he impaired it by his steady and disdainful repudiation of her authority, whenever it was brought to the test of submission."

But Ambrose, Bishop of Milan (375–398), was the most saintly of Western prelates—a true Roman born out of due time—and his reverence for the Apostolic See, during a long pontificate, summed itself up in the famous expression, imitated from the legists, "Where is Peter, there is the Church." On this classic sentence the policy of excommunication, interdict, and even deposition—which is the story of the Middle Ages—may be made to depend. The language of Jerome (342–420), most learned, lively, and provoking of the Fathers, is identical; and he who smiles at the frivolous elegance of Damasus or his clerics, yet cries out to him, "I am with thy blessedness, that is, with the Chair of Peter." When he undertakes his immortal work, the translation of the Bible, it is with the approval of the same Pope; and the Vulgate, which was the Scripture of the West for nearly twelve hundred years, might almost be reckoned among the genuine Decretals. Then came Augustine (354–430), whose inexhaustible fertility in dispute never drew him into controversy with Rome, though his deep or ingenious commentaries on received doctrine were, in the great break-up which we call the Reformation, turned against her by those most resolute enemies, Luther, Calvin, and Jansenius. But Augustine did more than all the Fathers to lift up the

Papacy as on a visible height—to idealise it as the new Jerusalem and the Christian Sion—when he put forth his vision of the City of God. There was no place known to men except Rome which could fulfil so large and sovereign a mission ; and that some distinct sanctuary it must be, the Middle Ages would have asserted no less confidently than the Greeks, who beheld the temple of the Sun, not in the open sky above them, but on the island of Delos or in the mountain-gorges of Delphi.

Marcus Aurelius, the crowned philosopher and Stoic (161–180), had in a touching apostrophe made invocation to the " dear City of God," which was to embrace all mankind. At that very time Christians were beginning to define their own society as the " Catholic Church," and to oppose against the multitude of Gnostic rites its mystic and divine unity. It was impossible that converts from heathenism should lose the sentiment, universal since Augustus, that Rome was the sacred capital of a world-wide civilisation, the meeting-place of all worships, and the centre of religion. This great idea can never have died out. Nor would it fail to be kept alive by the progress of the new creed, since it spread from the Imperial cities to their dependencies, and the Roman Province became the Metropolitan circle, with bishops occupying the rank of prefects, or subordinate to them, on the lines of the civil organisation. The primitive Church was the Empire taken a second time, but for spiritual and heavenly purposes. In every metropolis, says Bingham (whose evidence has stood the test of modern research), as there was a magistrate over the magistrates of each city, so there was a Bishop over the local bishops. That arrangement the Council of Nicæa confirmed. Constantine had new modelled the Empire. This first of the General Councils (325) acknowledged, in accordance with his dispositions, three great Patriarchates—Rome, Alexandria, and Antioch. The Bishop of Rome, it observes in its sixth Canon, already exercised his rights over "the suburbican churches," which are understood to mean the churches of the "Diocese of Italy." What the Popes did actually claim, as time went on, was a supreme right of interference in the "Prefectures" of Italy, in the two Gauls, which included Spain, and in Eastern Illyricum. Besides these particular jurisdictions, of which the last was frequently contested, they held, as appears from Athanasius, who cites a letter of Julius I. to this effect, that it was against the tradition to assemble councils and proceed to grave resolutions without their concurrence. All this betokens a close and increasing communion among the different local bodies of Christians. It is the old Roman vision of a world-empire expanding and realising itself as a Catholic Church, which if not yet governed by a Supreme Head, was by all its institutions calling for one.

The division of the Empire, which followed on Constantine's death, gave this problem a fresh turn. Of the Easterns it must be said, in general, that they were Erastians, if we may apply the language of the seventeenth century to the fourth. In the Emperor they owned a Divine right of superintending the

4

Church; he was a kind of lay Bishop, and it was impossible to say where his power ended. The secular arm executed the decrees of Councils, drove heretics into exile, and through all the controversies which tore Christendom wielded the sword of the Lord. It seemed a conclusion from this Old Testament view that the Imperial city ought to share in its master's prerogatives. Constantinople, which as Byzantium had been the suffragan of Heraclea, would not submit to be reckoned among the inferior churches. It aspired to independence; and though it dared not vie with "Old Rome" at first, it elbowed aside not only Antioch but the ever-orthodox Alexandria, and boldly insisted on taking the second place. Nor, as was shown in the sequel, did it pause when that was attained. Its Patriarch, John the Faster, wrote himself "Universal Bishop" in 590. His successors are still denominated "Œcumenical," which is the title he usurped; but neither they nor he establish their claim on a direct descent from one of the Apostles. The ground taken was frankly political; the city of the Emperor must be supreme.

In two General Councils, one held within the walls of Constantinople (381), the other in sight of its towers and palaces at Chalcedon (451), this demand was formulated as a Canon, or rule of law. The Popes, without losing a moment, raised the cry of alarm. They felt the danger which this Erastian principle would bring on their own policy of independence and freedom. Damasus, in a statement which might have been dictated by Hildebrand, asserts emphatically the idea to be henceforward echoed in every tone by the Apostolic See. To the temporal greatness of the Empire he opposes (381) the voice of the Lord Himself, who has given to Rome the primacy in Peter. It owes nothing to synods; it is above all other Churches, because of the text in the Gospels. Even Alexandria is "the second See," as being "consecrated in the name of Peter," through his disciple, Mark the Evangelist; on a like account Antioch is honourable, "for Peter took up his abode there, before he came to Rome."

In these declarations, and in the acts to which they were an answer, we note the beginnings of the great schism that has divided the East from the West. Constantinople is Erastian; Pope Damasus is Ultramontane. The answer to Constantinople was the Papal Monarchy.

Disputes concerning precedence among Bishops may seem the vainest of quarrels; but we cannot fail to perceive that the races of men and the systems of philosophy extant within the Roman Empire were struggling here mightily against one another, like the winds on the great sea in Daniel's vision. Egypt had been from of old the home of a mystical and ascetic religion, of which Neo-Platonism and the Christian teachers had borrowed as much as they would. Antioch and its vast dependencies were now covered with schools, in which the Greek spirit of reasoning and contention exercised full sway. To this side Constantinople was drawn by the habits of its indolent population; but though they welcomed a Syrian of genius, like St. John Chrysostom, in their Archbishop's chair, they would not submit to rank below

a provincial city on the Orontes. And Rome, which
was neither given with the Egyptians to ecstatic
dreaming, nor involved in the subtle syllogisms of
the Asian Greeks, but which held fast by law and
tradition, sided now with one of these parties and now
with another, as the interests of orthodox government demanded. The history of the fifth and sixth
centuries does but exhibit the three Eastern capitals
weakening one another by internecine wranglings,
with their accompaniments of riot and persecution,
until Syria and Egypt lay defenceless before Islam,
and Constantinople trembled within her sea-girt
fortifications. By the time of Gregory the Great,
the two Patriarchal Churches associated with the
name of St. Peter had almost run their course. Rome
was left as the sole Apostolic See, founded on the
rock.

We may watch this conception growing ever more
luminous in the utterances of the Pontiffs themselves.
It was to be strenuously acted upon, after the taking of
Rome by Alaric, in matters of Church government as
of dogmatic teaching, when Innocent I., Cœlestine, and
Leo the Great displayed their conviction that in them
and through them the Prince of the Apostles ruled.
Innocent (402–417) declared that all the Churches of
Italy, Gaul, Spain, Africa, and Sicily had been
founded by Peter and his successors; it was incumbent on them to follow the " use " of Rome. He
reminds the Bishops of Macedonia that they must
send an account of their proceedings to the " head of
the Churches." He takes the part of Chrysostom;
excommunicates the usurper of his See, Acacius; is

urgent against the Donatist schism in Africa ; condemns Pelagius, who brings into the fifth century such a modern air of " Naturalism " ; and strives to enforce upon the prelates at Carthage the power of receiving appeals which he grounds on the Canons of Nicæa. He was met, in this instance, with a counter-claim for verification ; the Canons (real or interpolated) were those of a Latin assembly at Sardica, now Sophia, in Bulgaria. But they took their place in the Corpus Juris, and helped, like the ever-growing pile of Decretals, to furnish precedents on which the medieval Popes were ready to act in every part of Christendom.

The fall of Rome in 410 was the destruction of Paganism. As a public religion it disappeared no less completely than the Jewish rites and sacrifices on the burning of the Temple. Innocent had saved the Basilicas of the Apostles from profanation, and Alaric remained only three days in the city. But, henceforth, sacred ceremonies, popular festivals, and the great days in the Calendar must all be Christian. The Prefect of Rome was a shadow of the impotent Honorius, cowering behind the marshes and walls of Ravenna. But the Popes in their Lateran palace, given them by Constantine, lived amongst the busiest throngs of the ancient Capital, which until the fires kindled by Robert Guiscard and his Normans (1085) spread out round the Palatine, Cælian, and Esquiline Hills. It was the duty of the Pontiff, as it had formerly been of the Emperor, to feed the people in seasons of famine ; to make good the losses occasioned by earthquakes, conflagrations, risings of the

Tiber, invasions of Goths or Vandals; to preside at the crowded Church festivals, which took the place of gladiatorial sports, abolished at this time; and to do what in them lay as mediators between the people and their conquerors. Alaric had besieged Rome three times; Italy was soon to be threatened by the strange figure of Attila the Hun (449), famous in history as the Scourge of God and in medieval poetry as Etzel, the hero of the Nibelung Epic. In 455 Genseric the Vandal took and plundered the city. Yet these reiterated misfortunes did but enhance the Papal greatness; since, whatever mercy was shown amid the prevailing cruelty, the faithful attributed it with Augustine to the power of the Christian name; and Innocent, but much more Leo, might take the credit of it as granted to the Holy Apostles at their intercession.

While, therefore, the Bishops of Constantinople were falling, like Nestorius, into heresy, or suffering deposition and exile; and while Alexandria was disgraced by furious partisans like Theophilus, or miscreants of the stamp of Dioscorus and his Monophysite successors, the Roman dynasty grew in strength, acquired influence with foreign and even hostile nations, absorbed into itself the renown of the Eternal City, and looked forward to subduing the whole West by missionary enterprise. Cœlestine (422–432), the Pope who put down Pelagius and the Pelagians in Africa, and who withstood their intrigues at the Imperial Court, was the same man that ordered the deposition of Nestorius at Ephesus, and is said to have dispatched Palladius, as afterwards he sent

GALLA PLACIDIA AND ST. LEO.

(*Mosaic above Triumphal Arch in St. Paul's outside Rome. Fifth Century.*)

39

St. Patrick, to preach the gospel in Ireland. Such missions were Roman in their language, liturgy, Canon Law, and cast of civilisation. They as truly implied a conquest to the legislation of the Church, as Cæsar's victorious campaigns in Gaul had brought with them the sovereignty of what was by and by denominated the Jus Civile over the vanquished barbarians. What was now attempted in the farthest Western Isle would be successfully carried out with the Franks before the century ended; with the Angles and Saxons a hundred years later; and at length with Germans, Danes, Norsemen, Wends, Poles, and Hungarians. The Papacy looked west and north. Its inheritance came to it from the old world; but during the next nine hundred years it appears in Europe as the principle of progress, expansion, assimilation, and novelty, disguised under the outward forms of law, which was continually enlarging its bounds by precedent.

Leo I., deservedly known as the Great (440–461), exhibits all the most splendid features of a medieval Pope, with no admixture of their forbidding or violent complexion. Like the eminent among them, he was a Roman by birth and breeding; yet we should not overlook the picturesque detail that he had personally made the acquaintance of Augustine in Africa during the troubles with Pelagius; he seems, indeed, to have risen up out of the pages of the "City of God," with his "noble aspect and spare youthful form," as though to carry their stupendous design into execution. He preached a majestic theology in language that no Papal briefs have surpassed,

though the best among them aim at reproducing it ;
for the Ciceronian amplitude of later and present
times is a lapse from the *cursus Leoninus.* But he
was more than a teacher in the schools. He laid
down the law with authority. Rome had now
" become, through the sacred Chair of Peter, head of
the world ; " its religious empire stretched far beyond
its earthly dominion ; and this was the work of
Providence. As already seen, the Roman Pontiff
did not stoop to argue with the time-serving Bishops
at Chalcedon ; they must subscribe his " Tome "
as he sent it ; and these men, who would fain have
exalted Constantinople, can yet flatter him in their
epistle as " keeper of the Lord's vineyard," and
" Archbishop of the world."

In Rome his action was no less decided. The
Manichees, who were now and all down the Middle
Ages to inherit the speculative tenets and bad name
of their Gnostic forefathers, had been condemned
to extinction by the Code of the Emperors. They
survived, nevertheless ; nay, they flourished exceedingly ; nor did the conversion of Augustine to their
sect, which they effected in his youth, ever pass from
the mind of the mature theologian. A discovery made
of them in the city (443) was followed by charges of
magic, and of gross crimes against morality—the usual
accusations, to be repeated with terrible consequences
in after times, whenever a Manichæan society came to
light. It is said that the evidence was strong and
conclusive. Some were admitted to penance. The
sect at large underwent exile and proscription ; but
none were put to death. Leo, whose share in dealing

with them is described by himself, wrote to the Bishops of Italy to make search after these pestilent heretics, and persuaded Valentinian III. to renew the severest edicts against Manicheism. The whole story reads like a chapter from the Albigensian campaigns of Innocent III.

The tremendous Scythian, or Hunnish invasion, which in 449 and the years following swept over Europe, had met with only the shadow of resistance from Theodosius II. It seemed likely to raze out the last vestiges of Western civilisation. With his innumerable hordes Attila laid siege to Constantinople, marched down to Thermopylæ, turned back through the Austrian and German forests, crossed the Rhine, and pitched his camp in Eastern Gaul. A battle of the giants was fought on the Plains of Chalons; on the second day Attila underwent a horrible defeat at the hands of young Thorismund, the Visigoth, not altogether without assistance from Aëtius, the Roman commander. The Hun retreated, but only to lay waste Italy as far as the banks of the Po. He might now have captured Rome, whither Valentinian III., last of the line of Theodosius, had fled for refuge. But on the reedy shores of the Lago di Garda, not far from Mantua, the Barbarian was met by a solemn embassy, Pope Leo at its head. To the petition of the venerable Pontiff he yielded. He would be content with tribute—it was called the dowry of the Princess Honoria, who had offered herself in marriage to this ogre—and would retire beyond the Alps. That he listened to Pope Leo's prayers is certain; his motives must remain a

conjecture. Was it disease in his army that held
him back ? Or a presentiment of approaching death,
excited by the speedy end of Alaric after he had
broken into the world's Capital ? Or did he behold
the Apostles in the air threatening him, while Leo
spoke with grave sacerdotal eloquence ? Later ages
put faith in the sublime legend. But it is doubtless
true that the wildest of Barbarian chiefs felt a
superstitious reverence for the name of Rome. Examples will be frequent of lawless freebooters who
turn aside even from sanctuaries known to be
wealthy at the word of saint or monk, and in dread
of the deities who dwelt there. Leo had saved the
city ; he was hailed on his return as a new Camillus.

Such noble achievements must have led him to
reply with scorn and indignation, as he did in three
letters still extant, to Anatolius the Patriarch who
claimed for Constantinople the second rank, as enacted in Canon 28 at Chalcedon. He would not
hear of it ; whoso pretended to be an Œcumenical
Bishop was Antichrist. Yet he not only received
questions from all over the West on points of discipline, but when Hilary of Arles in 445 had, in a
Council, deposed the Bishop Celidonius and the
latter had appealed to Rome, Leo annulled the
sentence and restored Celidonius. This was something new. Hilary, coming to the shrine of the
Apostles, pleaded the usages of the Gallic Church
and his own Metropolitan rights, in language of
remarkable violence, to which the Pope answered by
an epistle to the Bishops of his province, Vienne,
releasing them from their allegiance to the See of

Arles, and interdicting the offender from being present at future consecrations. Nay, more; Valentinian III.—a dissolute and cowardly prince, but devoted to the Church—issued at Leo's request a " Perpetual Edict " which recognised the Papal primacy as resting on the merits of St. Peter, the majesty of Rome, and the decree of a sacred Council. To resist the Pope's commands was treason; his decrees were law and did not need the Emperor's confirmation ; he was ruler of the Universal Church ; and all persons whom he summoned to him for judgment should be brought up, if they did not come willingly, by the Moderator of the province, that is to say, by the secular arm.

This establishment of the Roman Church as a supreme tribunal is attributed to the Empress Placidia, Valentinian's mother, and a staunch friend of the inflexible Pontiff. Regulations of a tenor not unlike, but without reference to Gaul, are quoted by a Roman Council of 380 in its address to Gratian and Valentinian II. " Following the precept of the Holy Apostles," say the Fathers, "ye have decreed that the Bishop of Rome should institute inquiries concerning the other priests of the churches." In these words we perceive that the ecclesiastical immunities were then allowed ; or, to quote St. Ambrose, " Priests (alone) were to pass judgment on priests." Quite another question was it whether the Pope could take appeals over the head of Metropolitans ; but the Perpetual Edict answered in the affirmative four hundred years before the False Decretals (about 850) made this principle the corner stone of a vast legal system. Hilary, it must be observed, was charged with tyrannical procedures, not with false doctrine. And the Gallican Church was already appealing from the Pope to its ancient Canons or customs—in vain now, as afterwards under Bossuet and the Assembly of 1682.

The crimes, follies, and murder of Valentinian brought Genseric with his Arian Vandals up the Tiber in 455. Rome could make no stand against him. Fourteen days were consumed in the pillage of the churches and plundering of the city. Pagan trophies were crammed on board ship, only to sink on their way to Carthage. The seven-branched candlestick and other sacred emblems brought by Titus from Jerusalem shared the same fate. The ladies of the Imperial house were made slaves, though not dishonourably treated. Leo might plead successfully with the Pagan Attila ; but the Vandals were heretics, and did not heed his expostulations. Yet they passed away suddenly as they came, while the Pontiff and his clergy remained, to console, to teach, and in some degree to preserve from the rising flood of barbarism a people who now saw in the Church their only ark of refuge.

If we extend our view over the ruins of the Western Empire, such is the spectacle that meets us on every side. Laws are broken up ; governors cannot defend ; the sword is the arbiter of public and private right ; the Pax Romana has ceased ; it is a universal confusion. But wherever a Bishop holds his court, religion protects all that is left of the ancient order. A new Rome ascends slowly above the horizon.   It holds within it the Hebrew and the Christian Testaments; it has never forgotten the forms of jurisprudence; it possesses an art, an architecture, curiously modelled upon the lines of happier days; it is even the heir of the religion which it has overthrown; it assumes the outward splendour of the Cæsars; but its reliance is upon a Creed they never knew, in which justice and mercy, qualities of the spirit, not of the flesh, are to serve as its strength and guidance.   The Emperor is no more; the Consul has laid down the fasces; the golden Capitol has seen its gods and heroes carried into captivity by a Wendish robber from the shores of the Baltic.   But the Pontifex Maximus abides; he is now the Vicar of Christ, offering the old civilisation to the tribes of the North.   He converts them to his creed, and they serve him as their Father and Judge Supreme. This is the Papal Monarchy, which in its power and its decline overshadows the history of Europe for a thousand years.

III

GREGORY THE GREAT, MONASTICISM, AND ST. BENEDICT.

(461–590–604)

THOUGH Leo I. had seen clearly the part which this New Christian Rome was destined to play, and himself had acted up to it magnificently, the next hundred and thirty years brought to the Papacy little honour and much tribulation. Not until we come to Gregory, best and greatest in the long line of Pontiffs, do we meet a ruler of powers equal to his task, while the unexpected revival of the Empire, due to Belisarius and Narses, but called by the name of Justinian, made the Pope subject once more to an Eastern Court. Obscure but embittered controversies led to a schism in spirituals between Rome and Constantinople which lasted thirty-five years (484–519). A Council, the Fifth General, is supposed to have cut off Pope Vigilius from Catholic Communion. But if the Greeks repudiated him, the Westerns revolted against him. Africa fell away; Ravenna,

47

Milan, Aquileia strove to be independent. The Goths were Arians; and three times under their rude heretical kings did they besiege the Eternal City. After the last sieges by Totila (546–549), the population, greatly diminished, fled from their houses; during forty days Rome lay desolate and silent.

TOMB OF THEODORIC AT RAVENNA.
(*Sixth Century.*)

The end had come of its greatness; even the old race was extinct or was lost among the Barbarian adventurers. A plague, returning with terrible frequency, almost as fatal as the Black Death long afterwards, spread from Egypt to Gaul. Earthquakes, floods, and a darkening of the air which seldom lifted, were taken to be signs of approaching doom. When the Gothic kingdom fell before the Lombards, when Theodoric, Boethius, and Cassiodorus were fading into memories of a past not wholly uncivilised, the ruin of the Western Empire was complete. At this hour of deepest eclipse Gregory ascended the Papal Chair, and the Middle Ages began.

In this noble and attractive person we may affirm that all which the ancient world could now bequeath to the modern was to be found. He sprang from the most conspicuous of late Roman Houses, the Anicii, who had long been Christian. The grandson of Pope Felix and son of Gordianus, at one time he was Prætor, if not Prefect, of the City. Then, in obedience to the strongest current of his age, he had become a monk. He turned his fine mansion on the Cælian into a monastery. He gave himself up to prayer, to reading, and to ascetic exercises. By Pelagius II. he had been sent to Constantinople as *apocrisiarius*, or *chargé d'affaires*—an appointment which, while the Byzantine Court governed at Rome, led up, as a rule, to the Papacy. Though not in the classic sense a scholar, and affecting some disdain for heathen accomplishments, he spoke and wrote a Latin which was far superior to the jargon now resulting from the wild intermixture of peoples and languages in Western Europe. In music and the arts that served for ritual or decorative purposes within the churches of Italy he was skilled to a degree which has made the name of Gregorians famous. Nor did he lack the qualities of a lawgiver and administrator. With ambition,

5

pride, or avarice — the temptations to which more than one Pope afterwards yielded—Gregory cannot be charged. His mind was not that of a philosopher; he shared in the beliefs so widely prevalent at his day, and by his book of *Dialogues* contributed not a little to spread them during the medieval period. His genius and character, direct, sincere, practical, yet over-laid with allegorising fancies (the common feature of decadence in thought), were altogether Roman.

Elected against his will in 590, he had no arms wherewith to resist the Lombards, whose Arian beliefs and barbarian race, no less than their burnings and plunderings, made them detestable to the older Italians. Yet on him it fell to feed and defend the city. The Imperial officers could do nothing. But the Church held large domains in the Agro Romano, in Calabria, Corsica, Sardinia, Sicily, and Dalmatia, which went by the name of St. Peter's Patrimony. It was a custom as early as Pope Soter (180) for the Roman Church to send assistance wherever Christians found themselves in distress. Now as then the Church fed the Roman people; to such elementary human offices had it come; but in thus stooping it laid foundations deep for the Pope's temporal power. Gregory acted as lieutenant of the Empire though not by designation. The Exarch came from Ravenna; took with him what was left of the garrison; and deserted the city against which Agilulf was bringing his wild followers. They were bought off by the Pope, who called himself with a smile "paymaster of the Lombards." When he was

rebuked by the Emperor Maurice, he could answer
that he was sharing in the dangers and warding off
the captivity of his own city. The sovereign power
was passing into his hands. He defends officials
who appeal to him from the violence of Byzantine
corruption and secular judges. He alone signs the
treaty of peace with Agilulf. He insists on the
freedom of soldiers who are desirous of becoming
monks, although the Emperor had forbidden it. If,
as Pope, he was the richest landowner in Italy, with
thousands of serfs and myriads of acres yielding him
a revenue, from these resources he nourished his
Romans at the doors of the basilicas. Neither would
he permit his *coloni* to be ruthlessly oppressed. He
maintained the churches, ransomed captives, set up
hospitals for pilgrims, and saw to it that twice in the
year a corn-bearing fleet from Sicily supplied Rome
with provisions at Portus. His tribune protected
the inhabitants of Naples from tyranny. He advised
or commanded military precautions to be taken in
Sardinia. Yet he would not exasperate the Lombards,
hoping doubtless to see them turn one day from their
heresy, as they came more and more under the
magic of the Roman name.

His relations with the Bishops and Emperors of
Constantinople were fluctuating. He had persuaded
Eutychius to give up the doctrine of a purely
spiritual resurrection. John the Faster, who styled
himself " Universal Bishop," was reminded of the
protest formerly made against this encroachment on
the rights of his brethren and of the Papacy ; but it
was a title which Gregory put from himself with

horror. The signature of his own predecessors, as the documents witness, had been " Bishop of the Catholic Church of Rome."

In 602 the Emperor Maurice was dethroned and murdered by Phocas, a centurion. That Pope Gregory had learned the details of this blood-stained revolution is not clear; but he acknowledged the usurper, received his portrait solemnly in the Palatine chapel, and wrote to him in terms of Oriental adulation. It is said that he resented various measures of unkindness on the part of Maurice; above all, his connivance in the ambitious designs of John the Faster. And confirmation is sought in the decree, put forth by Phocas in 607, which ordained that " the See of Blessed Peter the Apostle should be head of all the Churches." This undoubtedly was meant as a rebuke to the Patriarch and clergy of Saint Sophia. On the other hand, it does not appear that the Popes ever attached importance to the proclamation. In all their arguments they take their stand resolutely on the words of Scripture and their own Decretals, which had the force of law in Western Christendom.

The Bishops were fast growing into great temporal lords. Wherever a breathing time from war was given, men and women disposed of their wealth for spiritual blessings and benefits. Even unfit or youthful candidates now begin to appear, as the Sees of Christendom are worth coveting by noble families. But no Bishops can plead exemption from Gregory's jurisdiction. They are subject to his " forum." He deposes the Bishop of Naples, degrades him of Melita, threatens in severe terms the prelates of

Tarentum, Cagliari, and Salona. He abounds in remonstrances, which bore little fruit, against the scandals of the Gaulish Church, under Queen Brunhilde and the Kings Thierry and Theodebert. He has a certain power in Greece; but his directions, even in matters of dogma, find no acceptance in Illyricum. The West was to be Rome's peculiar province. There Gregory overthrew the failing squadrons of Arianism, reconciled Spain, and by means of his legate or missionary, Augustine, established in England a succession of Bishops, under whose ecclesiastical government the country was organised, as its inhabitants gradually submitted to the Gospel, and men like Theodore of Tarsus were sent from Rome to rule over it (597–668).

Had Arianism stood its ground outside the Greek Empire, a state of incessant religious warfare, ending at last in toleration, might have ensued, as when, long afterwards, the Peace of Westphalia (1648) set up a balance of power between Catholics and Reformed Christians. But the Arian creed was the product of a learned and disputatious temper, more congenial to reasoning than to simple faith; its home had always been the cultivated cities of Asia. From the Imperial Court it spread among the Goths. As they moved onward and took possession of Southern Gaul and Spain, the links which bound them to a Syrian system and a rationalising philosophy grew constantly weaker. Of learned teachers they could scarcely boast. Ulfilas, their Bishop, had translated the Bible into Mæso-Gothic; but schools of theology they had none, nor a centre of religious life, nor the logical refinement out of which this not very attractive heresy had sprung. In the lapse of time it was upheld only by Court favour.

Arian chiefs had reigned at Ravenna, Pavia, Arles, and Toledo; but the Catholic Bishops disdained to give way before them. And towards the close of the sixth century this political arrangement was breaking up. By a supreme good fortune, the Franks under Chlodowig (Clovis, Louis, Ludwig, are all forms of this Teutonic name) had accepted Roman Christianity at the hands of Remigius, Bishop of Rheims (496). It was a conversion equal in importance to that of Constantine, nor unlike it in its motives or its results. The mightiest sword wielded by a Barbarian was now at the disposal of the Roman Pontiff. The French King became " Eldest Son of the Church." He was destined to smite the Arian, to drive back the Mohammedan, to endow the Papacy with a kingdom of its own, to make the name of Frank synonymous with Christian all over the East for many ages, to found the Holy Roman Empire, and to lead the Crusades.

In its palmiest days the Arian had never been a popular creed. Against it the multitudes had risen in tumult; but its fiercest enemies were the monks, who swarmed out of their deserts and filled the streets of Alexandria or Ephesus with noisy protestations of the orthodox faith. Now, the whole world was turning to monasticism. It claimed to be the perfect, the Divine life. Its triumphs under Benedict, Columban, Boniface, of which we have soon to speak, were already assured in the conviction

even of the wild German tribes, on whom it exercised
an irresistible charm. All that was mystic, miraculous,
and beyond nature in the Christian teaching, found
its realisation wherever the solitaries planted their
staff in the wilderness. The Arian despised the
monk, and was vanquished by him. Something not
unlike the first age of the Gospel might be remarked
in this contrast between simple or enthusiastic
believers and the prelates, who were clothed in
soft garments and dwelt in kings' houses. If the
common people were to decide, the issue could not
be doubtful.

Thus the newly-baptized sword of France, and the
miracle-working rod of monasticism, were at the
service of a polity in Rome which had never
wavered since the days of Silvester and Athanasius.
To this array of forces the Arian host was quite
unequal. Law and learning, martial courage and the
enthusiasm of the cloister, were banded against it.
Burgundy, which had existed as an heretical power
since about 430, fell in 520 before the assaults of the
Franks, and with the dynasty its Arianism came to
an end. This was to be the tale everywhere. Spain,
under its feeble Visigoth rulers, abounded in crimes
and tragedies. Yet, unlike the Vandals in Africa, they
had given large toleration to their Roman or Catholic
subjects (the names are now used indifferently), and
had the Franks not come down upon them, Spain
might have exhibited the rare spectacle of a heretic
prince living in peace with his orthodox tributaries.
But in 507 the sanguinary Clovis wrested from these
Visigoths Toulouse and Aquitaine.   There ensued

hereupon a death-struggle between the Catholic party, which looked for assistance to the Franks or the Greeks, and the Arian nobles with their king, who were now hemmed about as in a circle of fire.

Leodevigild had two sons, Hermenegild and Reccared. Their mother was Greek and orthodox; the sons shared her beliefs. Against Hermenegild the charge was brought that, in conjunction with Leander, Bishop of Seville, he meditated treason, and was for calling in the Franks. His father began general measures of persecution; imprisoned Hermenegild, offered him the Arian confession, and on his rejecting it, had him put to death. All proved in vain. The young prince was revered as a martyr. Leodevigild died speedily (586), and Reccared, now King, held a tourney of argument between the contending Bishops at Toledo next year, which ended in his declaring himself a Catholic. Formal acceptance of the Nicene Creed followed in 589. Pope Gregory canonised Hermenegild, the story of whose martyrdom he has written with tender feeling. And in addressing Reccared, he spoke as though the Spanish kingdom were subject in a peculiar way to the Roman Church — a claim which later Pontiffs heightened into their suzerainty over the whole Peninsula.

As the Franks were instrumental in this conquest of Spain, so they took no insignificant share in the success of Gregory's mission to the Anglo-Saxons. Queen Bertha was daughter of Charibert, King of Paris. Frankish interpreters accompanied Augustine to Thanet; and St. Martin of Tours, whose shrine

ST. GREGORY THE GREAT.

(From an engraving in the British Museum Print Room.)

may be almost termed the cradle of the French monarchy, has to this day his church at Canterbury, founded by the pious Queen. Monks whose home was Iona or Lindisfarne, helped to make England Christian, from the Cheviots to the Thames. But Augustine, Paulinus, and Wilfrid of York made it Roman in hierarchy, ritual, and learning. The Saxon kings were constant pilgrims to St. Peter's shrine.

Four times has the Papacy won its triumphs over barbarians or heretics with the aid of men who had renounced the world only to conquer it. Gregory the Great was a monk and a Benedictine. Without these marching legions he could have done nothing for civilisation, and neither England nor Germany would have known the Gospel. St. Benedict is the Cadmus and Solon of the centuries which find their Cæsar in Charlemagne. But the Dark Ages follow; and four hundred and fifty years after Gregory, another of his name, the monk better known as Hildebrand, calls again to his cloistered brethren. With their help he reforms the clergy, sets free the Church, beats the Emperor to his knees, and dies feudal lord of Europe. Once more, under the most majestic of the Popes, Innocent III., Christendom seems to be falling in pieces, rent by factions, simony, clerical vice, popular heresy. And again the monks, transformed to friars by Francis and Dominic, but disciplined by yet another Gregory, charm the people back to their allegiance, put down the dissenters, subdue to their scholastic doctors the philosophy of Aristotle and the Arabians. Last of all, during the agony of the Reformation, Ignatius Loyola and his

Jesuits, taking to themselves the principle of utter self-sacrifice as a motive for combat and conquest, restore the day which had been all but lost, and cover the New World no less than the Old with churches, schools, universities, colonies. Medieval Europe can never be seen as it really was except in the light of that omnipotent monasticism.

Eastern in origin, it entered the West with Athanasius (340), captivated the impetuous Jerome, and was fostered at Milan by Ambrose. It flourished at Tours, Lerins, and Marseilles, and found a law-giver in Augustine, who cultivated its most austere virtues. But though Cassian sketched its heroes in his Fathers of the Desert, it was to derive from Benedict of Nursia its lasting form, at once more practical and more moderate than even the Rule of the lofty St. Basil. Romans or Barbarians would not endure the pillar-saints of Syria; and wildly picturesque as were the lives of Celtic hermits, the good sense which marked Imperial laws and ordinances tamed even these, when Columban's severe regulations yielded to the genius of a more considerate legislator. Not that Benedict had learning, or took on himself a civilising mission. His aim was strictly religious, ascetic, personal. But he framed a code upon which the life in community might be lived during ages of social confusion.

Thus the Christian republic began like some dream of Plato. Its celibate members were drawn from a world in which the sword alone had rights; where traffic had become piracy or brigandage; where libraries were but sheepskin, the fields a thorny waste, the Roman high-roads between city and city fallen into disuse, and all Europe lay in the gloom of a forest stretching unbroken from the shores of Brittany to the steppes of Russia. A few walled towns, calling themselves Roman municipalities, stood up as isolated rocks in the deluge. Over them the Bishops ruled as *defensores civitatis*, with phantom-officials at their elbow. But the question was, who would subdue the savage lands to the plough, and their intractable conquerors to a life not wholly warfare? After six hundred years of the strangest vicissitudes it was answered by St. Benedict's disciples. To all that is admirable in the Medieval centuries they lay a just claim, and the mighty figure of their hermit-founder stands aloft over modern civilisation as its author, if not its ideal. "The Order of St. Benedict," says Michelet, "gave to a world worn out by slavery the first example of labour done by the hands of the free."

His "legend," written by St. Gregory, takes us at a bound from the dead classic literature into the miraculous air and curiously painted lights of the Middle Age. Born near Spoleto (480), sent to study in Rome, he fled from the doomed city, and hid himself in the gorges of the Apennines, not far from a country house of Nero at Subiaco, where he lived three years in a cave, and where his twelve monasteries arose by and by, as well as the convent of his sister, Scholastica. The glory of monasticism was to be shared by illustrious women of genius, not Italian chiefly, but French, Saxon, Irish, German, whose institutes were adapted from those of the

sterner sex, while their industry in cultivating lands
or books was scarcely inferior. Thus began the
emancipation of woman in our Western world—
behind the safe walls of a cloister, in a sacred peace,
and under vows which Kings themselves could not
trample on without remorse and public condemnation.
Benedict, however, was to end his days at the yet
more famous Monte Cassino, which still towers above
the Garigliano, and which became a monastic Rome,
mother and mistress of the thousand communities
spread into every country where the Papal power
extended. Here the Saint encountered Totila, King
of the Goths, overawed him, and foretold his death.
Cassino was ruined in these perpetual wars; but
when Benedict and Scholastica passed away, almost
at the same moment, their work had been set on an
everlasting base, and time would prove this dream of
enthusiastic piety to be as enduring as the foundations
of Rome itself.

Much of the Saint's legend is romantic poetry.
What the man did and was we may contemplate in
his Rule. Its unstudied Latin lays down the sum of
discipline for monks, who are to spend their stated
hours in chanting the Divine service, in reading, in
manual labour. The brethren are to serve God with
their hands—*Laborare est orare*—a perfect idea, in
some magnificent degree fulfilled when the Order had
restored agriculture and the arts of life, had saved
from destruction the masterpieces of antiquity, and
"Eden raised in the waste wilderness." To the letter
they accomplished this word.

They were laymen, not clerics, **except the few**

needed for Mass and other ordinances. Abstinence from flesh, much fasting, silence, and the strictest obedience to command, were all means well suited to creating a peaceful, orderly temper, at once the marvel of barbarians and a check upon the universal *Faustrecht*, or rule of the strong hand. No one who had taken the vows could quit them at his good pleasure. Children were often dedicated before coming to years of discretion ; we must not suppose the modern respect for personal liberty in a time so rude and inchoate. A man belonged to his clan, his lord, or his community, unless he fled away to the wild wood and became a heathen or Christian Ishmaelite. But soon Maurus in Gaul, as the story tells, or at all events some follower of Benedict, was establishing the colonies which had swarmed from Monte Cassino. Houses multiplied all through Italy. The Lateran had its monks, and Gregory the Great, as we have seen, turned his mansion on the Cælian Hill into a cloister, from which he ascended the Papal throne, and England received its Christianity. The great lines of medieval Europe were drawn as on a chart, its problems designed, their solution foreshadowed, when the most Roman of the Popes died, after a reign of only fourteen years, crowded with memorable issues, on March 12, 604. He was not much more than sixty.

ST. BENEDICT ABBOT.

(From a portrait by Sassoferrato of Perugia.)

IV

ICONOCLAST EMPERORS AND LOMBARD KINGS

(604–739)

BETWEEN a dying system and one waiting to be born, the Pope stood, as it were, undecided for a hundred and thirty years after Gregory. His missionaries had gone out West; but he in the Lateran could not shake himself free of Constantine's successors, ruling by an Exarch at Ravenna, by a Dux Romanus in the Imperial City, and in the South by their military captains. On every side the Pontifex Maximus felt a power too strong for him. To rebel was not in his thoughts; still less would he or the citizens of Rome, proud though degenerate, exchange the tyranny of the Empire for the hated Lombard yoke. And what of the Franks? Their time was not come. Relations once frequent between the Pope and the Merovingians, seem to have died away in the seventh century. Councils were seldom called by the French bishops—only eight are recorded—and the petty kings, their wives, concubines, nobles, and serfs offer the *dramatis personæ* of a horrid, blood-stained play, in which scarcely a trace of human kindness is discernible. Clovis had given monasteries the right of sanctuary ; too often they were prisons into which reluctant but defeated royalty was thrust, its head shaved, and a gown instead of a soldier's mail upon its back, to meditate vengeance on the next occasion. From these kings, voluptuous, cowardly, and imbecile, nothing could be hoped.

Yet the Byzantine rule in Italy was doomed. With the Lombard invasion (569) the old order had come to an end. Always advancing, the new race drove before it to the sea, to Rome, Naples, and Otranto, what was left of the Imperial troops. In 650 the Lombard Duke of Beneventum held the South, while his lord the King reigned at Pavia ; the provinces were transformed into military departments ; instead of a Count there was now over the cities a feudal Guastaldo ; and above these rose the Dukes of Beneventum, Spoleto, Tuscany, Friuli. Venice behind its lagoons was independent, though it acknowledged the Empire. But in this falling state, when the Exarch was feeble and his officers corrupt, Byzantium looked to the Pope as at once its subject and representative, nor would be content unless he took on himself the burden of a defence which brought him only affliction.

In one hundred and twelve years (604–716), down to the quarrel about image-worship, by which this intolerable degradation was violently brought to an end, we reckon twenty-five Popes, a series rivalling in lack of historic greatness those who encumbered or

6

disgraced the tenth century. Two names are still remembered. Honorius (625–638), the victim of an imprudent answer to a captious question in divinity, was anathematised by the Sixth General Council, but was otherwise blameless. Martin I. (649–655), in repudiating the heresy charged upon his predecessor, fell into the hands of Theodore Calliopas the Exarch. He was hurried to Constantinople; stripped in the Emperor's sight before an innumerable crowd, who heaped curses upon the half-dead Pontiff; dragged through the city with an iron collar round his neck; and after eighty-five days of loathsome imprisonment was exiled to the Crimea, where he died. Such was the treatment a Pope might expect from Emperors who loved to be despots and theologians. His tormentor, Constans II., last of the Byzantines to visit Rome, spoiled the city in 663 of statues and works of art past reckoning, and took from the Pantheon its roof of bronze. The sea claimed this plunder, little of which ever reached the Bosporus. But it was clear that Monothelite and Iconoclast lords of slaves would sooner or later rouse the free West to break their bands asunder. The Churches were drifting towards separation. Ravenna, encouraged to brave Rome, as the story went, by Heraclius and Constantine, saw its Archbishop Maurus excommunicate Pope Vitalian, who retorted in kind. A dim shadow of Ghibelline Emperors and North Italian antipopes looms up out of this fog in which Latin erudition, and even the sense of history, appear to be failing from the schools of the Palatine. Agatho in 680 can but apologise for the ignorance of his Curia, and hope that

Theodore, Archbishop of Canterbury, a Greek and a philosopher, will come to his help. So low had the Imperial City fallen! "The very profession of the clergy is the knowledge of letters," says Cardinal Newman, reflecting on this correspondence ; " if even these lost it, would others retain it ? " Lombard and Greek were both enemies of the Holy See. What was to be the end of these things ?

Romans, Greeks, and even Syrians pass in the rapid and obscure Papal succession ; but Constantine, who died in 716, was the last undoubted subject of an Eastern Court. The dispute about images, a Puritan reform attempted by the rude Cilician peasant, Leo the Isaurian (717–741), suddenly transported into the church and the market-place a controversy which could not leave the people unaffected. Instead of abstract science, here was the practice of religion, the visible art and daily worship now a custom of centuries, called in question by the Emperor, defended by Pope Gregory II., by Germanus, Bishop of Constantinople, by John of Damascus (destined to fix the standard of orthodoxy for Eastern Christendom), and, above all, by the monks, the multitude, the very women and children who pulled the ladders from under sacrilegious officials bent on defacing the Cross or shattering the marble effigies of the Saints. What the Popes had longed for was given them—a support on which to lean against the hitherto unassailable majesty of Cæsar. With them now were the people of Rome, of every Italian city, of Ravenna and Byzantium itself. If Leo the Isaurian had learned his lesson, as has been affirmed, from the Moslems, then Mohammed may be looked upon as indirectly the occasion of the Pope's temporal dominion, with all that it involved during eleven hundred years.

Checked in their siege of Constantinople by Leo, a valiant soldier, the armies of Islam had triumphed in Africa; the Moors, a people not Semitic, beginning their career of romance and victory, had been converted to the Koran; and in 711 Tarik passed the Straits of Gibraltar, to which he gave his name. Thrice were the Berbers of the Atlas to conquer Spain, first from the Christian "infidels," and afterwards from their own fellows in the Mussulman faith. Not Saracens but Moors achieved this mighty enterprise, which in 720 brought them to the Pyrenees. In Languedoc, the old Roman city of Narbonne was their headquarters, whence in 725 they issued to capture Carcassonne, and destroy Autun, while they held Nismes to ransom. Their light horse swept into Burgundy. In 731 they gave the shrine of St. Hilary at Poitiers to the flames. Odo, Duke of Aquitaine, pressed hard, called in his natural enemies the Franks. Near Poitiers, South and North met in their first shock of battle (732); Abderrahman was defeated with unknown loss by Charles Martel, the Gallo-German chief, whose surname alludes to Thor's invincible hammer. A new royal race had come out from the Vosges mountains, and the Crusades had inscribed their great initial letter of crimson and gold on the chronicles of history.

St. Columban of Luxeuil, it is said in his *Life*, had warned Theodebert, a base Merovingian, that the ruin of his kingdom was at hand. From Austrasia, the

CHURCH OF SAN VITALE, RAVENNA. (*Sixth Century*.)

country between Meuse and Rhine, a pathway for invaders, that prophecy would now be fulfilled. Arnulf, Bishop of Metz, an Aquitanian, had been married before consecration. His grandson was Pepin, who defeated the successors of Dagobert II. at Testry, near St. Quentin (687), took the family of Clovis under his wing as Mayor of the Palace, and left a brave bastard son, more Pagan than Christian, this Charles of the Hammer. His wrestling was with Frisians, Saxons, Germans of every tribe, eager to get a footing west of the Rhine. Their Paganism devoured his; Charles found that the new Christians in Germany were his best allies; that Boniface, their Anglo-Saxon Bishop, would be the stay of the Franks and their unbought lieutenant; that to keep a hold upon Teutons he must join himself to the Roman Pontiff. At home he behaved as a despoiler of the clergy; beyond the Alps he seemed to defend the holy place against Saracens, and might prove to be a willing champion of the Pope against the not less intolerable Lombards.

It was in 726 that Leo the Isaurian published his edict for the destruction of images. Next year, when tumults had filled the streets of his Capital, the Exarch Scholasticus put it forth in Ravenna. Straightway, and without prompting, the people rose. Gregory II., whose character and abilities bore no proportion to those of his great namesake, watched the struggle from St. Peter's Chair. His own city, like Ravenna itself, was adorned with mosaics which depicted Christ, the Virgin Mother, and the Saints in glory. No one could dream that

the Pope, any more than the people, would relinquish
usages and traditions which might be traced on the
walls of the Catacombs almost to Apostolic times. But
the Lombards were now orthodox ; their King Liutprand swooped down on Ravenna, took the popular
side, drove out the Exarch, and overran Pentapolis. If
not the unexpected, this, to Gregory and his Romans,
was in the highest degree abominable. Scholasticus
had escaped to Venice. The Pope stirred into action
the fleet of these islanders, and under his direction it
combined with troops from the centre to get back
Ravenna, which Liutprand for a moment had
quitted. Such was the ancient policy of the
Lateran. Gregory himself, says Duchesne, had
maintained in its obedience Byzantine Italy, from
Istria to Naples. He now, in effect, set up the fallen
Exarch ; doubtless to keep at a distance the "unspeakable" Lombards—as the Pope terms them again
and again. But in requital threats of assassination
were made, or fancied by the excited populace, on the
part of Leo's officers against the intrepid Pontiff. He
was to be murdered, the images broken ; Paul the
Exarch was marching on Rome. A general insurrection announced that Italy was lost to the Emperor.
Eutychius, last Exarch, landed at Naples ; his predecessor had been slain in a riot ; and though
Gregory would not favour open rebellion, the Captains began to set up for themselves ; Lombards
joined with Romans in a common league ; and the
citizens pledged their oath to live and die with their
orthodox Bishop. In this act of spontaneous surrender
we mark the birth of the Popes' sovereignty over Rome.

" Their noblest title," says Gibbon, " is the free choice of a people whom they had redeemed from slavery."

Liutprand, however, was playing a double game. If the Pope, as it appears from his passionate epistles to Leo (729), had in view, chiefly or altogether, the defence of images, and did not aim at independence, the Lombard, a wily politician, enlarged his territory by the Dukedom of Spoleto, and was ready (or so he pretended) to let the Exarch have his Rome again. He came south; entered the Holy City; threw himself at Gregory's feet; dedicated sword, crown, and cloak on the altar of St. Peter's. A truce was patched up. The Exarch withdrew to Ravenna. In 730 a Council at Rome condemned the image-breakers and rejected Leo from its communion. But Gregory neither deposed the Emperor nor released his Italian subjects from their allegiance, though he may have winked at their withholding of the customary tribute. Leo, not very wisely, confiscated the Papal estates in Sicily and Calabria; tore Illyricum from the Western Patriarchate; and demanded a heavier capitation tax. At this juncture, in 731, the Pope died, and Gregory III., a Syrian, reigned in his stead. This was the man who, in 739, sent to Charles Martel the keys of St. Peter's shrine and filings from his chains, with the title of Patrician or Roman Consul, as a lure which might tempt him over the Alps. For Liutprand had come to the gates of Rome, and the lamps *ad limina Apostolorum*, in St. Peter's itself, were seized and borne away by his marauding troops. Would the Eternal City become the Lombard capital?

V

THE DONATION OF PEPIN

(739–772)

WE have reached the turning-point in Papal history. There had been a Duke of Rome, resident in the Imperial house on the Palatine ; an *exercitus Romanus*, which comprised the nobles who, however mixed their blood, fabled a descent from the Cornelii and the other Patricians of classic renown ; last, but greatest, the Pontifex Maximus held his court with its array of clerics about the Church of the Saviour. And how did he stand to Duke and nobles ? While the Emperor governed, he was a subject, his election not valid till confirmed from the Golden Horn ; and the "army," which claimed to be the Roman People, shared in his naming with the "venerable clergy." Now, was the Duke to continue when the Emperor had ceased ? If not, the whole of Italy might be absorbed into the Lombard Kingdom, and the Pope, exercising a purely spiritual jurisdiction, would still have been a subject, liable to the military chief at Pavia, whose government he would consecrate but never share.

Neither Pontiff nor citizens felt disposed to accept this solution. Religion, we are to understand, was not at stake. Lombard Kings, Liutprand, Rachis, Astolf, Didier, were as orthodox and pious according to the standard of the age as any Carlovingians. They founded monasteries and more than once retired into them ; in gifts to the sanctuary they were lavish ; their reverence for St. Peter did not fail, even when his keys were fashioned into spears to smite them by the invading Franks. But once admitted within the walls of Rome, they could not be thrust out. Their rule would not pass with transient expeditions ; they were at home in Italy, the Franks must always be foreigners. Intervention was one thing, conquest another. From Pepin to Napoleon III. French armies have come down into the Roman States ; but on the morrow they are gone, and Pope and people exult in their departure. With a Patrician whose centre of government should be at Aix-la-Chapelle, Paris, or Worms, Rome might be free ; then the question would arise whether the Pope was to rule the army, or the army to set up, pull down, pursue to death, or welcome in triumph its own Pontiff. Unaided, these turbulent sons of Romulus could not beat back the hardy Alpine mountaineers. At their bidding it was that Gregory III. and his successors, who shared the popular sentiment, called aloud to Martel, Pepin, and Charlemagne.

The majesty of Rome, although an Emperor no longer bore it up in the West, survived under the name of the Republic, and in the prerogatives of St. Peter. At a distance this wonderful charm, religious

and full of mystery, wrought its effect. What was a
Lombard captain of yesterday, when compared with
the shadow of Augustus, or with a living Pope?
Franks, in whom the Christian faith was now after
long eclipse coming to the light again, would have
looked on calmly while the Roman *exercitus* fled
before Liutprand. But if the Apostle sent for them,
his command would not fall on deaf ears.

Yet Charles Martel, with Germans and Moors upon
his hands, might have been unable, as he was perhaps
unwilling, to take the decisive step. Gregory's loud
laments had not been answered, when both the high
contracting parties died, within a month of each other,
in 741. A man of remarkable character, a Greek
named Zachary, endowed with no little share of that
firmness which we attribute to the Roman, succeeded.
He met the pious though aspiring Liutprand in 742 at
Terni, overawed him by a fervent appeal to the invisible powers, and won from him all the estates of
the Church in Sabine territory, as well as Narni, Sutri,
and Ancona. A truce of thirty years with the Roman
Dukedom was agreed upon. Zachary made a
triumphant march, on his return, from the Pantheon
to St. Peter's, amid the plaudits of his people. But
Liutprand assaulted Ravenna. Once more the Pope
stretched out his hand to save the Exarch; he
travelled in state to Pavia; confronted and subdued
his Lombard, who gave back what he had taken, to
die soon after with the reputation of a Saint. Rachis
followed him upon the throne. He too, in 749, broke
the peace, and invested Perugia. Zachary sought
him out, enlarged on the favourite medieval text,

"All is vanity, except to love God and keep His commandments," drew him from the camp to a monastic life, and saw him a votary at Monte Cassino. There he must have been the associate of Carloman, Charles Martel's first-born son, who had quitted the

POPE ZACHARY, A.D. 752.

Mayoralty of the Palace in favour of Pepin, his younger brother.

Now came to pass the momentous series of events which bound in everlasting alliance the French nation with St. Peter at Rome. Pope Zachary was to reap where Gregory the Great had scattered the seed.

During the Merovingian period, Christian and indeed natural virtues had seemed to die utterly away among the Franks. Queens like Frédégonde and Brunéhaut, Furies in mortal shape, had made even that generation pale with astonishment at their awful wickedness. Irish monks, of whom Columban was the most illustrious by his severity of life and strength of purpose, had thundered against the heathen vices which they could not extirpate. They preached to the Neustrians, the Swiss, the Italians; but they turned aside from the German folk, although Kilian at Würzburg, and the philosophic Virgilius at Salzburg, have left their names as Apostles across the Rhine. An Englishman of Devon it was, Winfred or Boniface, who now stood forth, a fine historic figure, to unite the Pope with the dynasty of Pepin and to create in these immense Teutonic forests the churches, townships, and Christian peoples that should later on come into view as the Holy Roman Empire.

Boniface (680–756) made several journeys to the shrine of the Apostles. He was submissive in teaching as in station to " St. Peter and his Vicar." When he founded the See of Mayence, which was to be supreme over Christian Germany, and that of Cologne, second only to Mayence, he insisted that they should always ask for the pallium—the token of spiritual authority—from the Pope. His orthodox mind could not endure the errors, as he thought them, of Scots and speculative dreamers like Adalbert, Clement, Samson, and the more learned Virgilius. The same frank English temper led him to remark on the venality and corruption of which he heard as prevailing in the Roman Court. Living as a Saint, he died a missionary and a martyr, among the wild Frisians, in 756. But his work was accomplished. Four years earlier he had anointed Pepin King of France in the name of Pope Zachary.

It was a deed without precedent. No Pope had hitherto given away kingdoms or adjudicated between the nominal sovereign, legitimate but helpless, and his lieutenant, who could only be a usurper if he mounted the throne. Pepin sent his priest, Fulrad, and Burchard, Bishop of Würzburg, to consult Zachary, before the nobles elected him. Then the Pope authorised what the nation executed at Soissons in their Field of Mars; he spoke a winged word, " Let the man be called king that in fact is so," and it was done. Childeric, stripped of the dignity to which he had been born, found himself a prisoner in a convent. While we bear in mind that the laws of succession were unsettled in a barbarous age; that the Merovingians had long lost their grip of the sceptre; and that Pepin's ancestors had rendered inestimable service to France as to Christendom, it is impossible to deny that this was a revolution, peacefully carried out, with the consent and consecration of the highest religious authority. Could the Pope give crowns? Then he could take them away. Such was to be the public law of Europe during the next six hundred years, never in principle resisted until Philip the Fair withstood and overcame Boniface VIII. It is significant that the same nation which now accepted a ruler at the Pope's hands should be the first to proclaim that kings are inviolable, and their crowns beyond the jurisdiction of the Canon Law.

Writing to the iconoclast Leo, Gregory II. had warned him that the Popes were the bond of union and mediators of peace between East and West. "The eyes of the nations are fixed on our humility," continued the Pontiff; "they revere as a God upon earth the Apostle St. Peter, whose image you threaten to destroy." Language as bold as it was affected, yet no fiction. In the memorable transaction by which Pepin's dynasty became legitimate and sacred, St. Peter had done his part. It remained that the Frankish monarch should do his. Constantine V., an able ruler who has come down to us in a dark and probably calumnious legend—for, like his father, he pursued images with a Mohammedan fury—still laid claim to Rome and the Exarchate. Had he not defaced the icons, he would have found an ally in his Roman Bishops, reluctant to face the unknown, counselling moderation lest a vigorous tyrant in Pavia should leap into the saddle and ride them down in their own city. But Astolf, the Lombard, saw in the abandoned provinces a desirable prey. He took Ravenna for the last time; extinguished the Byzantine government; and held all as far as Perugia (which escaped him) before 751. Not long afterwards Zachary left the Papal Chair to Stephen II., who made a truce of forty years with his Northern assailants, to be broken in four months. At this point we reach the Frankish descent upon Italy; the Donation of Pepin; and the establishment of St. Peter as a secular prince.

Southern chroniclers are never to be trusted when they speak of their foes. Violent terms, scarlet adjectives, which the facts will not warrant, appear to them as lawful in war as any other weapons. That the Lombards despised the Romans and called them liars and poltroons, full of lust and greed, we know from Liutprand. And that the Romans, though too probably the offspring of slaves or fugitives from every province of the Empire, scorned these tall, fair-faced men of the North as barbarians, is manifest in every line which Gregory the Great and succeeding Popes have left us concerning them. Had the Lombards told their own story, it would doubtless be still more evident than it is now that the quarrel which brought Pepin over Mont Cenis was on behalf of the Roman Republic, to which the Pope served as a figure-head, and that it did not originate in the high region of doctrine or discipline.

Astolf demanded once and again that the Imperial City should submit, pay a yearly poll tax of a golden crown, and leave him in possession of all he had seized in Central Italy. He could not win the city, but he dug up and carried away the bodies of certain Saints, to be laid in a shrine at Pavia. Some fruitless negotiations followed. The Pope sent urgent messages to the French King, and in return Chrodegang, Bishop of Metz, and the legendary Duke Autchaire or Ogier, were despatched as ambassadors to the Lateran. From Constantinople an injunction, which Stephen humbly accepted, bade him journey to the Lombard Court and there in person demand the restoration of Ravenna. With his Frankish protectors he set out, October 14, 753. The Imperial Legate was in his train. On arriving, despite Astolf's menaces, he spoke up boldly, offered gifts, and pleaded with tearful eloquence for the Greek Emperor's lost provinces. But his heart was with Rome, and only his words for the Exarchate. Astolf would yield nothing ; but he did his utmost to keep the Pontiff from prosecuting his expedition across the Alps. They separated ; the Byzantine Legate, with what nobles had accompanied him, went back to Rome, and disappears from history. Stephen and his clerks crossed the St. Bernard ; stayed a moment at the abbey of St. Maurice ; received a welcome from Prince Charles at Langres ; and on the Epiphany, January 6, 754, found themselves in the presence of Pepin at his rude Teutonic castle of Ponthion.

The King prostrated himself and held Stephen's bridle ; the Pope with his attendants, amid solemn chantings, knelt in sackcloth before this mighty protector, imploring his aid for St. Peter and the Roman Republic. Still the argument ran upon " restitution," but Pepin brushed it aside. He would neither defend the Eastern Emperor nor quarrel with him. He was all for peace and accommodation between the Lombards and St. Peter. So the winter passed. Stephen, in the monastery of St. Denis, sickened and recovered. Again he crowned the successful usurper, his wife, and his sons. From Monte Cassino an unexpected messenger had arrived to take part with Astolf—the royal monk, Carloman, Pepin's brother. It was a bootless errand. He could not be suffered to stand in the way of these great impending events; and in the seclusion of a religious cloister at Vienne he expired with almost dramatic propriety. After long debates, war was decided upon at Quercy-sur-Oise, in a popular assembly, or, as we should say, a Parliament, Easter 754. The passage of the Alps followed at once. Astolf was besieged in Pavia; without serious fighting he gave up his conquests, at least on paper; and the Franks went home. Stephen, distrustful but impotent, returned to his own place. His fears were well-founded. On New Year's Day, 756, the Lombard, with three divisions of a plundering army, was encamped round the Roman gates from the Salarian to San Pancrazio.

Fresh envoys from Stephen, at their head the martial Abbot Warneharius—a Frank who delighted in his armour and set the bad example of a fighting churchman, too frequent during the Middle Age—got clear of the Lombards, and crossing the sea reached Pepin. They bore three letters, couched in terms of deepest affliction; the third, addressed to king, nobles, and army, was written in the person of St. Peter, and already spoke of the *Gesta Dei per Francos* in terms which, if inspired, were flattering. Myth and history embraced; the battle was won. A second time Pepin descended with his warriors from the Cenis; once more Astolf yielded; the Greek Silentiary John begged for the lands, the cities which his master had not been able to conquer. He was answered with civil scorn. Devotion to the Apostle, and the hope of pardon for his sins, had been the motives which actuated the Frank who now, by right

of conquest, made over all his winnings to the Holy
See. Fulrad, another warlike Abbot, in command of
a small detachment, passed from town to town,
accompanied by the Lombard commissioners; he received their keys from a rejoicing people, and laid
them on the shrine of St. Peter along with the legal
document which conveyed them to their new lord.
This is Pepin's never-to-be-forgotten Donation.

Its text can no longer be found. But in Stephen's
Life, as told by the *Liber Pontificalis*, a catalogue of
the territories informs us that Comacchio and Ravenna
passed to the Pope with all the country between
Apennines and Adriatic, from Forlì in the north to
Jesi and Sinigaglia in the south—dead cities now,
not easily reached by the tourist, and with nothing
to show but antiquities. Ancona was not included
nor the rest of the March. Faenza, Imola, Bologna,
Ferrara lay outside the royal grant. Except Narni,
this so-called restitution comprised no more than
Astolf had taken—the Exarchate and Pentapolis in
their latest period. The Roman republicans still
wondered if they could get again what Liutprand
had borne away, and round off their possessions with
Bologna and Osimo.

Yes, it might be, when Astolf to their delight was
killed out hunting, and his brother Rachis, the monk
of Monte Cassino, called to succeed him, was opposed
by the Duke of Istria, Desiderius. Pope Stephen
sent Fulrad, the warlike Abbot, and his own brother,
whom we might describe as the Cardinal, Paul of Via
Lata, to this aspiring Duke. The Duke promised,
if he won the crown, to give back the remaining

cities, Ferrara, Ancona—whatever they demanded. Desiderius became king; Stephen wrote to Pepin with transports of joy; he was now, in a manner, lord paramount of Italy. Rachis, at the Pope's order, retired to his convent. But the crowned Lombard kept only half his promise, and fresh troubles came in sight.

At this stage a series of deplorable events in Rome, to be often repeated amid fury and bloodshed, must engage our unwilling attention. Stephen died in 757. He belonged, it would appear, to a noble rather than a clerical family—we will explain how much this meant in due course—and his brother Paul was elected, not without opposition from Theophylact, a name which recurs with tragic frequency in the Roman annals. Paul was severe: his exactions were large, his prisons crowded; and the Imperial Law, which he took over with his new dominion, inflicted death where Franks or Lombards would have allowed *wehrgelt*, or a fine. He began speedily to be detested as a tyrant; but his victims or enemies bided their time. No sooner was he elected than he wrote to Pepin, interposed between Desiderius and the rebel Dukes of Spoleto and Beneventum, sought for them (though they were clearly in the wrong) a French protectorate, and urged on the Lombard that he should fulfil his engagements. Pepin received these overtures with politic serenity. But he declined to cross the Alps any more. His envoys made peace on the principle, "Keep what you have got and be satisfied." Paul submitted, perhaps because the Greek Emperor was holding out a hand to France, where the veneration of images had never struck deep root. The French king steered a middle course ; he made Desiderius a sort of Vicar in Italy, left the religious question to the Pope, and kept the peace. We shall have occasion, not once or twice, to contrast the moderation of these French Constantines, when Roman affairs call them in, with the intense and blind fury which seems indigenous to the City on the Seven Hills. It was now to burst forth like a volcano, throwing up ashes and fire.

Paul was dying in 767 when Toto, Duke of Nepi, broke into the city with an armed band. He represented the nobles, who could not endure that a priest and his acolyths should rule over them. Toto would not have scrupled at murdering a Pope ; but Christopher, who had been Paul's Secretary of State, prevented this horrible sacrilege ; yet he could not hinder the monstrous Duke from seizing the Lateran (Paul had now expired) and proclaiming his brother Constantine Bishop of Rome. That the elect ruffian was a soldier and not a cleric; that George, Bishop of Palestrina, was compelled to ordain him on the spot; and that the Sunday afterwards he received episcopal consecration from this prelate and two others at St. Peter's shrine, throws a strange and far from heavenly light on the Roman world of the eighth century. Christopher still held out ; he was a captive, then he escaped—but not till a year had passed—to the Court of Pavia with his son Sergius, and came back, the Lombards helping him, on his errand of revenge. Toto was killed in the fight that ensued ; Constantine fell into the victor's hands. The atrocious Greek custom of blinding prisoners was now common, especially in Italian tumults. Constantine, his brother Passivus, and the Bishop Theodore had their eyes put out. But this was not until a fresh Pope, Stephen III., had been elected—a feeble, good man, who let Christopher execute judgment as he pleased. When no more victims were forthcoming, order reigned in the Lateran.

Pepin did not choose to acknowledge Constantine; and his sons, who succeeded him in 768, despatched no fewer than thirteen bishops to the Lateran Council, which was to cover up the irregularities committed by Stephen III. before and during his election. For he had earlier recognised Constantine as Pope. This unhappy creature, thrust on his knees in presence of the assembly, was reviled, beaten and flung out, and the acts of his Pontificate burnt. His ordinations were declared null and void—a fatal precedent which, one hundred years later, led up to the most ignominious of all the incidents that have darkened the history of the Popes. Stephen III., not relishing the species of tutelage in which he was held by Christopher, triumphant over the military faction, called in Desiderius, who came on pilgrimage—he was sincerely devout, though shifty—during the Lent of 771. A revolution was the consequence. Paul Afiarta, then celebrated, and a rival of the Secretary, served as a go-between to all the interests leagued against him. Stephen, a captive in the Lombard tents round St. Peter's, sent for Christopher and Sergius, to whom he had bound himself by solemn oaths; they came at his command; he celebrated

Mass in the Basilica, and at once entered Rome across the bridge with Desiderius, leaving these men to their fate. Gratiosus, the assassin of Toto, whom Christopher had raised to a dukedom, now turned traitor. From the Apostles' shrine the unhappy pair

POPE HADRIAN I.   A.D. 772.

were dragged out at nightfall by Afiarta and led to the bridge of St. Angelo. There, by a just but fearful judgment, father and son were blinded. As they had done to Constantine, so was it done to them. Christopher died three days afterwards; Sergius lived a year in the great prison of the Lateran. He was

drawn thence by Afiarta not many days before
Stephen's death, half strangled, and buried alive
under an arch in the Via Merulana. Stephen lay
helpless in the hands of Desiderius, who could, and
did, threaten him with the consequences of these
murders if he made appeal to the Kings of France.
In 772 the Pope went to his account, and Hadrian,
the future friend and counsellor of Charlemagne,
ascended the Apostolic Chair.

VI

CHARLEMAGNE, PATRICIAN OF ROME

(772–800)

ON an average, the duration of a Papal reign is less
than eight years. Hadrian I. ruled for twenty-three
(772–795). He stands out thus between Silvester in
the fourth century and Pius VI., who closed the
eighteenth, by his near approach to "the years of
Peter." Learned, as the age reckoned learning; of
illustrious descent; of pious and edifying morals; he
satisfied the military by his pedigree, and the clergy
by his devotion to their cause. Under Afiarta, the
Lombard interest had governed Rome by proscrip-
tions, exile, and murder. Young Carloman, the
French senior king, meditated vengeance on the
assassins of Christopher and Sergius; his brother,
Charlemagne that was to be, had married, or, at
least, had taken to himself, after divorcing a previous
wife, Desiderata, daughter of the Lombard chief.
But in a year the lady was sent home; Hildegard,
of a great Suabian family, took her place. Carloman

died, and his children were set aside in favour of their ambitious uncle in an assemby near Laon. Their mother, Gerberga, took the children and fled with them to the Court of Desiderius, who now staked all on a decisive throw. He lost, and his kingdom came to an end.

Before Gerberga's arrival, he had despatched an embassy to Hadrian, who replied by sending to him Paul Afiarta, as an easy means of getting him away from the city. Scarcely was the Chamberlain gone, when rumour announced that the Lombards had seized Faenza and Ferrara; that they were moving against Ravenna; and that Desiderius would insist on the coronation of the exiled French infants by Hadrian. Into this scheme Afiarta flung himself heart and soul. He boasted that, willing or unwilling, the Roman Pontiff should meet the King's wishes. But the Pope knew his man. A judicial inquiry was opened at Rome touching the circumstances under which Sergius had been half-strangled and buried alive. The guilt of Afiarta came to light. His accomplices died in prison or were exiled to Constantinople. The grand culprit, arrested by Hadrian's orders in Ravenna, confessed his crime, and before the Pope could deliver him out of his enemy's keeping, was put to death by the Archbishop and the Consular as a friend to the Lombards. Thus broke up in tempest the unnatural peace between Rome and Pavia. We seem to discern in Afiarta the strong man of action, unscrupulous and bloody, but a Roman patriot, whose alliance with the Italians of the North meant death to the foreign invader.

By his Dukes of Spoleto and Beneventum, the Lombard still wasted St. Peter's patrimony with fire and sword. Hadrian sent to Charlemagne at Thionville (now Diedenhofen, since 1871), and his appeal, which might have been unheeded, was enforced by Desiderius, who marched on Rome with Carloman's children in his train. At Viterbo he was met by three Bishops, charged to warn him off under the menace of anathema. It was an ominous expression, employed for the first time in a dispute concerning the Temporal Power. But for the moment it had an effect. The King returned to Pavia. Some idle negotiations led on to the expedition which, about Midsummer, 773, came down by the valley of Aosta and Mont Cenis, under Charles and his uncle Bernard. The passes were betrayed to them by old Italic natives who bore no goodwill to their Lombard chieftains. Adelchis, the Prince Royal, gained some advantages, but famine dispersed his troops ; he was compelled to take refuge in Verona with Duke Ogier and Carloman's children ; the road lay open to Pavia. Both the King and his son stood out manfully behind their thick walls. No resistance was made elsewhere. Spoleto, tired of its dukes, declared itself subject to the Holy See. Ancona, Fermo, and other cities followed its example. Hadrian was lord of Central Italy before Charles could grant it away to him.

Verona fell, and Adelchis fled to the Greeks. Pavia would not surrender. In the meanwhile, Charles came on pilgrimage to Rome and was received (Easter, 774) with the honours formerly given to the Exarch. At St. Peter's, Hadrian waited at the head of the great staircase to welcome his protector. Charles—a notable sight—ascended it on his knees, kissing the steps, as is customary still when pilgrims go up the Scala Santa. The Pope embraced him ; they entered the Basilica hand in hand ; the solemn chants resounded, and the ceremonies of Holy Week began.

On Wednesday after Easter (April 6, 774) was held the memorable meeting in St. Peter's which sealed this transaction, the birthday, in no questionable sense, of our modern Europe. Hadrian exhibited a document, drawn up, it was said, at Quercy-sur-Oise in 754, which, under the name and signature of Pepin and his two sons, made a present to the Pope not only of the Exarchate much enlarged, but of Spoleto, Beneventum, Tuscany, Corsica, Venetia, and Istria. In accordance with this more than royal donation, we are told, Charles had a new formula composed, copied, and solemnly ratified. One document was put into Hadrian's keeping ; another was left with St. Peter in his shrine. Then the French King went back to besiege Pavia. It unclosed its gates. Desiderius with his Queen Ansa retired from the world ; and at Corbey the last of the Lombards lived and died a monk, with the reputation of saintly virtues.

So extensive a donation as this of Quercy, though acknowledged by Charles in public assembly, takes away our breath. It was never fulfilled ; we ask whether it was really proposed. Did we possess the original diploma, we might judge for ourselves. But that parchment has long since disappeared ; and when we reflect on the manipulation of ancient deeds which

INTERIOR OF SANT' APOLLINARE IN CLASSE, RAVENNA. (*Sixth Century.*)

93

the legal conscience of those times indulged in and thought no crime, we can hardly take on trust a supposed engagement which would have made the Pope nothing less than King of Italy.

In any case, all that Charles yielded to Hadrian at this time were certain cities in Emilia; but even upon these Leo, the Archbishop of Ravenna, laid violent hands. He did so in the name of his Saint, the martyr Apollinaris. Ravenna claimed its share of the Lombard spoil. Its first Bishop, the story said, was a disciple of St. Peter; he could not be overlooked in the distribution of that Apostle's patrimony which was going forward. The late vassals of the Exarch were restive under what they called the Roman yoke. Neither in spirituals nor in temporals did they welcome it. Their Archbishop aimed at independence, like the prelates of Milan, Aquileia, and Grado, who had never been content to bow down before the Pope as Metropolitan or Patriarch of the West. Bishop Sergius in 756 had interpreted Pepin's donation as a gift of the Exarchate and Pentapolis to St. Peter at Ravenna. But Stephen III. had called him to Rome; kept him there until he submitted; and sent him back as his own Vicar. When Sergius died, Michael the Scriniarius was made bishop, despite the Pope's remonstrances, and held the See during a year. Then Leo came in, and his prompt execution of Afiarta shows what manner of man he was. While seizing the booty left after Desiderius had abdicated, he seems never to have lost credit with Charlemagne; it is possible that his death in 778 relieved Hadrian of an adversary whom he could not despise. Ravenna maintained its pretensions. Italy, like the ancient Greek world, was fated to be the battle-ground of civic strife, every little town against its neighbour, a prey to foreign foes because of its internecine and incurable factions.

Upon Ravenna and the adjacent territory Hadrian could now recover his purchase. He was continually adding parts of the old Sabine country, of Campagna and Capua, to his jurisdiction as a temporal prince. The Pope was henceforth to be a lord over many. He numbered his feudal retainers, who did him suit and service. He held a brilliant Court. He made generous donations to churches, charities, and especially to the city of Rome, which Hadrian restored and beautified. His kinsmen were to share in these unexpected honours. Paschalis and Campulus were nephews of the Pope. It is the first occasion on which we hear that word, destined to play a part as disedifying as momentous in Papal history. They became Primicerius and Sacellarius, heads of the Chancery and the Finances. There were always two sides, seldom if ever in agreement, of the Roman administration. On the Palatine resided the lay officials, who kept up the fiction dear to that proud people of a Republic, free and sovereign over Italian cities. At the Lateran dwelt their master, when he was not their slave or their victim, the Pontifex Maximus, with his twenty-five Cardinal priests and his seven Deacons, to whom we must add the seven suburban Bishops. The Papal Palace had its chamberlains, esquires, masters of ceremonies; it was already displaying the forms of Byzantine homage, the prostrations, enthronements, and studied acclamations which are yet observed in the Roman Court. An officer predestined to greatness was the Archdeacon, first of the seven Cardinal Deacons. In the Chancery writers were trained; a Latin style not altogether barbarous was preserved amid the frightful grammar and inflated diction of the period; and notaries superintended the archives, issued new documents, and edited old ones; nor was the library quite forgotten.

But the entire government devolved on the Pope, who, imitating the policy of Augustus, took no fresh title, and whose wisdom it was to veil the transition from serfdom to independence under well-worn phrases. Hence a confusion of terms, rights, laws, privileges, exemptions, and contradictory claims, which no acuteness of jurist or historian has ever been able to clear up. What were the limits of jurisdiction for the Pope, the Patrician, the People? Seek them in the direct power, the indirect influence that each was able to exert; when the waves mounted, the sands were covered; as ebb-tide came after flood, again the sands stretched out unbroken. Living forces, often conquered, yet in their essence unconquerable, struggled, and to this day are struggling, each for supremacy; but the Constitution, the Magna Charta, which would reconcile them, has not yet been written.

Only this we may affirm. Pope and aristocracy were opposed from the beginning. It was not on purely religious grounds that the Pontiff held or added to his temporal dominion, for how could religion be affected by his rule over Capua, Ferrara, and cities across the Apennines? Nor did the nobles, as a class, look up to him with reverence, or at any time take into account his relations to the Church at large. In their eyes he appeared like any other feudal sovereign, whom they would resist, dethrone, murder without scruple—it was the fortune of war—unless he were willing to purchase a doubtful immunity by leaving the government at their disposal, and sharing with them tax and tribute from the subject people. That divinity which, as we view the Pope's origin and venerable claims, should have hedged him above all men against sacrilege, never once hindered the Romans from proceeding to extremities with their ruler, alive and dead. In a ferocious time, they yielded nothing in barbaric violence to Franks or Easterns, and their outlook on the world was bounded by the walls of their blood-stained city. These factions, which often converted the Lateran or St. Peter's into a Colosseum where wild beasts tore one another, had sprung up long ago in the days of Pope Symmachus (501), and were to break out again after Hadrian's decease. Elected from a noble house, he satisfied the Roman "army" for a while; but did he satisfy the clergy? We may conjecture from the sequel that a sullen discontent brooded on their wrongs and waited for the day of reaction.

Outside Rome it was not likely that the princes and potentates overthrown by Charlemagne would keep still. Hildebrand of Spoleto, Rotgard of Friuli, Arichis down at Beneventum, were all stirring.

Adelchis, now in the South, urged them on; Beneventum was to inherit the fallen dignity of Exarch.
In 776 Charlemagne appeared on the plains of
Lombardy; he slew Rotgard in the first encounter,
and went back to his German wars. But he turned
a deaf ear when Hadrian spoke of the magnificent
promises made at Quercy and St. Peter's, which were
not yet fulfilled. When he came to Rome the
second time, in 780, a still more imposing Lombard
league demanded his attention. Arichis, the Bene-
ventine Exarch, son-in-law of Desiderius, and the
Patrician of Sicily, were laying waste Campania.
Much was attempted, little achieved, by the restless
Greeks. But, in the sequel, Hadrian gave up Terra-
cina; Grimbald contrived to secure the independence
of Beneventum; and the Holy See bartered its
claims on Spoleto and Tuscany for the tribute which
these Dukedoms had paid into the treasury of Pavia.
To make it quite clear that the Donation of Charlemagne would not be exceeded, his sons Pepin and
Louis were crowned Kings of Italy and Aquitaine.
Under a new form the Lombard monarchy was
revived. Nevertheless, at his third visit, in 787,
Charles gave his "friend and brother," for whom he
entertained a sincere affection, Viterbo, Orvieto, and
some other prizes in Roman Tuscany.

The sum appears to be this. Pope Hadrian
obtained for the Duchy (not the Province) of Rome
those limits which it preserved during the entire
Middle Age and almost down to 1870. He was
master of the Exarchate, Pentapolis, and the inter-
vening territories as far as Perugia; but Spoleto

remained independent. From Charlemagne he had gained the Northern provinces and those on the Eastern slope of the Apennines. But in Rome and Perugia his dominion, never precisely determined, was a substitute for that of the Greek Emperors, cast off by the people because of their image-breaking heresy. Towards the South, as Byzantium lost, the Pope won ; we shall see him putting forth claims by little and little to Naples, to Sicily, and to all the Italian islands. By way of recompense for this " pact of love and loyalty " on his part, Charles is made Patrician of the Romans. He was to mount higher yet, but not in the lifetime of Hadrian, who died on December 26, 795. The same day Leo III. was elected.

VII

THE HOLY ROMAN EMPIRE

(800–814)

SUCH headlong haste, which in later times was forbidden by regulations touching the obsequies of a Pope and the choice of his successor, must have been due to the still smouldering feud between clergy and army. Leo's election is described as unanimous; events showed by and by that it was not grateful to Hadrian's nephews, put down now from their high offices of dignity and emolument. At once Leo sent to Charlemagne, Patrician and Consul, the certificate of his election, with St. Peter's keys and the Roman standard—formalities hitherto not observed—which allowed or invited the Frankish ruler's interposition as a judge of appeal, were the electors disposed to make one. A legate even was asked for who might receive the popular oath of allegiance to Charles. Angilbert, a French Abbot, was sent, but no allegiance sworn. In the Lateran palace Leo built a triclinium, or dining hall, which he adorned with mosaics; Christ

giving the keys to Silvester, the labarum to Constantine ; St. Peter bestowing on Leo the pallium, and on Charlemagne the royal banner. Rome had two sovereigns, it would appear. But the Romans obeyed neither, except when they had no choice.

Arn, Archbishop of Salzburg, wrote to Alcuin in 798 from the city that discord was busy and the conduct of Leo himself not altogether apostolic. Paschalis and Campulus spread these reports or took advantage of them ; a conspiracy was formed, and on St. George's Day, 799, as the Pope rode out in procession, these discontented churchmen saw their chance. At San Silvestro he was pulled off his horse by a troop of armed men. Hadrian's Cardinal-nephews flung themselves upon him bodily ; they did their best to tear out his tongue and his eyes ; but not succeeding, dragged him into the church, beat him till he fainted, and left him for dead in front of the altar. Night came, and he was thrust into a cell at Sant' Erasmo on the Cælian. His assailants, no doubt, supposed that if he escaped death, a blind and dumb Pope could not be allowed to govern Christendom.

But Leo, as by miracle, recovered. The French legate, Wirundus, and the Duke of Spoleto, helped him to flee out of the city. Charlemagne commanded his presence at Paderborn, gave him a splendid greeting, and sent him back with a troop of German Counts and Bishops. His return was a triumph ; the insurrection went out in smoke ; yet charges had been made and must be met if the Pope's good name were not to be lost for ever.

In his own painted triclinium Leo confronted the Frankish judges ; Paschalis and Campulus were handed over to the royal power ; but, manifestly, until Charles himself appeared on the scene no conclusion would be reached.   He came once more to Rome.   On December 1, 800, before clergy and laity in St. Peter's, the cause was opened by their secular sovereign.   Yet who would accuse ?   And how was the Supreme Pontiff to be judged ?   He consented to purge himself by oath in another assembly on December 23—a humiliating and dangerous example, in which the majesty of the name of Leo underwent eclipse.

Two days later Christmas brought the people together again.   Mass had been chanted, and the King lay prostrate before St. Peter's shrine, when, at a given signal, the Pope, his suppliant of yesterday, took a diadem from the altar and set it on his brows, the choir breaking forth in acclamation : " To Charles the Augustus, crowned by God, great and pacific Emperor of the Romans, long life and victory !" His "lauds" followed, as in the triumphs of old ; he was already anointed, but on the head of his youthful son and namesake the holy oil was now poured ; the Empire of the West had come to life in a Frankish chieftain, after an abeyance of three hundred and twenty-four years.

Not the same as that which Augustus bequeathed to his successors.   For the first time a Pope had crowned an Emperor, on his knees before St. Peter's Confession.   This was the everlasting mosaic which all through the Middle Ages kings and nations saw

EQUESTRIAN STATUE OF THE EMPEROR CHARLEMAGNE IN THE
VESTIBULE OF ST. PETER'S.   (*Cornacchini.*)

above their heads when they looked up to Rome, the Capital of Christendom.   In their mystic view, which deepened as years went on, no man could be God's lieutenant over the people unless crowned and anointed like Solomon by the priests in the sanctuary. Who was equal in exploits or renown to Charles the Great? Yet he it was, and not another, that had received the insignia of royalty from a Pope in the attitude of feudal obeisance.   An age that delighted in symbols, that could not read, and therefore attached to visible ceremonies an importance we scarcely comprehend, gave to this Christmas pageant the value of those hieratic and wonder-working pictures in which its religion found so vivid an expression.   The new Roman Empire was, from its birth, a Theocracy.

But the Emperor could not be, as in Pagan days, Pontifex Maximus, and this distinction of persons should have warned Pope Leo that a Charter, or Concordat, was necessary to prevent misunderstandings.   None had been devised ; the act of Christmas, 800, has all the air of an impromptu suddenly got up and carried into effect as if to atone for the humiliation of two days previously.   A candid no less than ingenious writer, Duchesne, has reminded us that the False Donation of Constantine, dating from 774, alluded to by Hadrian, and probably the work of Lateran scribes, must needs represent the idea then favoured at Rome of an Imperial but absentee protector. The first Christian Emperor, said this lawyer's romance. had surrendered to Pope Silvester "all the provinces, places, and cities of Italy or the regions of the West." Could not, then, Leo yield on his own terms such powers as he might choose to a vicar in temporals, who would draw his sword always on the Pontiff's behalf, never against him ? Justinian's *Pandects* were forgotten in these barbaric Occidental nations ; and though Charlemagne legislated for many peoples, he could scarcely write his name ; he was no student of law-books, and had only monks for jurists. His actions demonstrate how little he was disposed to be merely a Papal legate on the throne. Yet even an Emperor must reckon with captains who would not always obey, and with a clergy to whom the Donation of Constantine speedily became a corner-stone of history and jurisprudence. Latin Christendom had assumed the form of a Teutonic Empire.

Natural, inevitable, under the conditions of the ninth century, this bold idea, however imperfectly realised, was alone capable of hindering a return to the tribal chaos out of which order had been slowly emerging. It enabled the Pope to act on all ranks and dignities throughout the West, as a spiritual teacher indeed, but with a two-edged sword at his command. It gave to the nations who have established their laws and carried their civilisation over all continents an outward and visible unity. When Byzantium turned more and more towards the rising sun, or shrank within the walls of Valens, it created an independent, homogeneous Europe, one amid all its dissensions, arrayed in a feudal, an ecclesiastical hierarchy, at the summit of which sat enthroned the Pope and the Emperor, fountains of law, justice and religion. In the august Œcumenical Councils at the Lateran, on the banks of the Rhone, or in the city of Constance, a Parliament of the peoples met: there was felt and acknowledged the claim of brotherhood among Christians, so far as an age of embittered and ignorant controversy could imagine it. The Popes, by their restoration of the Empire, but with the cross above its crown, were doing for our Western world that which Mohammed and his Caliphs attempted to do for the Arabs, Persians, Egyptians, and Moors. Nor is it possible to conceive that Europe would have held its own against the Moslem onset—which, had it been victorious, must have put an end to the Christian Church and what was left of the Roman inheritance—did not this mighty spiritual force, embodied in the successor of St. Peter, consecrate the Teuton, Norman, English, and Flemish sword, rouse up host after host of princes to a distant Crusade, and meet the fanaticism of Islam with an enthusiasm derived from Charlemagne and his paladins, the champions of Christendom.

It is time that we viewed more closely this extraordinary man, great in his achievements, his conquests, his laws and schools, his devotion to religious aims, weak only in his passions. The Charlemagne of legend and song is a prodigy, equal to Alexander. In the *Chansons de geste*, he is everywhere present, the King "à la barbe florie," whom that sweeping and stately verse appears to confound with Charles Martel, nay, even with Charles the Bald, ascribing to him all the victories, voyages, intrigues, events of the court, the field, the camp, which send him now to conquer Jerusalem, and now to perish with all his chivalry at Roncesvalles or Fontarabia.

The splendid "matter of France" had this Charles
for its hero, whom it handled with a lad's bold and
careless freedom, sometimes carrying him on uplifted
shield, anon plucking at his plenteous beard in the
mood of satire. Chief in a republic of princes, the
King must be as ready to strike as unscrupulous in
watch and ward against treason; he is a man of
blood and fire. But he has likewise a loud, eloquent
tongue, and the heart, or call it the sentimental and
amorous temper, of the troubadour, with a veneration
unbounded, yet hardly in our sense religious, for the
" Apostle of Rome."

Whatever date we assign to this epic poetry, the
figure thus drawn is not unlike Charles as history
paints him. Frank and Gascon by descent, akin to
priests on every side, prompt and far marching as
Julius Cæsar, with a touch (and more) of the native
subtlety masked by courage in arms which has ever
characterised the Gallo-French; an admirer of old
Teutonic ballads, yet willing to overlook treason in
Paulus Diaconus because he wrote an elegant
Latin; the Emperor added to these qualities an
imposing presence and stature, which the *Chansons*
exaggerate beyond human proportions. To them
he is a giant in size and in prowess—the defender
of the Cross, the enemy of the Saracens, who cannot
bear up against his onslaught. Allowing for perspective, the picture is grandly and not falsely
conceived. Charlemagne inherited from his ancestor,
Martel, the renown of the victory of Poitiers. In
establishing the Papacy at Rome on a basis of
temporal power, while he assimilated the Church

more than Dante would have approved to a feudal
or secular hierarchy, his acceptance of the Empire
was a step towards the making of Europe. Across
the Rhine he fought and subdued in thirty-three
campaigns another enemy, stubborn as the sons of
the Desert, and resolute in their hatred to the Latin
civilisation, the Frankish more settled life, the
religion which cursed their gods as devils, which cut
down their sacred oaks, and which burnt their forest
sanctuaries. The Saracens whom Charles overcame
were the Saxons. He did not win great victories,
but he harried and drove these heathen from his own
frontiers at Worms to the Lippe, the Weser, the
Elbe, the Baltic. Like Mohammed, he preached with
an army at his back. Death or baptism was the
choice offered, and to give it emphasis, in one batch
the Emperor massacred four thousand five hundred
Saxons at Verdun on the Aller.

Violence marked his conquests ; but the missionaries
who followed him were heralds of peace ; after
repeated efforts at independence Witikind descended
into the waters of baptism ; his barbarians submitted
to the clergy and paid them tithes, which was all that
the Frankish victor asked of them. As long as they
would be Christians, the Saxons might be compara-
tively free. From 787 onwards we trace the founding
of the eight chief Bishoprics—" religious colonies "
they have been rightly termed—Minden, Seligenstadt,
Verdun, Bremen, Münster, Hildesheim, Osnaburg,
Paderborn. There was a German Church, complete
in its appointments, richly endowed, and entitled to
the homage as well as the protection of the newly-

converted nobles, long before the German State could be said to exist. When we arrive at the period of Anti-popes and Anti-emperors, of Bishop-Electors arrayed against lay Dukes in the Diets of the Fatherland, it will not be unseasonable to remind ourselves that Mayence, Cologne, and Münster claimed precedence by their origin as much as by their ecclesiastical dignity of the great secular lords.

This twofold Hierarchy, of which Rome in Pope and Emperor set the example, arose over Western Europe under Charles's fostering legislation. Every district had its Bishop and its Count; a county was a Diocese, just as in England the ancient bishoprics were conterminous with the little kingdoms of the Heptarchy. At the base a widespread, almost universal serfdom; above that, qualified military charges, rank over rank, ascending to the Markgrave, Count, or Duke, who held of the King. To this pattern the Church conformed. Even a monastery must be a feudal tenure, and Bishops, though in vague and disputable fashion, held of the Metropolitan, who would fain have had no master. The False Decretals taught him that he must suffer appeals from his judgment to the Apostolic See—as indeed true examples dating far back were there to show. But, looking at this early medieval government as a whole, we may pronounce it to have been a confederation of freebooters with some semblance of law—a caste which disdained to till the soil, which would have thought commerce a degradation, and which lived and died with arms in its hands.

From such an aristocracy the Bishops were

taken as a matter of course; plebeian prelates, if by some happy chance elected, found themselves in society as uncongenial as that of an English mess to an officer raised from the ranks. Some Bishoprics, like Clermont, Metz, and it would appear Milan, ran in families. Royal blood had a claim on wealthy benefices, and thus what the Sovereign gave with one hand he took away with the other. Medieval Theocracy too often meant a Knight in armour who was consecrated Bishop that he might enjoy the revenues, and command the thousands of serfs, attached to a Saint's inheritance. The Abbot raised his troop of horsemen and rode at their head ; the Bishop received a training for the field, but little or none for the altar. When Europe was one vast camp—which is a true description of it during the centuries before Venice, Pisa, Genoa, and the Hanse Towns achieved commercial greatness—Ecclesiastics were military chaplains, inured to battle and bloodshed, who, even if they escaped and set up their abode in the wilderness, saw their Cluny, their Clairvaux, too soon endowed with lands, tenants, and public offerings, the price of which was always absorption in the feudal State.

Among barbarians, the tribe had claimed the man, but land was a fleeting possession. Now, every individual was *adscriptus glebae* ; the Church, tenant-in-chief of a third, a half, or two-thirds, of the whole country, had become a feud ; its Gospel character was strangely disguised in a parti-coloured garment, stained not unfrequently with sanguine hues. Its enormous and ever-growing wealth tempted Kings not so much to plunder as to appropriate these treasures, by the hands of their children, legitimate or bastard, and to trade in the selection of the unfittest to stalls, canonries, abbacies, mitres ; until the world rang with a sinister cry of " Simon Magus," the detestable and ubiquitous Heresiarch, who bought or sold for money the gifts of the Spirit in every Church throughout the West.

When he had overthrown the Saxons, Charles found fresh enemies behind them, the Wiltzi or Slavs on the Oder. From these he took hostages, and marched on the Huns, encamped in their wooden huts amid swamps, but gorged with the spoils of Constantinople. They underwent defeat at the Raab; it seemed that a Frankish Emperor would emulate the feats of Trajan, extend his dominion to the Danube, and appear as the neighbour no less than the rival or suitor of Irene, soon to be Empress of the East. He was recalled by troubles in Aquitaine, whither Hixem, the Moorish Caliph, had penetrated, and by a revolt of the Saxons. But his son, traversing the Theiss, defeated the Huns a second time, captured their ring, or stronghold, and sent home an incalculable booty. The Tartar Chagan professed himself a Christian ; his power was annihilated.

At Aix-la-Chapelle it might have been imagined that Rome in all its majesty was about to begin a second Augustan age. Vassal or suppliant Kings, Egbert of Wessex, Erdulf of Northumbria, Lope Duke of Biscay, flocked to the Imperial Court. Clement and Mailros, Irish Scots, came with the reputation of philosophers, and opened schools for the children of the nobles. Albinus, an Englishman, better known as Alcuin, the disciple of Bede, received from Charles the Abbey of St. Martin at Tours, and became first rector of the Studium, which grew by and by into the University of Paris. An all-embracing system of laws, the Capitularia, dealt with every class of the Emperor's subjects. It fixed the revenues, and insisted on the duties of clerics ; required an oath of fealty at their hands ; and commanded their appearance as feudatories at the Sovereign's muster, called Heerban. It might even, in a more settled age, have fulfilled the task which so perplexed his descendants, of coping with the Roman, Ripuarian, Lombard, Bavarian, Salic, and Canon Laws, under which his subjects were liable to every kind of conflicting obligation and justice bowed to the sword of the stronger.

But active and incessant as might be Charlemagne's efforts to create order in a chaotic world, his enactments fail in the large wisdom, they never display that mastery of principles, which the ancient legislation of Rome bequeathed for later times to apply or interpret. His advisers, who were Churchmen, gave to their own Canons an exorbitant place in his collection. But neither they with their tradition, nor the Emperor with his genius, could arrest on the downward slope a society which was too little versed in things of the mind to found a genuine civilisation, too far removed from the spirit of Christian freedom and equality not to have transformed it into a real and scarcely disguised system of caste, where industry ministered to pride, war was the only honourable profession, and not even monastic solitudes could follow after peace or ensue it.

On Charles's death, an Empire which had no inherent principle of life or unity, fell to pieces. The century and a half succeeding were one long interregnum; the Emperors move by like figures in a pageant; the sole reality was a feudalism which held its chief a prisoner, or which dethroned and murdered him, while fresh barbarian races came, saw, and conquered, to fall in their turn under the Church's influence. In 810, the victorious but fatigued Charlemagne was told that a fleet of Northmen had touched the coast of Friesland. With his own eyes he saw their light barks on the Ocean in a city of Narbonnese Gaul. "They are not merchants, but pirates!" he exclaimed to those around him. "I weep over the harm they will do to my sons and my people." Godfried, who happened then to be leader of the Northmen, had allotted to himself the German Empire. His kinsfolk were more ambitious; they became the masters of East and West.

VIII

CHAOS COME AGAIN

(814–867)

NOT unlike Augustus in his length of reign, extensive dominions, and combination of violence and cruelty with a charm which passed for good nature, Charlemagne resembled him also in the irregularity of his lusts, and the calamities which fell upon his immediate descendants. Pepin, his eldest and favourite son, died before him. With the consent of clergy and nobles, he named as his successor Louis, Prince of Aquitaine, whom we remember by his pretty old French title of the Débonnaire. But, as Michelet rightly observes, we should rather call him Saint Louis. The youth, bred up among priests, had learned piety, justice, tenderness, from their teaching rather than their example. Alone of the Emperor's sons he survived. That strong woman, Hermengard, the Empress, thought to govern him; as did afterwards his young second wife, Judith, mother of Charles, surnamed in his time the Bald. Yet, in the beginning, he acted on his own ideal principles ; he reformed the scandals of the Court ; he forbade his prelates to wear spurs and ride like cavaliers to battle ; he sent back into their cloister the intriguing Adelhard and Wala, royal monks, who had counselled Charles, not wisely, in his old age ; and he dreamt even of restoring the Benedictine Order to its former greatness, by the severe rule which Benedict of Aniane drew up. In his youth he had taken Barcelona from the Saracens. His heart yearned over the miseries of the serfs whom he tried to relieve. To the Saxons he gave back their right of inheritance. He would not, as his father did without scruple, appoint Bishops on his own authority; and in the Papal election he declined to interfere. Such was the man, simple, serious, chaste and merciful, whose virtues ruined the Empire, and whose multiplied humiliations have cast a shadow upon all, whether Bishops or Princes, that brought down his grey hairs to the dust.

He began his unhappy reign in 814. Two years later, Leo III. passed away. His end was not peace. Soon after Charles's death, a conspiracy of the familiar Roman type had broken out ; the conspirators were seized, a large company, and executed under the ancient Imperial law of treason. Louis, on hearing the tragic event, was shocked. His milder law had been disregarded, himself not consulted. Bernard, his nephew, the young King of Italy, was charged to intervene at Rome. He did so; Leo sent an embassy which apologized to the French Court. But rebellion on one side, evictions in Campagna on the other, and the need of fresh reinforcements from Bernard, testified that discontent was rife. Leo died, neither loved nor popular. A protégé of Hadrian's, noble, and of accommodating temper, was chosen, Stephen IV. He exacted an oath to the Emperor from the Romans, travelled into France, crowned Louis at Rheims with a consecrated golden circlet, took back the exiles, and died on his return, in 817. The same day Paschal I. succeeded to a thorny inheritance. He was destined to disgrace and the hatred of his turbulent people.

Meanwhile, the long threatened storm was bearing down on Louis. With his own hand he crowned Lothair, his eldest and most vigorous son, at Aix, in 817. It was the signal for Italy to rise. Bernard had never acquiesced in his uncle's succession; he reckoned now on the Bishops and cities of the Peninsula to support him against the Transalpine barbarians. But the enterprise came to naught: he was captured, saved from death by the Emperor, blinded by Heimengard, and expired soon after. This crime weighed heavy upon Louis. Yet he put down the Slavs and Basques who had revolted; he invaded Brittany; he beat the Danes, gave Hamburg its first Bishop, St. Anschar, and sent another to Sweden. All this could not turn his mind from its remorseful thoughts. He insisted, like another but willing Theodosius, on undergoing a public penance; he was scourged before the altar; and his feudal lords seized the occasion to revolt from an Emperor so feeble. The movement was headed by his three sons, who shut him up in a cloister. Then his people at Nimeguen restored Louis, and Lothair, with the leaders of the revolt, was in his power. Louis forgave them (830).

Paschal, it is said, like the Bishops of Milan and Cremona, had favoured Bernard's stroke for Italian independence. In 823, when Lothair was in Rome,

CHURCH OF SANT' AGNESE OUTSIDE ROME, A.D. 625.

he crowned the young Emperor, whose hand the Popes were to feel more than they liked in the sequel. Obscure causes led almost immediately to the blinding and murder of two high Roman officials—Theodore the Primicerius and Leo the Nomenclator—an act charged upon Paschal by his enemies, from the guilt of which he purged himself by oath before the

Imperial Commissioners. But he added that these traitors deserved to die. When his own turn came, in February, 824, the people, who hated him, would not suffer the Pope to be interred in St. Peter's.

A contested election followed. Two candidates were proclaimed ; but, thanks to Wala, the French monk and politician, Eugenius II. won the day ; and Lothair now intervened to some purpose. He issued his famous diploma (824), with its five articles, which guaranteed all persons who were under the Emperor's protection — thus defeating the sanguinary law of *lèse-majesté*, under which so many horrors had been perpetrated. The Romans could henceforth choose to be tried by Lombard or Salic law. Again, their magistrates, though not appointed by the Emperor, must present themselves to him on being nominated. Two Missi, or Residents, one Imperial, the other Papal, always at Rome, are to report on the administration annually, to hear plaints, and to notify miscarriages of justice. And the election of the Pope is to be in the hands, not only of the clergy, as decided in 769, but of the laity as well ; the elect, before his consecration, will take an oath in set terms and in presence of the Residents. It was a victory for the nobles, otherwise called the Roman People. Still more did this Constitution, as acted upon, enhance the suzerainty (no other word will express it) which the Emperor was now to exercise over the Holy See in its temporal concerns. When the next Pontiff succeeded in 827, the nobles insisted on their rights, and chose Gregory IV.

It was an age of impotent kings, national dissensions, and haughty, but far from enterprising nobles, when whatever courage or learning was left had taken refuge in the Church. Louis acts like a monastic saint; his kinsman, Wala, whom he had exiled from the Court to his cloister and imprisoned in the Castle of Chillon, is a politician, all-powerful with Lothair and now the adviser of Gregory. This Pope, therefore, followed the Italian King when he rebelled once more against his father. Judith, famous for her beauty, but more than suspected of infidelity to her husband, was always bent on securing to the infant Charles that Empire which, as an aged man, he obtained during a few troublous years. His step-brothers reckoned him the adulterous offspring of Bernard the Aquitanian; they would share among themselves the dominions of Charlemagne; and, in 833, Pope Gregory entered the Imperial camp at Worms as a mediator, but left it only when Louis had been betrayed. Judith, a captive in Lothair's hands, went her way to the Castle of Tortona; Charles, too young for vows, was imprisoned in a German abbey. This tragic intervention of the Pope and clergy was long known as the "Field of Lies," equal in disgrace to the still more famous "Day of Dupes." Gregory went back to Rome, and that is the last we know of him.

But Louis, in the Church of St. Médard at Soissons, was compelled to utter a confession in which he took on himself the guilt of this long civil war. Stripped of crown and armour, clad in a lugubrious garment, he acknowledged his sins, and submitted his conduct to Ebbo, Archbishop of Rheims, whom he had raised

from a servile estate, and to Agobard of Lyons, the
apologist of his sons, the accuser of his wife. This
penance, which the Bishops inflicted on a meek if
incapable Prince, called forth a speedy reaction,
especially among the Germans and the lower people.
Lothair's chief partisans died ; a crowded assembly
at Metz annulled the Diet of Compiègne ; and
Agobard was deposed, with some other great prelates.
New treaties and more partitions filled the remaining
years of Louis with sorrow ; they were death-tokens
upon an Empire now breaking up irrevocably. In
840 he died himself; in 843 the agreement of Verdun
divided France from Germany for ever.

The documents which attest this memorable event
were drawn up in both languages. Charles signed as
King of the French, Louis as King of the Germans.
Lothair was Emperor, holding a middle and transient
domain which extended from the Meuse to the
Mediterranean ; but his Imperial dignity seems to
have depended on his possession of Rome and Italy.
All three were weak and failing powers. Northmen
laid waste their maritime cities, burnt their abbeys,
and sailed up their rivers, with a gay insolence which
sang of war as a summer pastime. Saracens or
Moors, above all the Aglabites from Kairouan
(Cyrene), infested the seas, attacked Sardinia ; in 831
they laid hands on Palermo ; Sicily was almost
colonised by these Africans. Yet in 840, two miserable pretenders to the Duchy of Beneventum called
them in as allies, and the Peninsula lay open before
them. On August 23, 846, they landed at the mouth
of the Tiber. Ostia was abandoned ; the children of

Ishmael came up to Rome, occupied and profaned St. Peter's, devastated St. Paul's, and went off with their booty. Some indecisive battles appear to have taken place, and the story ran that a tempest, overtaking these miscreants on the shores of Africa, had buried their sacrilegious spoils beneath the waves.

Though Europe lay under a cloud of ignorance and imbecility, an outrage so deplorable stirred the public conscience to its depths. People charged Lothair the Emperor with criminal negligence; the Pope, they said, was a simoniac. Sergius II., elected in 844 without consulting the Franks, had raised his brother Benedict to the See of Albano and suffered him to buy and sell in the courts of the temple. Even the monasteries were spoiled by this Mayor of the Palace, who contrived to get into his hands the civil no less than the ecclesiastical authority. The shock was great. Lothair ordained a reformation of the clergy; despatched his son Louis with an army against the Saracens of Beneventum; and levied a collection for the building of walls and towers to defend St. Peter's. A fresh Pontiff, Leo IV., carried out this project in the still surviving Leonine City. Beneventum was conquered and divided. For the next twenty-five years, Louis II. is paramount in Italy (850–875). He combats the Saracens in Calabria; attempts Bari, which they had made their place of arms; interferes between the Pope and his own Missi or legates, threatened with death by Leo IV.; and prepares the choice of a Pontiff less unfavourable to the Franks by naming as Legate Arsenius, Bishop of Orte, whose son was the learned but unstable

Cardinal of St. Marcellus, the secretary or librarian Anastasius.

This young man, it seemed likely, would occupy the Papal Chair as an Imperialist when Leo passed from it. On grounds which we cannot ascertain,—but the Iron Age possessed no historians and has left only meagre chronicles and a few scanty, not to say, partial documents,—he had been excommunicated and was living in exile. The year 855 saw a new election; Benedict III. became Pope; but he was not the French candidate. Anastasius returns with the Emperor's legates, is master of the city and the Pontiff. The Roman clergy hold out; a compromise, a second election, the degradation of Anastasius to lay or monastic rank as Abbot of St. Mary across the Tiber, carry us on to 858, when Louis could appoint a man of his choice. It was the Deacon Nicholas, who shares with Leo and Gregory in the Roman line, and not without reason, the epithet of Great.

His reign, which lasted only nine years (858–867), was marked for remembrance among the obscure Popes of this period by three momentous and critical transactions,—the deposition of Photius, intruded Patriarch of Constantinople; the attempted but unsuccessful divorce of Lothair II., King of Lorraine, from Theutberga; and the putting down of quasi-independent prelates, who aimed at something like a national Church, whether in Ravenna or in Rhineland, but whose efforts and defeat have attained undying celebrity through the False Decretals. Each of these chapters fulfils the condition of a great and tragic history. The Greeks, hitherto on strained but not schismatical terms with Rome, now stereotype as differences of dogma what had been thus far regarded as variations in discipline. Christendom is rent in two not long after the Empire of Charlemagne falls to pieces. On the other hand, the Popes reserving to themselves the matrimonial causes of Kings, ascend a tribunal from which they depose sovereigns and give away sceptres. By a simultaneous stroke, the Church, instead of breaking up, as Charles's monarchy had broken, into petty and opposed principalities, is centralised in the West. A supreme Court of Appeal is set up in the sight of mankind, its charter the Bible, its weapons spiritual, but entailing penalties in this world. For deposition, interdict, excommunication greater or less, carry in their train forfeiture of dignity, goods, or life, and the Holy See can reckon on sentiments which become the foundations of order, in the State as in the Church.

Whenever, as now, the Pope seemed a man of genius and character, his great office made him supreme over all causes; the higher the ground he took the more implicitly was he obeyed. Though Nicholas had an Emperor at his doors, he upheld the independence of the Holy See in language not to be surpassed by Hildebrand. He began with the Archbishop of Ravenna, who was vexing in his neighbourhood certain Papal subjects. Summoned to Rome, protected by Louis II., and disregarding the mandate, he fell under excommunication in a Lateran Synod (the Pope in Council), which went on to forbid the intermeddling of strangers in elections to the Chair of Peter. At last the Archbishop came with Imperial legates,—but too late. Nicholas, during a journey northwards acted like a sovereign in Ravenna. Louis gave up his man ; a forced but absolute submission was the consequence ; and the city of the Exarch was once more humbled before Eternal Rome.

But Nicholas bore on his shoulders a double burden, under which it may be said that he sank, though victorious. The King of Lorraine, brother to Louis, had repudiated on a monstrous charge his innocent wife Theutberga. And at Constantinople Cæsar Bardas, after a similar act, was living in open shame with his son's widow. The prelates of Rhineland, including Treves and Cologne, had not scrupled to bless Lothair's wickedness in solemn Synod ; his concubine Waldrada was enjoying the honours of a Queen. More melancholy still, an accomplished, eloquent, and not unamiable scholar, the layman Photius, had suffered himself to be caught up in a scheme of revenge, devised against the lawful Patriarch by Bardas ; in six days he had been carried through all the degrees of the priesthood, and was now seated upon a usurped throne. Ignatius, the deprived and persecuted Bishop—a Saint in the eyes of his own generation—who had rebuked the Cæsar and brought these evils on his head, was a prisoner in Mitylene. And Photius, by the hands of four prelates, sent to Nicholas a letter which did not tell the truth, and which sought recognition for himself from the Apostolic See.

But in Rome the facts were suspected ; these Bishops returned with a cautious answer in which the Pope demanded a free Council, the unforced resignation of the canonical Patriarch, and the restitution of ancient rights over Illyricum, Epirus, and Thessaly. For bringing a message so insolent, the Emperor—that is to say, Bardas—threatened the Roman legates with violence; and they yielded to menaces or bribery. A Council was held; the legates suppressed what their master had written; Ignatius, tortured or under fierce compulsion, was made to sign (if he did sign) a blank paper, which his enemies filled up with a confession of guilt and a formal resignation. The judgment of this Court assembly Photius then despatched to the Holy See, with a letter of his own in which there is some beautiful but hollow writing. But Nicholas disowned his legates, refused to acknowledge the layman, and called on the other Eastern Bishops to execute his decrees. Early next year (863) Ignatius found means to acquaint him with what had really taken place, and with his own sufferings. The cup was full, it was running over. Sentence of excommunication was launched against Photius and Gregory of Syracuse, who had consecrated him. His acts, his ordinations, were pronounced null and void. Those who would not recognise the true Bishop were threatened with the woes of Judas and Canaan. All this Nicholas put forth in St. Peter's name, and from it no appeal was lawful.

A violent interchange of threats and anathemas filled the ensuing years. Photius kept his See, charmed the multitude, convoked a Council in 867, and secured nearly a thousand signatures to the

manifesto in which he upbraided Rome with apostasy
from primitive faith and usage.   Bardas had come to

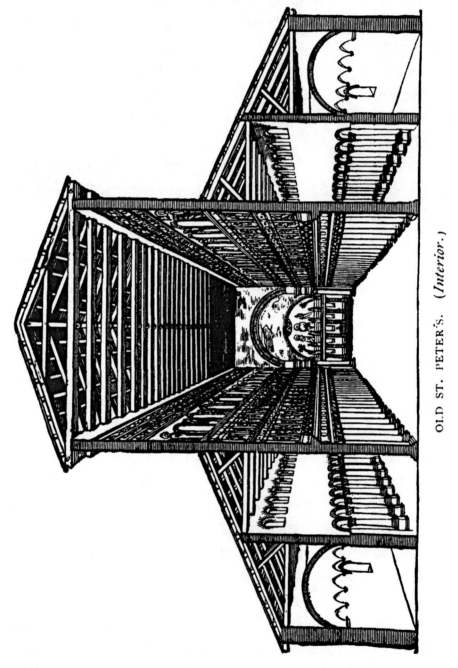

OLD ST. PETER'S.   *(Interior.)*

a bad end ; Michael the Drunkard still protected the
intruder.   But scarcely was the meeting dissolved

when a revolution in the palace led to Michael's assassination, and his murderer, Basil the Macedonian, deposed Photius, who had formerly crowned him as co-regent, and now perhaps would not condone his regicide. Ignatius was restored, and began a fresh reign of ten years.

By this time Nicholas was dead. The Eighth General Council, as it is reckoned in the Western Church, was celebrated in 869 under Hadrian II. Though Photius had been degraded in a tempest of obloquy, it does not appear that any one proposed to take his life. A student, he might have been happy in his exile could he have carried his books with him. On the death of Ignatius, he persuaded Basil to receive him into favour once more ; and in 879 he mounted the shaking throne of Sancta Sophia, with the consent of that fiery Pontiff, John VIII. Again expelled by Leo the Philosopher, tried for high treason and acquitted, he withdrew into solitude and ended the schism of thirty years by his death,—perhaps in 891. To scholars and critics he has left in his *Myriobiblion* a feast of learning, which testifies to his insatiable and omnivorous appetite. To the divided Churches of East and West his more dangerous legacy has been the Eight Articles which, on grounds too frivolous for a smile, too trivial for refutation, have set Latins and Greeks in everlasting schism. Doubtless, the one sufficient article, not named among these, was the Papal Supremacy which Constantinople never would admit, except when the enemy was at her gates.

Photius, Hincmar of Rheims, and Nicholas I., all three contemporaries, light up the dull anarchy of their age by learning, force of character, and some of those qualities which entitle men to rank in universal history. Had they been united, France, Rome, and Constantinople might have offered a far-shining and formidable front to the Mohammedan, who was exacting tribute from Italians and Greeks; the Norsemen would have been subdued by a civilised world at peace within its borders; and centuries of confusion need not have vexed mankind.

But the ambition of a literary and not over-scrupulous Byzantine led Photius to scorn and reject the Roman Church. Nicholas would never consent to abandon his claims on the ecclesiastical provinces of Bulgaria and Western Greece. Hincmar, who ruled the French King, behaved towards Pope and people, towards his suffragans and Charles the Bald himself, with the insolence of a high-bred noble who held the crozier in his left, but was ready to strike with the sword in his right. Pretensions, real or fictitious, were bolstered up with forgeries. None of the scribes could be trusted not to interpolate or mishandle official letters; laws were invented as well as evaded; violence was the order of the day. Yet this perpetual turbulence did not imply strength of head or of arm. Invading Danes or Norsemen found the cities defenceless, the country open. Islam, which in our eighth and ninth centuries rose to splendour, and could boast of its art, science, literature, philosophy, and chivalrous manners, had lost in vigour what it gained in luxurious refinement. But it was yet able to put armies of Christians to flight. Like a crimson cloud it hung over Bosporus and Tiber simultaneously. Nothing save its internal divisions, the weakness of the Caliphate, and the sudden ascent of the Turks to greatness, while these had their eyes turned in the direction of India rather than Europe, prevented the conquest of Christendom in the years before us.

IX

FEUDAL HIERARCHY—FALSE DECRETALS

(847–882)

IT has been observed that the French Kings by their matrimonial disorders gave the Popes an authority in the Gallican Church and realm which might otherwise have been difficult to maintain. With them this was the standing quarrel, as with German princes the investiture and feudalising of clerics. Lothair, who had inherited the middle kingdom of Lorraine from his father and namesake, married Theutberga, daughter of Boso, Duke of Burgundy. But there was an Anne Boleyn, named Waldrada, whom he desired to raise to the throne. Horrible and false accusations were made against Theutberga ; she was cleared by the ordeal of boiling water to which her champion submitted. Nevertheless, driven wild by persecution, the unhappy lady acknowledged crimes that she had never fallen into ; and in three synods at Aix-la-Chapelle, the cowardly Bishops, including Treves, Cologne, and

Metz, annulled the marriage and proclaimed the concubine their lawful Queen.

Hincmar of Rheims, a learned and masterful prelate, was disposed to take advantage of Lothair, whose dominions Charles the Bald coveted, as in the sequel he annexed them. The Archbishop had been watching this bad business. He drew to it the attention of Pope Nicholas, who, in a reply addressed to him, quashed the proceedings at Aix, ratified the marriage with Theutberga, rebuked the King in scathing terms, and deposed Günther of Cologne as well as Theotgand of Treves, the leading sycophants. These Bishops, after corrupting his legate, had been foolhardy enough to appear in Rome before the Pope. They even brought down on him Louis II., whose mixed and lawless soldiery entered the city, scattered a procession of clergy and people, and threatened the Pontiff himself (863). Nicholas crossed the Tiber from the Aventine in a boat, and spent two days and nights at St. Peter's shrine. The Emperor fell ill. There was always something fatal in the Roman air to these Northern princes. Terrified and ashamed he made peace by abandoning the two Bishops, who fled home in disgrace, but pretended to excommunicate the Pope, and would not resign. Then Lothair deserted Günther, professed repentance, and would come as a pilgrim *ad limina*. The Pope scorned his pilgrimage. He ordered him to take back his wife. He sent Arsenius, who had long administered the Roman Chancery—an able but covetous man—to keep the peace between these Carlovingian phantoms, to restore Rothrad, Bishop of Soissons, over the head of Hincmar, who had deprived him, and to see Theut-berga crowned.   His victory was complete ; historians agree that it was well merited.

Not that Lothair yielded once and for all.   He could not give up Waldrada.   But judgment was awaiting him at Rome when he should finally appear in his pilgrim's garb under Hadrian II.   Meanwhile, as the Chronicler says, Nicholas " tamed kings and tyrants, and ruled the world like a sovereign."   When he dealt so inexorably with the Archbishops of Treves and Cologne, putting them out of place by his simple decree—not remitting them to the sentence of their brother Bishops—he was acting a part which, even more than his language to the miserable Prince of Lorraine, implied œcumenical power from which none were exempt.   We have come to the False Decretals.

It is a singular story of fraud and Nemesis. Bishops who had been transformed into Barons, and had themselves divided the Empire at Verdun; who by the Capitularia of Epernay shared the civil jurisdiction equally with Counts ; who elected, tried, and deposed Kings; were now arrogating an independence such as the Polish nobility claimed and exercised down to 1772.   Charles the Bald was their humble client. Hincmar writes to Louis III., " I and my colleagues with the rest of the faithful have chosen you to govern the kingdom, on condition that you keep the laws."   Charles, on the ground that he was anointed by Wenilon, Bishop of Orleans, pleads that to depose him without trial by the Bishops, who are " thrones of the Divinity," would be a sin.   Contrast the language of Henry VIII. to Cranmer when giving him leave to proceed in his great matter of the divorce: "Albeit, we being your King and Sovereign, do recognise no superior on earth but only God, and (are) not subject to the laws of any earthly creature." The real King was at Rheims, where Hincmar raised troops against the Normans, and held Parliaments attended by the spiritual and temporal lords. Except where a Bishop controlled the city, little or no order was observed. Even the Abbot, says Chateaubriand, was merely the old Roman patrician, with his vassals, farmers, villas, towns, and territories, and an enormous income. Louis le Débonnaire had raised plebeians to sacred heights, but the affront was bitterly resented; an aristocracy of birth did in fact rule in Church and State.

These overweening prelates, rich and often dissolute, ambitious, hard, quarrelsome, could not brook the judgment of Metropolitans who, no better than they in morals and not more than their equals in blood, were ready to depose their suffragans, to sequestrate properties, to intrude favourites in the episcopal seats. From this peril deliverance must be found, and obviously appeal to a supreme yet distant Court was the way of escape. Rome might curb the Metropolitans; and a strict or almost impossible form of procedure, sanctioned under the Apostolic name, derived from primitive ages, would shield the Bishops when accused by their subjects of rapine or violence. To manipulate ancient writings, to edit history in one's own favour, did not appear criminal if the end in view were otherwise just and good. It is admitted on all hands that the famous Charter of Clovis, renewed by Dagobert, which bestowed on the Church of Rheims possessions in Champagne, Austrasia, Burgundy, Auvergne, Touraine, Poitou, and Marseilles, cannot have been genuine. The larger Donation of Pepin exhibited to Charlemagne by Hadrian I. is open to serious doubts. We might continue the list. Now, at the Synod of Quercy (857), a whole volume is suddenly produced which, under the venerated name of Isidore, Canonist and Bishop of Seville, claims a place in the Church's legislation, and while defending the hierarchy against every attack from below, leaves it in the Pope's unquestioned and unlimited jurisdiction.

It is what Milman calls it, "an elaborate and most audacious fraud." Dionysius had collected the Pope's Decretals, which began, as we have seen, with Siricius to the Archbishop of Tarragona (385). Sixty new epistles, from Clement to Melchiades, and the Donation of Constantine, now are published as authentic in addition. The old Isidorian collection included the Councils from Silvester onwards ; thirty-five false decrees, and the acts of spurious synods, were introduced by the unknown forger. Who was he ? Experts and critics are divided on the question.

Not a Roman, certainly. Perhaps we should distinguish a shorter and a longer form of the fiction, which cannot have been devised in a day. The Church of Mayence, Otgar its Archbishop who died in 847, and his Deacon Benedictus Levita, have been singled out as the place, the patron, the instrument by earlier writers ; their connection with the imposture seems undeniable. When many of the higher clergy stood between Louis le Débonnaire and his rebel sons, it is thought that Ebbo, the confederate of these, and Otgar, might have invented Decretals which would shield them from the Emperor's vengeance by cutting the ground from under his jurisdiction and that of his Metropolitans. On the other hand, West-Frankish or Neustrian elements are discerned in them ; and Hincmar began by accepting the collection as genuine. Spanish it was not, nor Roman, nor yet Italian. And with its manufacture the Popes had nothing whatever to do.

The compiler's aim was, first, to set up an entire spiritual immunity ; no secular power should call a Council or condemn a Bishop without the Pope's consent. Lay courts were not to adjudicate upon ecclesiastical causes ; nor might laymen appear as accusers or witnesses against the clergy. But from secular tribunals to spiritual there was always the right of appeal. No Bishop was to be tried by the Metropolitan alone. He must be cited before a Provincial Synod, summoned at the instance of the Apostolic See. When thus on trial, the only witnesses allowable against him are his peers, of whom seventy-two are the lowest number whose testimony can be received. From this office the law excludes not only laymen but priests ; and the culprit is free to appeal to Rome, enjoying meanwhile, though deprived by conciliar sentence, his property and privileges. Between the Pope as Supreme appellant Judge, and the Bishops as his " men " in a strict feudal signification, the ancient rights of synods, Metropolitans, clergy, and laity were, by this reading of Church history, swept into oblivion.

By those who would apologize for Benedict the Levite (if such was the forger's name), it has been pointed out that he did not ascribe to the Holy See rights which were without example. Of the Decretals a considerable number are authentic, though antedated ; others embody the contents of lost documents.   Julius I. (342) had protested against holding Councils where the Pope was not invited ; he called it an unheard-of thing.   To this Pontiff the greatest of Eastern Saints and Patriarchs, Athanasius, had appealed from local synods.   Chrysostom had been protected by Pope Innocent ; and at Chalcedon Dioscorus was deposed on the ground that he convoked and held an assembly of Bishops against the Papal ordinance.   St. Leo had deprived the Metropolitan of Arles, and rearranged his province.   With Milman these apologists might observe that " the new code was enshrined in a framework of deeply religious thought and language " ; that " the whole is composed with an air of profound piety and reverence ; a specious purity, and occasional beauty, in the moral and religious tone " ; and that " there are many axioms of seemingly sincere and vital religion."   In this key wrote the pious Möhler, who bids us make allowance for a child-like age, not precise or literal, which did no more than magnify an idea of the Papacy that could still be derived, though these false documents were not extant, from what is legible in Fathers and Councils

But a forgery they were; and Hincmar, who relied upon their authority in his Synod of Rheims, could not demur to it,—though he roundly called it a trap for Bishops,—when Nicholas turned it against him, received the appeal of his suffragan, Rothrad, and restored him as above described. Could, then, the Lateran Chancery bear witness to this grand array of Apostolic letters and legislation? That has never been pretended. The insignificance of the Papal archives we learn beyond dispute from Gregory the Great. What were the sources to which False Isidore betook himself? It is conjectured that the work has been pieced out in mosaic fashion from Rufinus, Cassiodorus, the West Gothic *Breviary* of Alaric, the *Liber Pontificalis*, and other materials, wrought up into a definite pattern. Yet Nicholas and those who came after him cited the spurious Decretals no less freely than the genuine. They made their way into the official collections; they became a part of Gratian's *Decretum*, and were embodied in the Canon Law under Gregory IX. At the Renaissance, Nicholas of Cusa suspected them; the centuriators of Magdeburg, De Moulin, and Blondel convicted them of falsehood. They are now universally given up. But with the Donation of Constantine they formed a juridical romance which in the Middle Ages took the place of law and history.

Hadrian II., who came after Nicholas (867–872), was a man of venerable age, austere morals, and the highest Papal doctrine. Before taking orders, he had been married. His wife was living, probably in a convent; his daughter seemed now, though not in her first youth, a tempting match to the Romans, who were beginning to court the alliance of the Lateran. For there was always a strong Church interest, and these elections betray signs of clanship among the chosen.   Arsenius, the greedy legate and Home Secretary, had two sons; one, Anastasius, whom we have known as a defeated candidate for the tiara, and the other Eleutherius, not in holy orders.   The lady in question was betrothed to some one else when Eleutherius, in the violent Roman fashion, carried her off with her mother and compelled her to marry him.   Hereupon, Arsenius fled with all his treasure to the Emperor Louis.   Hadrian demanded back his wife and daughter; Eleutherius murdered them both.   He was caught and executed; his rapacious father died suddenly.   Anastasius fell under Hadrian's wrath, but perhaps could vindicate his innocence, and died in power.

Soon after these tragedies, Lothair II. came to Rome as a pilgrim.   He was ill received.   But at length Hadrian consented to his reconciliation, and under the most fearful warnings, administered communion to him and his attendants.   They took the pledges required.   Within a month the perjured King died at Piacenza of the plague; the others, it is said, did not outlive that year.   Charles the Bald seized Lorraine which, by all rights, belonged to the Emperor Louis; and Hadrian, in language as haughty as Nicholas had ever used, maintained the Frankish-Italian claims.   He threatened the nobles and bishops of France and Rhineland; nor shrank from holding the sword of interdict (a word hitherto

not pronounced on kingdoms) over Charles's head.
There was one man who could have secured the
triumph of Hadrian and Louis—the Archbishop
Hincmar. But Hincmar came boldly forward with a
Gallican demand that the Pope should not meddle
in State affairs. He refused to leave Charles's Court;
nor, he said, should the Franks of Austrasia be slaves,
encumbered with an absentee King unable to defend
them from the Pagans. Charles and Louis the
German shared the spoil of Lorraine between them.
Louis the Italian had none of it.

By way of retaliation, the Pope supported against
Charles his youngest son Carloman, who had been
monk, abbot, highway robber, and in open warfare
with him, but who appealed to Rome from his
deserved chastisement. The Bishops, in spite of
Hadrian, proceeded to degrade him. Hincmar of
Laon, whom his uncle at Rheims had advanced,
would not sign the document. He, too, was a contumacious cleric. The great man at Rheims had
many quarrels with him; so had the King. The
climax was reached when young Hincmar, to protect
himself, laid under interdict his own diocese. His
uncle, the Metropolitan, took off what the Ordinary
had laid on; the Ordinary quoted False Isidore;
defied Hincmar of Rheims and three provincial
Councils; and asserted the immediate unqualified
jurisdiction of the Pope. Hadrian summoned him
to Rome. But conceive the situation of the
other Hincmar. He now fenced with the False
Decretals, and argued that the Holy See was used
to pass laws only by conciliar authority; that it

ought to respect the Canons (as Bossuet spoke long afterwards) and not to rely upon compilations or forgeries. In a vehement letter drawn up by the Primate of Rheims, Charles was made to affirm that the King of France is no vicegerent of Bishops but lord over his own land. He quoted none save the genuine Decretals. Hadrian lost the battle. Carloman was tried, condemned, deprived of eyesight ; his accomplice, Hincmar of Laon, suffered the same fate. But the Decretals of Benedict Levita had acquired fresh force. Meanwhile, Rome and Italy were plunging into a mad confusion which would spread its waves over the next two hundred years.

John VIII., a Roman (872–882), has been described with some truth as a lofty spirit ; but he was born out of due time. The Italian Louis II. died without children (875). By right of birth, Louis the German should have succeeded. But neither the Pope nor his subjects desired to see the wild Teutons in Rome. Then and always what they preferred was a French Emperor as the head of Latin civilisation. " France," says Muratori, "has been the refuge of persecuted Popes." The German language, customs, harshness, perhaps honesty, did not win the Southern heart. Now, accordingly, John held out a sign to Charles the Bald, who came in haste, and at Christmas, seventy-five years after Charlemagne, was crowned in St. Peter's. " We have elected and confirmed, with the consent of our brothers the Bishops, the Ministers of the Roman Church, the Senate and People of Rome, King Charles as Emperor of the West,"—such was the Papal intimation, not welcome in France, as substituting an absolute for a limited monarchy; nor to the Bavarian Counts and Bishops, who held that Louis the German could not thus be put on one side. It mattered little. In two years both competitors were gone. Charles the Bald expired in an Alpine village. Carloman of Bavaria marched down into Italy. His ally or lieutenant, Lambert Duke of Spoleto, seized the Leonine City; threw the Pope into prison; and exacted from the Romans an oath to the Teuton. But he could not hold this dangerous Capital, in which every house had become a fortress. When Lambert retreated, John VIII., after paying a round sum to the Hagarenes or Saracens to keep them away from St. Peter's, fled to Genoa, to Arles, and to Troyes.

Every town in Southern Italy at this time was menaced by the infidels, or had entered into alliance with them, except Bari and Tarentum, now held by the Greeks. Naples, under its Duke or Bishop, admitted a Moslem garrison. Gaeta did the same. Marauding bands infested Campania. Pope John, in 874, had fitted out a fleet on the Tiber with Greek sailors; he engaged the Saracens, captured eighteen of their vessels, and released six hundred Christian slaves. He built likewise an enclosure round St. Paul's; obtained some advantages at Amalfi and Salerno; but could not break the alliance between Naples and the pirates of the South.

His flight to Louis the Stammerer did not mend matters. The Church was in dire need of a strong secular arm, but where to find one? Charles the Great was perishing in his imbecile descendants.

Their names, which historians feel bound to recite,
had better be forgotten. In 884 the mighty house
was represented in France by an infant, Charles
the Simple; across the Rhine by Charles the Fat;
—these nicknames well denote the contempt into
which royalty had fallen. At Ravenna, in 880, the

SANT' APOLLINARE, RAVENNA. (*Exterior.*)

German was accepted as Emperor by John VIII.,
and for a short three years seemed master of the
Western Empire. Then he was flung aside. The
Pope went back to Rome, after launching in his
ten years' reign some three hundred letters of
anathema, and attempting to depose the sovereign
Archbishops of Milan, Ravenna, and Naples. He

had acknowledged Photius; confirmed the Council of Constantinople; and driven from the Lateran Formosus, Bishop of Porto, with his adherents. But enemies were never wanting to John VIII. If we may believe the *Annals* of Fulda, the conspirators belonged to his own household. They endeavoured to poison him; this not succeeding, one of them beat out his brains with a hammer. Many Popes had suffered martyrdom; of John VIII. it is customary to say that he was the first assassinated (December 15, 882). Unhappily he was not the last. From this hour we shall see the Papacy going down as into the Valley of the Shadow of Death, to ascend by miracle from its deeps, and exercise a yet wider dominion, when the worst had been endured.

X

THE HOUSE OF THEOPHYLACT

(882–964)

UNTIL Otho the Great appeared in Rome (961) it is impossible to deal with the Empire as any longer a reality ; and the Papal succession bears almost as ghostly an appearance. "Come like shadows, so depart," is the summons at which these spectres, often dabbled in blood, pass over the stage in a lugubrious masque of anarchy. Yet the new world was slowly forming ; to the tenth or eleventh century we must ascribe that greatest of all transformations by which the Normans, Danes, Prussians, Hungarians, and Muscovites bowed their necks under the Christian yoke ; put from them a Paganism steeped in superstition and cruelty ; began their studies in the Gospel, which are not yet ended ; and chose Christ instead of Mohammed. This, so far as we can learn, was an apostolate never inter-rupted, though Popes, Bishops, and Kings fell into the wildest disorders. As a spiritual movement, it seemed to go on of itself, or in the words which we still read on the Arch of Constantine, *Instinctu Divinitatis;* Providence was its only guide.

But the Carlovingians had disappeared. In France, Odo, Count of Paris, descended from an obscure family in Anjou, which had been rallying the centre against the Normans, opened a succession of thirty-three Kings, and an era that lasted nine hundred years. Arnulf, the base-born son of Carloman, who actually closed the Carlovingian dynasty, received the Empire in 896, and fled from Italy fifteen days after, never to return. The Popes, such as they were, had now to deal with an Italian power at Spoleto; with another, more distant and less hostile, in Friuli; but above all, with a Roman aristocracy, the most unbridled that even those centuries knew. With Guy of Spoleto master in Milan, the Lombard kingdom had risen to life again. It was a line of Machiavellian princes, leagued by marriage with Tuscany or Beneventum; not shy of the Saracen alliance, much less of the Greek; calmly desecrating the churches in Rome; but affecting, when it suited them, the pious ways of Charlemagne, though prepared to dethrone the Pope as if their meanest vassal. Into such hands did the fall of the Empire commit the venerable Father of the Faithful. Almost every year beheld that ideal defaced and trampled on which, in *Titus Andronicus*, is so happily bodied forth as the Rome of devout imaginations :—

> " Suffer not dishonour to approach
> The Imperial seat, to virtue consecrate,
> To justice, continence, and nobility;
> But let desert in pure election shine,
> And, Romans, fight for freedom in your choice."

II

Two score years were taken up with the lamentable tragedy of Formosus, "the Pope Beautiful," who was persecuted living and dead ; and with the shameless records of Theodora and Marozia, in whose feminine usurpation of the Holy See Gibbon's fancy detected the origin of Pope Joan. Then comes young Alberic, Senator and perhaps Saint, a lay impropriator of the Papacy, under whose rule the Pontiffs are chaplains, and who might have founded a succession in St. Peter's Chair, could public opinion have looked with favour on a married clergy. But his foolish son, Octavian, who was Prince and Pope at sixteen, outraged every rule of his order, and when he called in the German King Otho, he was preparing his own act of deposition. The lay dynasty yielded, though sure to revolt again, before Northern good sense and simple piety. Such is the ignominious period we have now to sketch as rapidly as possible. Intrigue, unreason, violence, and murder furnish its dominant notes.

Formosus, if we may believe the scanty evidence, was of blameless and even austere character. As Bishop of Porto, his diocese was little more than a name ; but he had been consecrated, and Nicholas I. sent him as legate to the Bulgarian King. Boris, or Michael, was a convert to Christianity through his wife and the illustrious missionary Cyril, who evangelised the Slavs. He desired to see his Church independent, with an Archbishop at its head. He asked of the Pope to appoint Formosus, much loved of the Bulgarians. Hadrian II. refused on what seems to us the idle pretext—it proved a spark to set the world in a blaze—that Formosus was a Bishop already and could not be translated. This ancient rule, now set aside, was intended to curb the ambition of prelates, aspiring to rich or metropolitan Sees. Formosus came back, was a candidate in the election of 872, and was regarded by John VIII. with an evil eye. There is no proof that he favoured the German as against the French interest. But he belonged to an opposition which included Gregory the Nomenclator as well as other high persons, who fled from Rome lest a worse thing should happen to them, on the death of Louis II., their protector. John summoned them to no purpose; and all, including the Bishop of Porto, were excommunicated in a synod held at the Pantheon (875).

But when Marinus came to the throne in 882, he restored the exiles, and among them Formosus. The latter had sunk into lay communion. He was under an oath to Pope John that he never would reclaim his episcopal dignity. Marinus, however, absolved him from these engagements, as he surely could according to Canon Law. In 891, this much enduring prelate himself became Pope, not without tumult and popular acclamations. His immediate predecessor, Stephen V., had crowned Guy of Spoleto in this very year as Emperor, but under constraint. Formosus, in like extremity, crowned his son Lambert the next year. Meanwhile he implored Arnulf of Bavaria in private letters to come to the deliverance of the Holy See. Arnulf did come in 894; he was also crowned, and set out to besiege Lambert and his mother Agiltrude in their castle above Spoleto. A stroke of paralysis ruined all his plans. He was carried in a litter across the Alps; and Formosus died of grief and vexation in 896.

His death gave rise to the most astonishing disorders. Boniface VI., an excommunicate, and Stephen VI., already Bishop of Anagni, consecrated by Formosus, passed away before the year was out. Stephen, however, in his brief Pontificate, served as the instrument of the Italian faction and of Agiltrude, now in Rome, whose advisers must have been sufficiently at their ease in Canon Law to deduce a warrant from it for the dreadful scene that followed. On Arnulf had been poured by Formosus *unctio illa barbarica*, which robbed of Empire the Spoletan family. Though dead, he must be made to expiate his crime. A Council was held in St. John Lateran. Stephen VI.—himself a translated Bishop on whom Formosus had laid hands—ascended the judgment seat; and the corpse of the late Pontiff, dragged from its tomb in St. Peter's, was solemnly set up as prisoner at the bar before the assembled Fathers. Charged with violation of the Canons, it made no reply; neither did the deacon, assigned as counsel for the defence, dare to open his lips. Sentence of guilty was pronounced; the Roman ordinations of Formosus were annulled; his body was stripped of its vestments, down to the hair shirt which this austere man wore next to his skin. The corpse, thrust into a nameless tomb, was taken thence by the populace, who sided with their Italian masters against the German Arnulf, and flung into the Tiber. Some fishermen brought it to shore in their net, and after many wanderings it was at length laid to rest in the atrium from which it had been torn.

Within no long time, the Lateran Basilica, polluted by this horrid sacrilege, fell to the ground. Friends or partisans of Formosus, when Agiltrude had gone home, lay in wait for Stephen VI., caught and stripped him of his garments, and strangled him in prison, fifteen years after John VIII. had been murdered. We have no means of tracing in detail the next events. Romanus occupied the throne four months, Theodore twenty days. Then two Popes were elected—Sergius III. and John IX. Young Lambert declared for John; his rival escaped into Tuscany. The succession to the priesthood was in danger if ordinations could be annulled on grounds so precarious; and John held several large synods, attended from every part of Italy, in which Stephen's monstrous acts were done away. It was felt (and no wonder) that some public security should be taken against disorderly elections. Henceforth none were to be valid except in presence of the Imperial legates, as had been ordained by Lothair in 824. Lambert, who would have united the nation, died and left his kingdom at the mercy of Berengar, who in 898 occupied Pavia. Then John IX. quitted the scene. He was followed in four years by three Pontiffs, two of whom, Leo V. and Christopher, were murdered in their prison by the ever-memorable Sergius III. With him enters the house of Theophylact.

Sergius, like Stephen, had received the consecrating oil from the hands of Formosus; at whatever date elected by his faction to the Papacy, he was then Bishop of Cervetri in Etruria; and we run little risk of falsehood in describing him as "malignant, ferocious, and unclean." For seven years he had eaten the bread of exile at the Tuscan Court, where Marquis Adalbert II. the Rich, married to Lothair's illegitimate daughter Bertha, reigned as the ally or the enemy of Louis of Provence. With Tuscan soldiers the self-styled Pontiff returned in 904 to Rome, had his two predecessors murdered, and held out for another seven years. In Liutprand, Bishop of Cremona, he has found an inferior and possibly ill-natured Tacitus. But fragments remain from the lost documents of this dark age, that bear out his allegations touching the vices and servility of Sergius III.

Over the Papal treasury presided a "vestiarius," who in this period was Theophylact, Duke and Master of the Horse, sole Consul and Senator—in modern language, Prime Minister, as well as Commander-in-chief. His wife, Theodora, led Roman society, and their two daughters, Marozia and Theodora the younger, seem to have inherited the haughty licentious qualities which are so frequently observable in great Italian houses early and late. Theophylact held a charge over Ravenna, where his imperious wife attached to her party the Archbishop, afterwards John X. Thus it may be said that all the powers of Central Italy were combined, first, against intruders from the North like Berengar of Friuli, and second against that section among the Roman clerics who leaned to a German Emperor.

HOUSE OF THE VESTALS IN THE FORUM (ROME).

151

We now perceive what was likely to happen under such a Pontiff as the miscreant Sergius. Theodora ruled supreme. "She won the Roman princedom," says Liutprand between rage and admiration, "and like a man she wore it." Formosus had drawn upon him the wrath of Agiltrude; he did not escape that of Theodora, whose favourite Sergius, if the rule against translations of bishops were enforced, could never have been Pope. How to evade this law was the question. Casuistry of a scandalous sort had been invoked by Stephen VI., and was adopted by Sergius III. If when he consecrated them Formosus were not lawful Pontiff, they had never been true bishops; as unfledged ecclesiastics they might be promoted to the Supreme Chair. This reasoning will give us the measure of their genius and their probity. Again a Council; again degradations, anathemas, re-ordinations, the Hierarchy thrown into confusion, the Apostolic Succession threatened. Naples and Beneventum resisted; Auxilius and Eugenius Vulgarius (the latter less constantly) wrote in defence of Formosus. If Canon Law fell into contradiction or absurdity, what would be the fate of those high prelates who governed the West? No more shameful, no more perilous moment had occurred in the Latin Church, where heresies, seldom or never of an abstract kind, concerned themselves at once with action and led straight to secular divisions.

But Sergius held his ground. Rumour declared him the paramour of Marozia, though twice her age, and the father of John, afterwards Pope John XI.—a tale which Muratori challenges but the Papal catalogues accept. On his death in 911, Anastasius III. and Lando pass over the scene. If they belonged to the foreign faction their speedy removal would be explained. It is certain that John X., who came next and lasted fourteen years (914–928), endured or welcomed the patronage of this quasi-royal house. A translated Bishop by the grace of Theodora, he would not recognise the Formosan ordinations; the *Invectiva in Romam*, a manifesto from Naples, treats him as a usurper; but in any case John X. displayed remarkable though not priestly qualities. The Saracens, strong on the Garigliano, had spoiled and occupied the noble Abbey of Farfa in the Sabines. They put a zone of fire and pillage round the Apostles' tomb. Pope John called to his aid Berengar, whom he crowned Emperor in 915, and the Imperial vassals of Tuscany and Spoleto, commanded by Alberic Marquis of Camerino. A league was formed; the Pope marched with his captains, charged at their head (an exploit in which he glories), and himself or his generals beat the infidels at Baccano and Trevi. With certain Apostolic lands he bought off Naples and Gaeta from their unholy alliance. The Greeks joined in; a fleet was contributed from along the coast; battles ensued by sea and land under Theophylact, Alberic, the Lombard princes. In two months the last of the Saracens was killed or taken (August, 916). And Alberic received the hand of Marozia.

The world was changing again. Berengar had called in the savage Hungarians to help him in his

quarrels.   He was murdered in 924 at Verona.
Landing at Pisa, Hugh, King of Provence, accomplished, dissolute, but full of respect for the clergy,
hastened to Pavia, and found the Archbishop of
Milan and the Pope himself eager for his ad-
vancement to the Imperial throne.   The great
Vestiarius and his wife lay in their gilded tombs.
Marozia had lost her husband; but perhaps the
splendid widow, wealthy, popular, energetic, and
only thirty-four, was more powerful than in his
lifetime.   Hadrian's gigantic Mole, a miracle of
strength, formerly adorned with marble statues,
which the besieged garrison hurled on the head
of Vitiges and his soldiers, was now the Castle of
St. Angelo and the den or refuge of every Roman
tyrant.   This enterprising woman seized upon it, and
from the Emperor's tomb offered herself with her
treasures to Guy, Duke of Tuscany, son to Adalbert
the Rich and half-brother to Hugh of Provence.   If
John X. had been Theodora's *cavalier' servente* we
perceive that a family quarrel was at hand, its prize
Italy, the Popedom, the Empire.   To such base
uses may great things come!

John had a brother named Peter, Count of Orte
and his mainstay in the contest, a very unequal one,
which he attempted with Marozia.   But she, *for-
tissima Tyndaridarum*, an unconquered virago, was
a match for both of them.   Rebellion, at a sign from
her, invaded the Lateran; the brothers were seized,
Peter slain before the Pope's face, John flung into
a dungeon and smothered (928).   Europe and the
Papacy, it may not be unfairly observed, could have

bishops, down to the days of Gregory VII. Manasses, Archbishop of Arles, was a pluralist who bought or appropriated Trent, Verona, Mantua. Hugh's own base-born sons were bestowed at Piacenza, or thrust into the Sacred College. Abbey lands, nay, the abbeys themselves, went to Court favourites. The rank and file of the clergy no longer observed those Canons which forbade them to marry; the prelates were soldiers, sycophants, traitors by turns to Hugh and Berengar, keeping their wives in state, alienating Church property to their children. Actual robbers, as Waldo at Como, held the Sees of Christendom. And Manasses, who had won Trent from King Hugh, opened the passes of the Alps to his enemy, the German Otho.

In comparison with such unholy men of God, Alberic was a saint. But he had usurped the Patrimony of the Apostle, and retribution lay in wait for the crimes which have given his House a dreary fame in Roman annals. His son bore the name, almost the title, of Octavian. Might he one day be Augustus? The lad was hardly ten years of age, when Otho, like a sudden re-appearance of Charlemagne, glittered on the Alpine horizon, swooped down to Canossa, where Queen Adelaide was undergoing a siege from Berengar of Ivrea, and set the garrison free. It was a warning of change to all Italy. Alberic had his boy tonsured; the fatal instance of young Theophylact was there to urge him on ; gathering the Romans in St. Peter's, he made them swear that, on the death of Agapitus, they would choose Octavian. Perhaps the lay nobles did so

willingly; the clerics, held down for fifty years, cannot have ceased to whisper Otho's name. Alberic
was in the prime of life, but the Middle Ages
were times of scant vitality, when no one except
hermits in the wilderness came to three score and
ten. At forty the Patrician was dead (954); Agapitus
followed him in less than a twelvemonth. Octavian,
now John XII., at sixteen was Imperator, Consul,
Pontifex Maximus. In his scarlet mantle Elagabalus
occupied St. Peter's Chair.

A medieval Elagabalus, who donned his armour
against the Southern Lombards and was put to flight;
who hunted, drank, gambled, and converted the
Lateran into a *lupanar;* who sold abbeys and bishoprics, ordained lads for money, mutilated prelates,
and mingled jests and cruelty with his wanton
sacrileges. Several years passed before the monstrous
career of an ungovernable youth was interrupted.
Italian affairs had thrown up froth and confusion like
the sea. Otho ruled in Germany; Berengar of Ivrea
and his son Adalbert were detested, but still they could
deprive the Archbishop of Milan, and menace Pope
John. We do not know the particulars of an obscure
transaction; yet who can doubt that sooner or later
the German King would have taken on himself to
regulate the condition of Rome and Italy? John XII.
perhaps forestalled his indignant subjects. He and
the deposed Bishops, with many Princes, entreated
the royal aid. In 961 Otho received the Iron Crown
at Pavia. Next February (962) saw him in St.
Peter's; "by his valour," says Otho of Freising, "he
had translated the Roman Empire to the Eastern

Franks." They were to hold it, under many vicissitudes, for eight hundred and forty-four years, down to 1806. Otho was the first, as he was among the greatest, of German Kaisers.

John XII. anointed him, and the Emperor swore to protect the Roman Church, give back her possessions, and make no change in her government without the Pope's leave. The people and their Pontiff then took the oath of allegiance to him. On the body of St. Peter they swore to abandon all connection with Berengar and his son. When Otho retired, the mad young man entered into immediate correspondence with Adalbert, who fled soon after to the Saracens, and then took refuge in Rome. Otho left the siege of Monte Leone where Berengar was straitly shut up, marched to the city, and was told that Pope and King, despairing of support, had taken to the open country. A Council was at once called. The charges at which we have hinted were brought against the absent Pontiff. Liutprand of Cremona, in the Emperor's name (Otho could not speak Latin) warned the Bishops that clear proofs must be forthcoming. John was summoned, an Imperial safe-conduct offered him. The youth replied in a crude Latin message that provoked shame and laughter when it was read out, " We hear that you mean to elect a new Pope. If you do, in the name of Almighty God I excommunicate you, and forbid you to ordain or say Mass." Instead of coming to the Council, he went out shooting at Tivoli.

What should be done according to the Canons? It was a perplexed situation. But the Emperor's pre-

12

lates perplexed it more.   They deposed John (Dec. 4, 963), and elected Leo, who was not in orders, but who held the position of Chief Secretary to the Holy See. Within a month the Romans were up in arms.   They fell on Otho's diminished troops, barricaded the bridge of St. Angelo, and had to be put down with immense slaughter by the Germans, now thoroughly exasperated.   The Emperor, compelled to resume his blockade of Berengar, marched away to Montefeltro, leaving his Pope behind him.   Immediately, there was an insurrection of women, said to be high born, in favour of their Alberic's son and heir.   Leo contrived to get off in time ; John returned, mutilated the leaders whom he could catch of the Imperial party, and in a Council which was doubtless popular asserted his rights.   This took place in February, 964.   In May, while pursuing some intrigue, he died suddenly, by the judgment of Heaven or the dagger of an injured husband.   His decease cut an entangled knot.   The Romans, however, disdaining to wait for Otho, and not recognising Leo VIII., elected a Pope of their own, who was called during the next unhappy days by the ironical designation of Benedict V.

XI

ROMANCE OF THE OTHOS

(964–1003)

MEANWHILE, Otho had taken Berengar and Willa, his wife, at Monte Leone—a couple stained with every crime, who had played Macbeth and Lady Macbeth to the Queen-widow Adelaide, by this time married to her German hero, now in consequence Italian King and Emperor. When these miscreants were despatched over the Alps, Otho drove straight at the Romans, struck them helpless, and saw their Benedict V. in his robes crouching on the ground before him,—a spectacle which drew iron tears down that Pluto's cheek. Degraded, exiled to remote Hamburg, the true or false Pope is seen by us no more. Leo VIII. confirmed anew the diploma which, in some uncertain shape, John XII. had granted. This " Privilegium Othonis" compels the Romans to swear that they will never elect a Pope except with the Emperor's consent, and the candidate is himself to take an oath of allegiance. In fact, as Liutprand says, they surrendered their right of election to Otho and his successors. But had they not done as much during the sixty years before? The House of Theophylact was the Great Elector, yet with this difference, that Theodora, Marozia, Alberic were flesh of their flesh, bone of their bone. If they submitted to a stranger they did so unwillingly, and not a moment longer than they could help.

When the Barons, Counts, or whatever they styled themselves,—these brigands of a mixed pedigree now encamped all over Rome,—wanted a pretext to rise, they put forward the banner of the Republic, and S.P.Q.R. became their superb device. Against Otho in person they dared not rebel; when Leo VIII. died in 965—it seemed impossible that any Pope should reign long—they humbly begged a Pontiff from the German soldier. He sent them a kinsman of their late Elagabalus, in the hope to keep them quiet, the Bishop of Narni, John XIII. Yet in three months they blazed up once more, took the miserable puppet, mishandled him, drove him from the city. John collected troops in the Campagna, returned, and was admitted with hymns of rejoicing. The Barons had heard that Otho was approaching for the fourth time to his restless capital.

Christmas came (966); Pope and Emperor dealt a fearful vengeance on the rebels. Their twelve Tribunes were hanged; their dead Præfectus Urbis was dug out of his grave and dismembered; their living one hanged by the hair to the equestrian statue of Marcus Aurelius, then set upon an ass, scourged, and cast into prison. Even the Greek Emperor cried out at such enormities. Liutprand answered for Otho that it was the law, Theodosian, Justininian : *Jugulavit, suspendit, exilio relegavit*; what else should be done to sacrilegious wretches? John XIII. was now in the saddle again. He went with his patron to Ravenna in 967, and got

OTHO I. EMPEROR " THE GREAT," A.D. 973.
(*From a print in the British Museum.*)

from him the lands, cities, and lordships of these Adriatic regions, so long withdrawn from the Holy See In acknowledgment he crowned Otho II. After seven years Pontificate his place was empty. Otho named Benedict VI. in January, 973, and himself expired in May of the same year.

He is termed the Great ; with reason if we take

into account his marches, fightings, victories over many combatants, his honours achieved, and extent of sovereignty nominal or effective. Once more there was an Emperor of the West. Hugh Capet, Duke of France, and Lothair its *fainéant* King, were Otho's nephews on his sisters' side, Hedwiga and Gerberga. His brother, St. Bruno, Archbishop of Cologne, was also Duke of Lorraine and the Low Countries; with him for lieutenant, Otho governed as far west as Brittany. The Saxon House which had risen upon the ruin of the Carlovingians was predominant in the Latin, German, and Gallic territories. Such a reward had fallen in less than sixty years to Henry the Fowler and his lion-hearted offspring. Henry (919–936), says Carlyle, was "a very high King, an authentically noble human figure, visible still in clear outline in the grey dawn of Modern History. The Father of whatever good has since been in Germany." Twice he beat the Huns, at Sondershausen and Merseburg; twice the Wends; besides these, the Misnians, the Czechs from whom he captured Prague; and the Danes under King Gorm the Hard. He set down the Dukes of Suabia and Bavaria; appointed six Wardens of the Marches; saw that his burghs had walls round them; instituted a town militia; founded Quedlenburg Abbey and many others; and carried St. Michael the Archangel on his standard. " A right gallant King and Fowler," says Carlyle.

Undoubtedly; nor did Otho quite come up to his level. We have seen how fierce and vindictive he could be; yet, as Thietmar affirms, "never since Charlemagne did so mighty a ruler and guardian of his country hold the Imperial seat." For thirty-six years he battled strongly to put down rebellions in Franconia; conspiracies of great Bishops with Lorraine; incursions and alarums of Bohemians, Wends, Danes; and the House of Ivrea, which might have grown into the dynasty of Savoy and Italy. Then his son Ludolph revolted with many prelates; Duke Conrad beckoned to the Magyars; and they fell upon the German lands savagely. Otho had to pacify his people, and to beat the Magyars till they went away for good, leaving him with that Italian coil to disentangle which kept him so many years south of the Alps. He was buried at home in Magdeburg, an Archbishop's seat of his creation. The Emperor did as he pleased with Bishops and their estates; but his policy aimed at making the Church wealthy, as a counterpoise to his revolting Dukes and Margraves. He is well named the tenth-century Charlemagne (936–973).

After his decease the sanguinary Roman records yield "no light but only darkness visible," in the gloom of which we perceive Crescenzio, son of Theodora, and brother of John XIII., rising up to snatch Benedict VI. into St. Angelo and there strangle him. Under such auspices Franco, the Archdeacon, a national or anti-German choice, calls himself Boniface VII., is overturned by the Imperial Resident Sicco, and flies to Constantinople, carrying with him the sacred vessels from St. Peter's. A grandson of Alberic was appointed, surely to content the partisans of that still indomitable race. Benedict VII. lasted nine years. Otho II., a man of war, not always fortunate, refined and somewhat unsteady, had come to Rome in 980. His marriage with a Greek Princess, Theophano, gave him rights over Apulia and the Far South. But in 982, the Saracens, encamped in those parts, defeated him with terrible slaughter, and he escaped them only by flight. His heart, we may suppose, was broken. Four years earlier he had beaten his French cousin Lothair, led sixty thousand Saxons and Flemings to Paris, and chanted Te Deum on the heights of Montmartre. Now he retired to Rome, where a new Pope of his making awaited him—John XIV., late Italian Chancellor and Bishop of Pavia—almost, the Romans would have muttered, a German. He assisted the youthful Emperor to die. Otho was not yet thirty when the atrium of St. Peter's received his worn-out frame. A child of three represented the Saxon Kings. Theophano, his mother, took him to Germany ; until he grew up, she would be Emperor. John XIV. must have shivered when he was left alone in his palace.

Crescenzio had kept up a correspondence with the absconding Franco, protected by Court influence at Byzantium ; for the Easterns would not give up their claims on Magna Græcia. His return was speedy ; his acts according to the usual pattern. He had soon thrust John XIV. into the *oubliettes* of St. Angelo, where the wretched North Italian perished, it is said, by hunger. Then Crescenzio died, and his epitaph, dated 984, may still be read in Sant' Alessio on the Aventine, where he lies till the Judgment Day. Franco followed him next year. But his body was outraged and left naked in front of "Constantine's horse," that is to say, of Marcus Aurelius and his steed, then set up in the Lateran piazza. Young Crescenzio II. stepped forward as Patrician; he did not contest the Imperial authority. There was a Pope John XV.; perhaps also an Antipope; we feel about in the dark of history for persons and events at this time. It would appear that John underwent sufferings which compelled him to retire into Tuscany. It is certain that when Otho had reached his sixteenth year the Pontiff invoked his aid. But in April, 996, this poor shadow slipped away, and the German youth of genius, halting at Ravenna, was called to Rome by Crescenzio, acting as head of the Republic.

No story in the Middle Ages wears upon its brow more beauty and sadness than this royal boy's descent to the South. His pure young enthusiasm, his accomplishments, friendships, misfortunes, and piteous death, fill us with an interest which belongs to lyrical tragedy. One pictures him as Euphorion—half Greek, half German—with his fair features and golden locks, his eyes alternately piercing and dreamy; under that almost feminine tenderness the wild Teutonic rage looks out; he is dowered with the love of love, the scorn of scorn; he is adventurous, detached, a pursuer of fame and learning, always in quest of greatness. We shall not look upon his like again till Frederick II. reminds us, in his perfect moments, of the youth he could never have excelled and would have done well to imitate in that fervent devotion to ideals, which not even the smoke and horror of certain cruel or infatuated deeds have been able to tarnish.

Time it was that an end should come to the Roman anarchy, now more than a hundred years prevailing—a scandal in the eyes of Christians so huge that it has never ceased to loom upon the page of history like a thundercloud. Otho, brought up by an admirable mother, felt as young men do when they set out on their adventures, capable of the noblest things. At Ratisbon he gathered the Bishops round him—among them Gerbert, lately deposed from Rheims. A crowd of high German prelates led him on his way; he confessed and was absolved by St. Romuald, Abbot of Emmeran. The Lombard Princes did homage at Pavia; for who could resist the armed host descending from the Alps? Soon after he learned that John XV. was no more; in accordance with his grandfather's "Privilege," the Emperor must choose the Pope; but a thrill of astonishment passed over Europe when news came that Otho, a lad of sixteen, had named his cousin Bruno, who was but twenty-three, to the Chair of St. Peter. The Romans were ousted; in Church and State a German held the sovereign power.

Bruno, son to the Duke of Carinthia, and Otho's bosom friend, had the intense purity, and not a little of the stern temper, which we remark in young Saints. He took the name of Gregory V. Rome threw wide its gates; the two noble kinsmen were enthroned, one at the Lateran as Pope, the other at St. Peter's as Augustus. Then Otho held a Court before which Crescenzio II. appeared to expiate the misdeeds of his ancestors, the Theophylacts, and his own. He was found guilty; the Pope begged him off, not aware that Italians never forgive. Crescenzio left the dock to spread sedition in the castellated dens where his fellow-nobles lurked. Otho dreamt that his quest had been accomplished; he set out for Germany and war with the Slavonians. But Rome was not reformed in a day.

Three months had scarcely elapsed when the weary old scenes of blood and massacre were enacted again. Crescenzio struck an attitude which some might imagine sincere—freedom, the Republic, and no doubt Junius Brutus, furnished his eloquent themes. That Rome, if the capital of Christendom, owed any duty to the world which acknowledged it, none of the Crescenzi have ever supposed. But mark the first appearance of the Tribune, who was to culminate three hundred and fifty years after in Rienzi. The severe young Saint, Gregory V., had made few friends. He saved his life in the tumult; but when he fled to Pavia he was destitute and almost alone. He could simply excommunicate the Patrician, which he did in February, 997. Crescenzio replied with an Antipope, Philagathus or Lovegood, a Calabrian Greek, just then on his way home from Constantinople. The Empress Theophano had made him Bishop of Piacenza; this was his gratitude. He called himself John XVI.—John had grown to be the rallying-cry of a party which descended from Marozia and her son, and which gloried in its Roman patriotism.

Large schemes, it is said, occupied the wealthy Antipope and his Consul when Otho, having broken the Slavs, turned down to Rome, entered without resistance (the cowardice in battle of these street-rioters is remarkable), and set up Gregory V. again. We would fain blot out the next page in his life. German wrath had now got the upper hand of Christian meekness. Pope Lovegood, seized in the Campagna, was frightfully mutilated, his eyes and his tongue pulled out, as Thietmar declares, by Gregory's own orders. The gentle St. Nilus, Archimandrite of the Greek convent at Grotta Ferrata, interceded for his countryman in vain. Philagathus, a horrible sight, was paraded through the streets of Rome, and then banished to a monastery. Yet he survived until 1013, when he ended his days at Fulda.

St. Angelo was still a refuge for Crescenzio ; and, as it seemed impregnable, the story ran that Otho, by a feigned proposal of easy terms, lured the Patrician to his doom. We will hope, as another account tells us, that it was taken by assault. The Republican hero suffered death by decapitation on the battlements ; twelve othe perished with him ; their bodies were hung, head downwards, on gibbets erected above Monte Mario. These are not German customs ; but in Italy traitors have been so dealt with, in fact or in effigy. St. Nilus warned Pope and Emperor that their deeds would come in judgment against them. Crescenzio, with his golden halo of martyrdom, had left a son to avenge him. And though the Emperor made Rome his residence, he could not defend his cousin's life in that world of subtlety, treason, and dark dissimulation. Gregory was poisoned, or somehow done to death, on February 18, 999.

Romans would now, they probably thought, behold a Pope of their kith and kin, after an intimation so decisive. The musing Emperor thought otherwise. He could light upon no Cardinal in the Lateran precincts who would do such honour to Rome, the world's golden head, as befitted a new Augustan era; but there was one whom he had in view, a miracle of learning, his virtues unimpeachable, his piety sincere and fervent. After the German Pope, a French philosopher, a man of letters, acquainted with Saracenic universities and European Courts, was to mount the Apostolic throne. Gerbert, a name which reminds us of Æneas Silvius Piccolomini and even of Erasmus, became Pope Silvester II. by an Imperial decree. "Rome," said Otho, "was the world's capital, the Roman Church mother of all Churches; but her Bishops, ignorant and careless, had pulled her down, made her riches over to the basest of mankind, stripped the altars, given up their lawful rights to usurp those of the Empire. Constantine and Charlemagne had been foolishly prodigal in their Donations. A moderate patrimony was now bestowed; a worthy Pope created."

This language, these visions, the youth had learnt from a man whom he was exalting to dangerous eminence. Gerbert started so low down and mounted so high that he was called a necromancer by his contemporaries, accustomed to see Popes and Bishops of noble or kingly pedigree. A poor lad of Auvergne, he was bred up in the Cluniac house at Aurillac. Chance made him known to the Count of Barcelona; he travelled into Spain; learned mathematics from

Arab texts or teachers; visited Cordova and saw the Caliph, Hakim II. It was the splendid noon of Moorish erudition, philosophy, poetry, and chivalrous knighthood—a contrast in brilliant colours to the Latin world, which seemed to lie on its death-bed in frenzies of convulsion, weak, moon-struck, imbecile. Gerbert felt the charm; when he went up to his high place the illiterate Westerns asked if he were not a Manichæan, in league with powers of darkness. Count Borel took him to Rome in the last days of John XII.; he was remarked by Otho I., and sent to the Archbishop of Rheims, Adalbero. From the second Otho he received the once edifying but now degenerate Irish-Italian monastery of Bobbio. Its corrupt monks and litigious lay usurpers drove him thence to Rome, where he could get no satisfaction, and to Rheims, where he taught with success during ten years. He wrote the Archbishop's letters, corresponded with Adelaide and Theophano. His patron, Adalbero, dying, left him the See. It was not likely that an obscure student could make good his claim while Arnulf, a side-slip of the fallen French royalty, stood by to be elected. Hugh Capet had seized the crown. Perhaps by way of conscience-money his vote was given to the Carlovingian, who, as soon as he held Hincmar's crozier, plunged into treason; he was betrayed by another miscreant, Bishop of Laon, to Capet; and was tried in solemn council of prelates and nobles, with a view to his deprival (July, 991).

Gerbert laid down the law to these by no means reluctant Bishops. They brought Arnulf to a public confession, deposed him, and, lest he should appeal to Rome and John XV., declared by anticipation their attitude towards Popes who were "full of all infamy, void of all knowledge;" in bold words they threatened to break away, as Africa, Asia, Constantinople, had done. They would not hear of a popular election; and Gerbert, their master or mouthpiece, was chosen by them for Archbishop.

Thus the Manichee, necromancer, half-Moslem, had shown his ambiguous colours, and was a Gallican —nay, should we not call him a Protestant and Reformer, some centuries too soon? The traitor of Laon envied his eloquent friend's good fortune; he persuaded the German Court to back up the Pope, who was nettled and alarmed by such severe denunciations, the more stinging because they could not be refuted. To the French prelates again in meeting came Abbot Leo, as Legate *a latere*. His first charge was to undo the Synod of Rheims; his second to deprive and interdict Gerbert. Hugh Capet had no desire to provoke the clergy, at home or abroad, by whose connivance and favour the crown passed from Louis le Fainéant to his own almost sacerdotal dynasty. He suffered the great scholar to be put down at Moisson. Gerbert's household forsook their fallen chief, and he set out alone for the Court of Adelaide and young Otho, from which had come his misfortune.

He possessed the art of making friends, and, it would seem, of fascinating even his enemies. At all events he conquered the hero-youth, and filled him with dreams of a miraculous Roman

Renaissance so soon as the first Millennium of
Christianity should be accomplished. The Auvergnat
became Archbishop of Ravenna and Supreme Pontiff.
His pupil had built a palace in Rome on the Aventine; there he saw in vision the Fifth Monarchy
ruling a peaceful world, Pope and Emperor united
as the hope of mankind. Silvester II., who could
subdue every one he addressed, did not, however,
subdue the Romans. They shared none of his
apocalyptic dreams; they abhorred the wise French
Pontiff; they conspired against the German Emperor.
We may imagine Rome as the hungry, untameable
wolf, chained but defiant, whose effigy then, as in our
own days, the citizens regarded with a love which
was hatred to everything not Roman. In two years
they had rid themselves of Gerbert and Otho.

How it was done remains a mystery of iniquity,
for we cannot doubt the wickedness, although its
agents, like their victims, died and made no sign.
Legends were plentiful in so credulous a world.
This one which tells how young Otho met his
doom has been disputed, yet survives with stories
of the House of Atreus and is of a strain as
melancholy. When Crescenzio II. was beheaded on
the St. Angelo terrace, his beautiful wife, Stephania,
it is said, fell into the hands of the wild Germans.
She suffered like Lucretia; unlike Lucretia she
would not die, but waited with preterhuman endur-
ance till she could get her revenge. In the tale she
is always surpassingly fair, a witch in cunning, and
able to move with her young son, Crescenzio III.,
among the Court ladies and gentlemen whom Otho

entertained. She is Delilah and catches him in her silken nets, though he is a spirit of fire and purity, pilgrim to shrines far and near, but at last "effeminately vanquished," as greater men had been. At some banquet the woman, true type of Vittoria Accorombona and other Roman "white devils," to speak with our English tragedian, gave her lover a poison which did not kill him instantly, but which acted in slow corroding effects upon a system never too strong. He drank and knew not that death was in his veins.

Thus far the legend, which Milman believed to rest on convincing evidence. What history tells, yet as a confused babble, may agree with it. Tivoli, in the gorge of the Anio above Hadrian's classic villa, was a town belonging to cadets of the Marozian dynasty. It had become a rival to shrunken Rome, and was now in revolt against Otho. He marched, in 1001, with soldiers from the city, to make an end of it, taking with him Pope Silvester, who never would be left alone in his unguarded Lateran. The Tivolese, persuaded by a foreign Pontiff, laid down their arms and accepted the pardon which Otho held out to them. But where were the spoils which the Romans had hoped for at starting? On his return with empty hands, the Emperor, as he sat in his house on the Aventine, saw a furious mob attempting to batter in his doors. He escaped by a postern; carried away the Pope to Ravenna; and never set foot again in Rome. Yet he passed its inexorable gates more than once on his expeditions to Calabria. He had gone on pilgrimage to expiate his former deeds of violence, not only to Monte Cassino, but to far-off Gnesen in the Polish land, where his friend St. Adalbert lay in a celebrated shrine. He did a thing yet more characteristic of the age and himself: he opened the crypt in Aix-la-Chapelle where dead Charlemagne sat in his chair of state, bearing his crown and sceptre; from the dead man's neck he detached a cross of gold and wore it as a relic or Imperial charm. His days, it is said, were now spent in prayer and almsgiving. But nothing could save Otho, and we seem to hear a muffled sob as the chronicler of that unpitying time records how he died at Paterno, in sight of Rome, and was borne back over the Alps, until he came to Charles the Great once more, to be laid at rest by the side of his heroic predecessor. He was only twenty-two.

Gerbert followed him in three months. Poisoned, says the Saxon monk, by Stephania; in any case, struck dumb; broken by his long wanderings; not suffered to reform the Church he had so magnificently exalted in his prophesyings, or to lead the Crusade and recover Jerusalem, over whose captivity his letters seem to weep. Crescenzio III. is Consul; half a century of Tusculan oppression throws Hildebrand's reform into far perspective.

THE GOOD SHEPHERD—EARLY BYZANTINE MOSAIC AT RAVENNA.

179

XII

TUSCULAN SUCCESSION—PAPACY BOUGHT AND SOLD

(1003–1048)

TUSCULUM is a spur of the Alban or Latin Hills, about sixteen miles south-east of Rome. It had still Greek remains scattered in its glades and thickets when Gregory, Captain of the Fleet under Otho III., restored its ancient citadel, ascribed to Telegonus, and made of it a strong castle. He was connected with Tivoli ; but now that the Crescentine branch of his ancestors had blossomed, envy, the Italian vice, prompted him to cut it down ; he affected a devotion to the Empire ; and from his rocky nest we may see the Ghibellines descending over Latium, Tuscany, the whole unhappy land. Crescenzio III., his cousin of the elder stem, lasted only nine years, in which time he had appointed three Popes, John XVII. and XVIII., and Sergius IV., son of a cordwainer. These and the Consul being dead, who should succeed ?

There was an Emperor of the Saxon House, a Saint and warrior, Henry II., who had to fight for his Iron Crown with Arduin, Marquis of Ivrea— the Alpine mountaineers wanted no Germans in Lombardy—and he was busy winning the great prelate-princes; he could not previously attend to Roman affairs. Gregory the Tusculan had three sons, Alberic, Romanus, Theophylact; the last a Cardinal. By gold or intrigue he contrived the election of his clerical son, though not without opposition; and, in fact, Benedict VIII., as he was styled, had to take refuge at the Emperor's feet in Germany, nor did he come back until peace was made with Crescenzio IV., the city Prefect, who held St. Angelo for his family. In 1013 Henry defeated Arduin; with his Queen, Cunegunda, he arrived in Rome, where the usual ceremonies of coronation took place. Whether Benedict VIII. lived up to his sacred character we do not know; what we do know is that he cut to pieces a Saracen army which had disembarked at Luni in Maremma, and sent to the Republics of Genoa and Pisa vehement letters, urging a naval Crusade for the recovery of Sardinia, which was accomplished. The Pisans maintained that he had given them the island. No dignity seemed secure unless ratified, even in those degenerate days, by a Papal grant, which carried with it, as Hergenröther observes, not so much dependence on the Holy See as independence of all other lords.

Gerbert had raised Poland to the rank of a kingdom and consecrated the Hungarian crown of

St. Stephen. The eleventh century was beginning
with a group of Saints on the throne—Otho, repentant
and a pilgrim ; Robert of France, who lived far more
strictly than his own Bishops ; this Henry II., a
monk in all but name ; and the Apostolic Stephen,
who converted his Magyars with sword and crucifix.
The restoration of monasticism had been undertaken long ago at Cluny. Rome was the dark spot
in a brightening sky. Yet of Benedict VIII. we
hear no evil, but rather good ; and his friendship
with Henry, whom he visited in Bamberg, accompanied to Monte Cassino, and joined in an expedition
against the Greeks of Capua, must count in his
favour. Note that Henry II. made a grant of the
city and bishopric of Bamberg to the Holy See ; this
was afterwards exchanged for Beneventum, a treaty
which appeared to invest the Popes with dominion of
an Imperial sort over Naples. It was an unlucky
transaction, prologue to an Iliad of woes in times not
far distant.

Twelve years passed ; Benedict and Henry went
to their graves in peace ; and Romanus the Senator
took or bought the vacant Chair. In one day he
was Prefect and Pope. The old abuses flourished ;
John XIX., bred a layman and a Tusculan, was not
likely to end them. In 1027 he crowned the
Emperor Conrad, in presence of Rudolph, Duke
of Burgundy, and the Anglo-Dane, Knut, otherwise
well known to English readers. Knut, a pious
traveller to St. Peter's shrine, cannot have been
edified when a tumult broke out in the very church
between Milanese and Ravennates on the question

of precedence. That was not the only fighting which disgraced a high festival. " Undisciplined Germans, turbulent Romans," both were to blame, we will say. But the sure thing is that whenever a Teuton came to be crowned, blows and bloodshed drew a crimson arabesque about the glowing page. Always the citizens attacked the soldiers and got beaten for their insolence, this time with great slaughter. Conrad insisted on their leaders appearing before him with naked feet and cords round their necks, which would be remembered, not to his advantage, when he was gone. Neither did he reform the Church in head or members. The clergy in almost every part of Europe were marrying or giving in marriage, against the Canons which Nicholas I. had promulgated, which Silvester II. and Benedict VIII. had tried to enforce. But the evils were felt; they were named; simony and concubinage must be rooted out; if the clergy would not cleanse the holy place, then their rivals and adversaries the monks would do it. A scandal yet more gross than the reign of John XII. precipitated the reformation.

Still the House of Tusculum. John XIX. went to his account in 1032. His brother, Alberic, made one son " Consul Romanorum," another, the last Theophylact, Pope. This was a lad ten or twelve years old, who had the title thrust on him of Benedict IX. An hereditary but irregular succession had thus kept the cross keys for well-nigh a hundred and fifty years in the hands of Theodora's descendants.

At a distance the Papacy was ringed about with a halo in which the individual Pope, good or bad, seemed lost. So rapid a transit of unknown men left the faithful indifferent. Pilgrims, indeed, were plundered ; monks groaned in their prayers over the Church's captivity ; but official routine never quite ceased ; and the average Italian learnt to distinguish between the man whom he despised and the priest who was minister of the Sacraments. When Abbot Leo replied to Gerbert's terrible indictment at Rheims, he admitted all the charges—corruption, venality, uncleanness, bloodshedding—nor was he a miscreant personally ; but still he quoted, *Tu es Petrus*, still he warned his audience against the impiety of cursed Ham. We can hardly suppose that Henry II., had he been living, would have found no flaw in the election as Œcumenical Pastor and teacher of a child who did not know his catechism. Unhappily, Conrad was engaged in deadly strife with Heribert, the married and magnificent Arch- bishop of Milan—another real Antipope, forerunner of King-Cardinals and Protestant Hermanns of Cologne. He let the nomination pass, though contrary in letter and spirit to the Canon Law. When Benedict was old enough to travel alone, at seventeen or there- abouts, he joined the Emperor, and on two occasions, at Cremona and Spello, pronounced the ban of the Church against Heribert—not, we may be sure, because he lived as a disorderly Bishop, but to chastise the rebel or the patriot. However, a change was at hand.

For, in Rome itself, Benedict lived up to his pre- decessor John's example ; he was a bandit, not a priest, stained with adulteries, homicides, the vices of his bringing up and his youth, but unopposed while Gregory his brother held the Consulate. A tumult at length, in 1044, which we need not ascribe to religious indignation, drove him from the city and St. Peter's. His Tusculan guards held Trastevere; street-fighting led to no decisive results; but the opposite, which may have been the Crescentine, party met in St. Peter's, assembled in conclave and, not without bribery, elected John of Sabina, who became on these terms Silvester III. Seven weeks of confusion followed, and Silvester was compelled to flee into his native mountains.

Triumphant Benedict was again lord of Rome. But on May Day an event to which no parallel can be found in Christian records, startled the city and the Curia. Benedict had sold the Papacy, for money down, to the wealthy Arch-priest of St. John at the Latin Gate. The document was signed and sealed by which Apostolic succession, keys of St. Peter, and all thereunto belonging, were conveyed to John Gratian, henceforth to be Gregory VI. in virtue of hard cash. Every one writing since on this unspeakable bargain has alluded to Didius Julianus who bought the Roman Empire. Simony had achieved its masterpiece. A Pope selling the Papacy, a Pope buying it, that, as the French say, had yet to be seen. Electors (if in the chaos of law we could tell who were, and who were not, entitled to the office) had taken their bribes many a time, and were to do so again; in such wise that the eminent modern historian Pastor is compelled, with a blush, to remind some critics that, until Julius II. ordained otherwise, simony did not vitiate an election to the supreme seat in Christendom. But could a Pope dispose of it like a worn-out cloak or a pair of old shoes? That was a new point for Canonists. One might parody St. Jerome, *Ingemuit totus orbis et se esse simoniacum miratus est* : Simon Magus had conquered.

Motives have been guessed at on either side. Benedict, like the Cardinal Cæsar Borgia in days to come, was meditating a splendid marriage, and wanted to be secularised. John Gratian was a simple, pious man, who devoted his riches to buying out a

INSCRIPTION IN SANTA SABINA ON THE AVENTINE.
(Fifth Century.)

scandalous intruder, not otherwise removable ; or he intended a larger profit, for it seems certain that the moment he was master he attempted at the sword's point to get possession of estates held by lay usurpers in the Campagna, and undertook the safeguard of pilgrims bringing gifts to St. Peter. Be that as it may, Gregory VI.'s reputation owes no small debt to a monk then residing on the Aventine in Alberic's monastery del Priorato, whose name was Hildebrand, and who became his chaplain and chief counsellor. A second monk, Damiani, wrote to him with unconscious sarcasm from Fonte Avellana (where Dante would one day brood over his unearthly visions), that now the reign of simony had come to an end. These were his friends; but he was still Didius Julianus.

And now Henry III., another saintly Emperor (one cannot forbear a blessing on these good Teutons) arrived. In 1046, at a numerous Synod in Pavia, his voice was lifted up against the traffic which bought and sold, not only in the Temple, but the Temple itself. Gregory VI. hastened to meet him at Piacenza. Benedict, who seems to have missed his intended bride, lay behind the Cyclopean walls of Tusculum. Silvester had got back St. Peter's. There had been a moment when all three Popes held their court in Rome— at the Vatican, St. Mary Major's, and St. John's. The Emperor advanced to Sutri. Historical parallels have their use. We are reminded here of the Council of Constance, Sigismund the Emperor, and the trio of doubtful Popes in 1415. Was any one of these valid? Henry began by deposing Silvester, who retreated into a monastery. John Gratian acknowledged his "shameful and simoniacal heresy, which was the work of the devil," and decreed his own deposition. Benedict would not come down from his fastness. Yet, as he seemed legitimate, Henry went through a more solemn procedure against him in St. Peter's, and only then appointed his man, Suidger, Bishop of Bamberg, by whom in turn he and the Empress Agnes were crowned. The Romans looked on in sulky silence. They would have preferred even a

Tusculan to Clement II. It might have been wiser to maintain Gregory VI., which was no doubt Hildebrand's judgment.

When the Emperor is crowned, it is time for him to go. Henry went south, broke the rising power of Salerno, took under his protection Melfi and Aversa, Norman colonies with a great future before them, and returned by the Eastern coast, where Clement expired at Pesaro, October, 1047. Benedict IX., it was whispered, had given him a deadly drink, and the dissolute young man was in Rome again. He had won help from Boniface, Marquis of Tuscany ; he meant to be Pope after all. Such an act of rebellion to the Empire, of dishonour to the Church, did that noble Boniface share in, whose grandfather Azzo, Lord of Canossa, sheltered Queen Adelaide, while his father Tedaldo had received large benefices from the Saxon house, including Mantua and Modena. Boniface himself held possession of Tuscany by a like privilege. Hereafter, his only child, the Countess Matilda, would make up for this disloyal dealing, and spend her life in service of the Roman Chair.

John Gratian was in far-off exile with his chaplain, Hildebrand. The last of the Tusculans held his court of misrule nine months ; but on hearing that Marquis Boniface would not support him against Henry, he fled and was seen no more. The Bishop of Brixen, who took the name of Damasus II., had been appointed without so much as the form of election, by the Emperor. He came in the midst of German soldiers, and in twenty-three days was dead (August, 1048). Again the sceptre designated a

Roman Pontiff, cousin to the royal house, of stately bearing, famed for virtues and miracles, who had stooped to the lowly Bishopric of Toul. Bruno called himself Leo IX., and when he set out for Italy Hildebrand went with him. From that moment down to 1085—some thirty-seven years—the monk from Cluny and the Aventine governed the Church.

XIII

HILDEBRAND

(1048–1073)

LOWER than Benedict IX. it was impossible that the Papacy should fall ; and higher than Hildebrand in fact, hardly perhaps in idea, it could never soar. Humanly speaking, three different ways of escape from degradation might be imagined for it in the eleventh century. One was that opened by Gerbert, but which death hindered him from advancing upon —the way of an intellectual new-birth, not without Arabian influences, or even Greek and classic revivals, such as, long after, the Renaissance under Nicholas V. was to bring forth. A second was the road of the Emperors, which some would call Ghibelline, Erastian, or merely secular ; but Otho III. is the most convincing proof that it need not have fluttered a plume in the crest of religion, while upholding the rights and dignities of a Christian State. The last, which turned out to be the destined course of things, divided itself for nearly two centuries from Gerbert's philosophic ascent; and it came almost immediately into conflict with the Imperial power. It was the way of monastic reform.

Monasticism had separated from the world. If it cherished learning, or did not put science under a ban, yet its own aim was not knowledge, but the perfect life—*summa Quies*—as expressed in vows of poverty, purity, obedience. It could not transform society at large into a cloister, but it could and did make a cloister of the Church. It reformed the Papacy by seating in the Chair at Rome a succession of monks. During the best part of a hundred years the Capital of Christendom was Cluny. St. Benedict avenged himself on Benedict IX. by ruling the faithful in his stead.

That is no figure of speech. When Rome, under baleful enchantments, had lost the very shadow of holiness, wisdom, and spiritual greatness; when her fine gold was dim, her sanctuaries held by brigands or adulterers, far away on the banks of Saone and Loire a movement was beginning, to live the life which Christ had lived, in silence, labour, detachment. The Benedictine Rule, made by Witiza of Aniane (817), too sharp and vexatious for daily use, had long been forgotten. Monasteries, like bishoprics, fell into the hands of lay lords, their concubines, children, and retainers. Soldiers clank about their courtyards; hunting dogs give tongue in sacred solitudes. Monks and nuns break their vows; infants receive the abbot's crook; lands are alienated, buildings fall to ruin; learning, of course, is neglected. Not universally, for exceptions might be found in the worst of times ; but monastic wealth was tempting, and the feudal convert scarcely more than half a Christian. Between him and the Norman pirate how little was there to choose ?

At this dark period, in 910, William, Duke of Aquitaine, set Berno to rule over his foundation of Cluny. Now had monastic life its second spring. The gentle and comprehensive method of St. Benedict prevailed once more in a multitude of houses, old and new. Many were derived from the great French centre, others independent. Dunstan, Abbot of Glastonbury—statesman, artist, recluse, reformer of abuses—took his inspiration from it in the *Concordia Regularis*. Hanno, Archbishop of Cologne, saw it enforced. Würzburg, Einsiedlen, Hirschau—abbeys all over Europe—discovered in the Great Rule a code of civilisation as well as of piety. Three hundred churches, colleges, and monasteries looked to Cluny as their mother-house. Its abbots, in a long line, were men renowned for the austerest virtues. Peter the Venerable is worthy of his name. St. Hugh, the friend and ally who never forsook Gregory VII., built himself a monument in the church at Cluny, which remained the largest and most imposing in Christendom till St. Peter's excelled it. Lands, revenues, privileges of every kind were showered upon the monks, who for a good while used them as they were meant, to the public benefit. But now a contest was breaking out of a kind hitherto scarcely known. The parties in Hildebrand's first period, down to Henry IV.'s manhood, were on one side a corrupt Hierarchy which would not be reformed, and which could rely on its kinsfolk among the nobles and all the clergy tainted with concubinage; and, on the other, Pope, Emperor, and monks, animated by the genius of a single captain. For Hildebrand's "imperial mind," as Newman justly terms it, directed the whole series of campaigns which at last issued in the victory of monasticism.

This remarkable man, the Julius Cæsar of the Papacy, was, like Gerbert, a plebeian; his birthplace is not positively ascertained. His father is said to have been a carpenter of Saona in Tuscany, and that he had German blood in his veins we may well believe, since there were few of his country that had not. His uncle Laurence had become Abbot of Sta. Maria on the Aventine, and called the lad to him. In self-restraint, watching, and study he passed his youth. Some uncertain years he spent at Cluny, under Odilo, the illustrious reformer. He loved solitude, but duty recalled him to Rome before Gregory VI. had purchased the tiara; and if he consented to be this Pope's minister we can only suppose him ignorant of the transaction, or persuaded that a subsequent election had made it good. Historians will always perhaps take different sides when they write of Hildebrand; none would charge him with hypocrisy or time-serving. He followed Gregory across the Alps. When his patron died he went back to Cluny; there Pope Leo IX. found him and carried him to Rome. Henceforth he is Gregory VII. in all but name.

The most Petrine of Popes bore a striking resemblance to St. Paul. His letters, of which we possess

14

nine books, were weighty and powerful, but his bodily presence was weak, his stature small, his delicate frame racked by frequent sickness. In friendship he showed himself passionate and exacting. He needed sympathy, yet exercised imperious control over every one; learning and elegance he disclaimed, and spoke slightingly of his "rustic style"; but who could be more daring or adventure upon a new line of action with more confidence than Gregory VII.? Again, like St. Paul, he brought into the religion which he exalted a revolutionary idea; the Apostle freed it from Judaism, the Pope from Feudalism; in their hands it became something universal, not bounded by race, kingdom, colour, prerogative. What has been called the essential Democracy of monasticism appears in both these master-spirits, to whom rank was an outward show, the powers of the world vain or transitory. But in natures so vehement thought is flame rather than light; nor have they ever ceased to stir up enemies as fierce as their partisans have been devoted.

It was afterwards told that, on meeting Leo IX., Hildebrand counselled him to put off his Papal insignia, enter Rome on foot, and solicit the votes of a genuine election. We cannot be sure; and it signifies little. The new Pontiff had been chosen in Germany. He was a graceful, energetic presence wherever he went—the first of those Apostolic pilgrims who travelled over Europe, holding Councils, correcting abuses, receiving the homage of Kings and crowds, Popes truly Œcumenical. He restored St. Peter's, visited Monte Cassino, which was then

ST. PAUL'S OUTSIDE ROME, OF WHICH HILDEBRAND WAS ABBOT.

(Fifth Century—restored.)

195

growing to its height, and the picturesque St. Michael's Mount in Calabria, from which those others, French and Cornish, take their name. But his task lay before him. Hildebrand summed it up, "to take their wives from the clergy, their investitures from the laity." A celibate ministration, freedom of election, security of the Church estates, such was the programme. Towards its fulfilment hardly a few in the episcopal ranks would lend a hand; the highest were its resolved opponents. Leo might count on St. Hugh of Cluny, on Hildebrand, on St. Peter Damiani; and popular opinion, which reveres a virtue it cannot equal, took part with the monks against disedifying secular canons, married priests, and high-born tyrannical prelates. In 1048 Leo began his visitation of the churches of Europe. Rome must be reformed from the circumference. It had lost its savour, though Hildebrand has in later times been held up as a Roman. But he never was a cleric, and the school of the Lateran could lay no claim to him.

At Pavia Leo held a Council; he crossed into Germany, met the pious Archbishop Hermann of Cologne and Henry the Emperor; excommunicated, subdued, converted Godfrey of Lorraine, a freebooter who now lost his Dukedom, and, after public scourging, humbly rebuilt with his own hands the Church of Verdun, which he had burnt. So mighty was religion when a Saint wielded its power in the ages of faith! Leo passed on into France. He dedicated Rheims Cathedral, not yet the exquisite and sumptuous Gothic which we know; he gathered the Bishops next morning, and charged them as at the **Great Day** to confess if they had bought their consecration. Treves, Lyons, Besançon, professed their innocence. Four others allowed themselves guilty. Hugo of Rheims, a notorious simoniac, kept silence. But he could not escape a summons to Rome. The Bishop of Langres, convicted, took flight; others were deposed; absentees, who would not join the Pope in council on French territory, underwent a similar fate. The Papal primacy, endangered by all we have recited, was proved from the Canons. Leo had undone the Gallican measures of Gerbert.

Scenes not less decisive were witnessed in the Council at Mayence; the Metropolitans bowed before the Pope; Sibico of Spires underwent his trial; and Leo, as he returned towards Italy, visited Fulda and confirmed the privileges of many German convents, acting as supreme Lord in spirituals. In five years he crossed the Alps three times. He would not endure that even German Bishops, who now filled North Italian Sees, should lift their heel against the Papacy. Humfred of Ravenna was put down, restored, and died suddenly. By Leo's appearance in the camp at Presburg (1051) and his persevering efforts, the Emperor was induced to offer Andrew of Hungary a peace which the latter refused. At Worms, next year, he made an attempt to get back for Rome thirty-one churches and forty-seven monasteries north of the Alps which had been taken away, including Bamberg; and now it was that in exchange for the latter Leo accepted Beneventum, the fatal heritage.

Antipapal enmities, smouldering beneath the
ashes of simony, burst into lava-floods, as he
seemed to grow more Italian and less German. The
troops which had been promised him were denied.
Still he marched from Mantua, with Suabian knights
and condottieri, a loose array, to combat the Normans
under Robert Guiscard. He received Capua, which
had thrown off its Prince. He dreamt of conquering
Sicily. Peter Damiani raised his voice in loud
reprobation of a militant Pontiff; such acts were no
better than the Apostle's denial and David's adultery.
Judgment soon followed them. June, 1053, saw the
Normans victorious at Civitella and Leo in their
hands a prisoner. He forgave them, returned to
Beneventum where he did penance for his late martial
exercises, arrived in Rome, and ordered his open
coffin to be set in front of St. Peter's shrine.
With deep solemnity, he uttered over it a dying
speech, not unlike those words of the Emperor
Severus, *Omnia fui et nihil expedit.* He had been a
monk in his cell, a Pope in his palace; all had shrunk
to this narrow stone. Then he died in a transport
of religious exaltation, April 13, 1054.

Hildebrand, without a moment's delay, hastened
from France. Archdeacon of the Roman Church, he
had been sent to quell the subtle rationalising heresiarch, Berengar of Tours, who disputed or denied the
Catholic view, maintained by Lanfranc, and said to
have been imperilled by Scotus Erigena, of the
Eucharist. We are not to dwell on this controversy.
Enough that Hildebrand, assailing the lion in his den,
held a Council at Tours, which he would doubtless

ARCH OF TRAJAN AT BENEVENTUM.

have carried to an orthodox conclusion did he not hear or suspect that Leo was dying. From Berengar he took a declaration, ambiguous, seemingly sufficient, which was afterwards made a charge against himself, and broke up the Council. Then he assumed the government of the vacant See. The interim lasted a whole year.

Boniface of Tuscany had been murdered. His large dominions, which embraced so much of Central and Northern Italy, went to his wife, Beatrice, and she chose to marry the brigand-Duke of Lorraine, now under Henry III.'s Imperial ban. His brother Frederick had been made Cardinal by Pope Leo. This combination of rival powers was unendurable to the Germans ; and, it would appear, to Hildebrand. He invited, nay compelled, Gebhard, Bishop of Eichstadt, to ascend the Papal Chair ; for Gebhard, though hostile to Leo, was a reforming prelate, the Emperor's trusty counsellor, and yet, in the language of later times, a true Guelf. The Bishop accepted reluctantly ; he became Victor II. ; and Henry followed him with a formidable host. The usurping Duke Godfrey fled—but into German quarters where he could stir up rebellion. Beatrice and her daughter Matilda the Emperor kept in his hands. A Council at Florence forbade (how vainly !) the alienation of Church lands to laymen. Victor, just or severe, narrowly escaped poisoning at the altar. In 1056 Henry, worn out by insurrections, expired at Goslar, leaving his son and the Empire to Victor's tutelage.

A strong Pope, by the confession of all, he made peace among the Germans, did not offend

Godfrey of Lorraine, and restored the Cardinal Frederick who had been in exile as long as Henry III. lived. He held his court at Ancona, his synod in Florence; he despatched Hildebrand a second time to France that he might depose, reform, reclaim on the lines of Ultramontane policy. His least defensible act, the setting aside of Abbot Peter, and installing Frederick of Lorraine at Monte Cassino, is ascribed by Tosti to the bold Archdeacon. It was hardly done when Victor passed away at Arezzo (July, 1057). Godfrey and Beatrice ruled as Imperial lieutenants in Italy. The Romans, their master away in France, clamoured for Cardinal Frederick. He yielded, whether from ambition who shall say? No churchman could go beyond Stephen IX. in zeal or austerity. As Legate in Byzantium he had excommunicated the Patriarch Michael and his Eastern colleagues. He now raised Damiani to the purple; proposed immense schemes to Godfrey; took for the Crusade, but sent back again, the treasures of Monte Cassino; and in March, 1058, was dead at Vallombrosa, where St. John Gualbert attended his last moments. Stephen IX. is a strange and splendid apparition, enigmatic to us, but not easily forgotten in the Papal gallery.

They say that he was poisoned. The familiar Roman factions sprang on the stage; Crescenzio, the Tusculans, the Count of Galeria chose Benedict X.; clearly they felt no shame in calling to memory Benedict IX. The Emperor was a child, the Archdeacon still away; and they wanted no reform. Their candidate was a Crescentine, Bishop of Velletri.

He made lavish donations to the people; St. Peter's ornaments were coined into money. Peter Damiani protested; Hildebrand made a league with the Empress; and, in virtue (it must be supposed) of rights granted to Otho, Henry II., and Henry III., persuaded her to name the Archbishop of Florence, a Burgundian, Gerard, who advanced under such support to Rome, and was recognised as Nicholas II. His rival, degraded, taken by Hildebrand—yes, with Norman help—shut up in the convent of St. Agnes, figures yet as Pope in the catalogues. A crisis had arrived. Was not the Roman Archdeacon acting as a Ghibelline? The Chancellor, Guibert, who represented the Empire—could he legitimate this new election? Either Rome must henceforth sink to be, in spirituals as in temporals, a fief, an investiture, on a level with Mayence and Hamburg, or every secular lord, including the Emperor, must withdraw. When he lay dying at Salerno, in 1085, Gregory wrote that his aim had ever been to make the Church, "free, chaste, Catholic." And was *this* freedom?

In the Lateran, meanwhile, under his guidance, a Council proceeded to draw up rules which, allowing the Emperor some shadowy right of approbation, vested in the seven Cardinal Bishops and their fellow-members of the Sacred College the real election. At Rome, if circumstances would permit; otherwise, wherever a peaceable choice could be made. The Roman laity, no less than the German Cæsar, thus forfeited powers which, as our history demonstrates, they had seldom exercised with discrimination, never once in view of the Church at large. Seventy Bishops signed.

They also compelled Berengar, who was brought before them, to abjure his doctrine, or, at least, imagined that he had done so, in terms which he afterwards explained away.

Robert Guiscard and his Normans, still excommunicate, had overrun Apulia ; the last Greek official had sailed to Byzantium. Robert's policy had never been inflexible—Guiscard means "the Cunning "—and he now sent messengers begging of Nicholas II. to take away the ban. In the synod of Melfi it was done. Nay more, the Pope made Richard Prince of Capua ; to Robert he gave Apulia, Calabria, Sicily (when the island could be got from its Moslem invaders), all to be held as fiefs of the Holy See. This bargain ratified, he took a Norman guard with him to Rome. Before long they were treading down the old nobility ; they laid waste their lands and subdued their castles as far as Sutri. Nicholas died in 1061. To exclude Hildebrand, the barons named young Henry IV. their Patrician, and were prepared to take a Pope of his choosing. The Archdeacon looked on scornfully. By way of compromise the Cardinals elected an Italian, but a Lombard, Anselm of Lucca, who was known as Alexander II.

We enter now on a period of Antipopes. The secular Roman party, whom their enemies described as Simonians and even worse, persuaded the German Court to fix on Cadalus, Bishop of Parma, who was at once acclaimed by the Lombards of Milan and the neighbouring regions as Honorius II. What had taken place in the ancient city of St. Ambrose to render this feasible, shall be told by and by. In the

spring Benzo of Albi, his agent, who likewise represented the Emperor, arrived in Rome, scattered his
bribes right and left, drove out Alexander, and warned
the Senate that a Pope could not be elected by monks
and Normans—in a word, by Hildebrand.　Soon after
Cadalus, with troops and treasure, came to Sutri; he
was at Tusculum, and the Alexandrian forces cowered
inside the walls of Rome.　Godfrey the Duke appeared as a *Deus ex machina*, with more soldiers
than either party.　The candidates must retire and
submit their claims to examination.　Scarcely had
they done so when news was brought of a revolution
in German affairs.　Hanno of Cologne had dared to
kidnap Henry IV. from the Empress Agnes.　Godfrey
joined him; Damiani left his cloister, appeared at
Augsburg, pleaded in his quaint yet passionate way
for Alexander, and won the assembly.　But still two
Popes divided the capital of Christendom; at St.
Angelo, the Parmesan with his secular Barons; at St.
John Lateran the Bishop of Lucca.

For two years (1063–1065) this unseemly spectacle
continued.　That ill-fated lad, Henry IV., was tossed
from one hand to another; the Archbishop of Cologne,
whom his monastic friends called a saint, had given
way to Adalbert of Bremen; a war of churchmen
ensued, with abbeys plundered, monks despoiled—it
was the heyday of insolent and greedy feudal Bishops
intent on their own aggrandisement.　At length a
conspiracy of princes and prelates in the Diet of
Tribur flung Adalbert down.　Henry must abandon
him or yield his sceptre.　He attempted flight, could
not manage it, and saw the Archbishop fall.　That

was the signal of Hanno's triumph; with him the monastic party returned to power; Cadalus heard the news in St. Angelo, and paying his gaoler Cenci three hundred pounds of silver, he escaped to the North. At Mantua the Germans recognised Alexander in 1067; Cadalus assailed the city and was driven off by the Tuscan Godfrey, after which he did nothing memorable and died in obscurity. Meanwhile Guibert accepted the wealthy See of Ravenna. In 1073, after a stormy reign of twelve years, Anselm of Lucca died. Hildebrand, who seemed to choose Popes and to bury them, was performing the funeral obsequies in St. John Lateran when the acclamations of the people and Cardinal Hugo's eloquence summoned him to the vacant place. The crimson mantle was thrown about him, the tiara set on his head. He wept, refused, fell ill. But he could not escape the burden; and he announced his election, it is said in words of grave warning, to Henry IV.

XIV

HENRY IV. AT CANOSSA

(1073–1076)

NEVER did man embark on a voyage so seemingly desperate as that to which Gregory VII. was now committed, body and soul. What did he propose? To reform the Church, cleanse and renew the corrupt Hierarchy, set it free from its bondage to kings and nobles, and in doing so, to abase the Empire, which until of late had been his stay. Such a policy, straight as an arrow to his own apprehension, appeared crooked, subtle, and devilish in the eyes of many, and those not always depraved. Against him stood up, rank after rank, the thousands of clergy who would rather forego their livings than their wives. On the Bishops, gorged with plunder and open law-breakers, he might count for a determined opposition. Nor did the people, who like himself, were little better than born serfs, rise to that view of Church or Papacy, pure in its angelic brightness, with its gleaming sword unsheathed to smite even royal vice, which, as his letters testify, was habitual with him. "To forsake righteousness," he said, "is to make shipwreck of the soul"; and with Æschylean energy, "All the attempts of mortals are but straw and stubble against the rights of St. Peter and the power of the Most High."

His Bible he knew by heart. In all his epistles it overflows, as in St. Bernard's sermons and correspondence; it shapes his thought, enforces his argument; no Puritan lived more habitually in the atmosphere of Psalms, Prophets, Old Testament Theocracy. He did not pretend to be a scholar; but the "rustic style" in which he gloried is a tesselation of Scripture phrases; he wrote and spoke as a Prophet to the degenerate House of David. His favourite word — it was the last he uttered — is "righteousness." But he is often weary of the sun; in writing to his dearest friends, the Countess Beatrice of Tuscany and her daughter Matilda, he lets fall the strong expression, "I was desperately ill, now I am well again, and sorry for it." Elsewhere, he says to Hugh of Cluny, "An immense sadness, sorrow without a break, encompasses me round about. I have lived twenty years in Rome against my will." He calls it, "this Rome, to which the Almighty brought me back in chains"; had Providence laid so heavy a burden on Moses or Peter, they would have died under it; his own days are a living death; he is always fainting and crying, "Lord, take me away from this world; make no long delay!"

Those who would resolve Gregory or men of his

temper into ambitious hypocrites, make no allowance
for the strength of a reforming passion, kindled in the
cloister, fed upon deep and secure beliefs.   Hildebrand led a mighty movement which carried him

ST. GREGORY VII., POPE A.D. 1085.
(*From an old engraving.*)

along at the same time.   It was not of his creation.
When he proposed to abolish lay investiture and
clerical marriage, he was summing up an idea which
during the last hundred years had been silently

gathering force. His raptures, fasts, vigils, scourgings, while they bore witness to the man's sincerity, disclosed an ascetic, unworldly type of the Christian life, in which thousands believed perfection to consist, while none could less resemble the ways of the beneficed priest or his patron and tyrant the military Prince-Bishop. Could celibacy, instead of being the rare exception, become the rule, it would reform the clergy as by a magic stroke. And if laymen, including the Emperor, ceased to traffic in church-livings, the scandal of a luxurious, negligent, feudal Hierarchy would come to an end. That this Reign of the Saints might turn, as in other times, to an all-embracing, irresistible despotism—to Florence under Savonarola, to Geneva under Calvin, to Presbyterian Scotland or Puritan New England—Gregory did not imagine. He spoke always of the Church's freedom.

In the first authentic Decretal, Siricius had insisted with the Archbishop of Tarragona, and through him to the Spanish Church, that every bishop, priest, and deacon must be celibate. A Council of Carthage in 397 calls this an Apostolic law; and though Vigilantius protested, Innocent I. (417) renewed the enactment; St. Leo extended it (440) to sub-deacons; and such has ever been the discipline of the West. If a married man took orders, his wife entered a convent or abode under his roof as a sister. Thus we meet the curious names of *presbytera* and *episcopa* in Church history, and we read of priests' or bishops' children. In the East, however, custom, which had always been acquainted with a married clergy, per-

mitted matrimony to stand with orders in the lower
ranks. It would not suffer it in bishops, who were
to be chosen from the monasteries. And in the
West it should be observed that orders were not
conferred till the age of thirty and upwards; that
various Councils appealed to Nicæa on behalf of a
milder rule: and that, as the learned Thomassinus
expresses himself, the earlier practice had been
undecided or fluctuating. Even in the eighth
century Paul I. rebuked, and was on the point of
deposing, the Archbishop of Ravenna for living
publicly with his wife. Nicholas I. renewed the
laws of his predecessors, and was charged by Photius
with infringing the Nicene Canons on this very
account. Children born after their father's ordination
were reckoned illegitimate or even slaves; but the
repeated injunctions of Popes and Councils prove that
the rule of celibacy had fallen into disfavour almost
everywhere during the ninth, tenth, and eleventh
centuries. When Gregory began his reform, says
Montalembert, " the whole clergy, with the exception
of the monks, and of certain bishops and priests
quoted as marvels, lived in permanent and systematic
concubinage."

Such is the witness, such the language, of Peter
Damiani, who in this long and sanguinary contest
played the part of St. Jerome against Vigilantius,
with a strength of resolution, and, it must be added,
a coarseness of terms, not to be imagined by those
who have never studied his writings. Himself rescued
and brought up by a priest's consort, the kindest
return he could make, after his monk's profession,

was to set the clergy free from these dangerous help-meets. And with the marriage of ecclesiastics certainly were bound up the sale, the transference, the secularising of benefices. Priests and deacons, said Desiderius, Abbot of Monte Cassino, are not ashamed to marry and leave children as heirs in their wills. What could they bequeath except what they had plundered? "These women," said Atto of Vercelli in 956, "rule the house, and when master is dead, inherit what the priest has left of the Church's goods and the alms given by the faithful." The people sold the election to livings, continues Desiderius, the priests sold the consecration and the gift of the Holy Ghost. It would be easier, exclaimed Damiani, to turn the heart of Judas than to convert a Bishop—heretic and robber as he is—from his poisonous heresy. Bishops, even in Rome, kept their concubines and called them openly their wives. In 1040, says Bonizo, it would have been hard to find in the Eternal City a priest that was neither illiterate, nor simoniacal, nor living in disorder.

Monks had at first been laymen, solitaries or united in a common life, but by rule they were "continent," that is to say, unmarried. Since the resurrection which began about the middle of the ninth century, their great leaders had been ousting the wedded secular canons and enforcing the strict Western discipline, as we may read in the trials and triumphs of Dunstan, the English Abbot. Nevertheless, it is patent from the large area over which opposition sprang up, from Apulia to Ireland, that the clergy in general neither observed the law nor

wished it to bind them.   Under Leo IX., and in his
despite, French bishops were publicly married, prelates of great Sees like Rouen, of smaller ones, like
Le Mans and Quimper.   In 1059, Damiani reproaches
Annibert of Turin for allowing his clergy to take
wives.   Long before this, St. Boniface had brought a
similar charge against the Germans ; and Leo VII.
wrote to Gerard, Archbishop in Bavaria, " It is
deplorable that the priests in your country are
openly married and ask to have their sons ordained."
St. Adalbert gave up his Bishopric of Prague because
he could not endure a clergy which declined to be
celibate and a nobility which was polygamous.
Evidence to the like effect could be multiplied ; but
there is no reasonable doubt that clergy and bishops,
left to their own devices, would have abrogated the
law and converted their benefices into hereditary
fiefs, on the pattern set them by their secular
neighbours.

Of this movement the centre was Milan, never at
rest under the Roman supremacy, as proud of St.
Ambrose as though he had been an Apostle.   Ruined
by Attila, greatly restored under Archbishop Anspert,
the city flourished when Pavia decayed, and in 1018
Heribert governed it with a magnificent liberality, a
show of learning, and a resolution of character, which
made him the foremost prelate in Italy.   He crowned
Conrad II., and himself joined in the Emperor's
Burgundian campaign.   But he was something of a
tyrant and his people rebelled ; Milan underwent a
siege at the hands of Conrad.   The Archbishop defeated his Emperor ; he set up the famous Carroccio ;

he gave Milan freedom, but made it amenable to his own government. The Milanese, when Heribert died, invoked him as a Saint; yet he had been married to Useria; and on the election of Guido, the long-expected conflict broke out between reformers and Epicureans (1057).

These turmoils in the Italian cities of the Middle Age cannot fail to remind us of similar, but hardly more violent, scenes in the small republics of Greece. They did, in fact, spring from causes economic as well as political, and religion was often a mere pretext. Guido's rival, Anselm of Badoagia, could influence the vavasours, or base tenants, the "Minores," as they were termed elsewhere, whose debts burdened them, and who felt keenly the impositions laid on their shoulders by the Archbishop, his nobles, and his ministers. The monks would side with a discontented, suffering multitude. Gregory VII. always speaks as the champion of the down-trodden. And a sincere desire to end abuses may have actuated Landulf, the eloquent, high-born preacher, and Ariald, the man in the market-place, who were Anselm's lieutenants. The reformers appealed to authority, the relaxed to ancient Canons; and both parties to St. Ambrose. But Ariald drove the married clergy out of church. They were forcibly separated from their partners. Guido, on the other hand, held a Council at Novara, and dared to excommunicate the leaders of reform. He brought down on himself (1059) Peter Damiani, now a Cardinal, with Anselm of Lucca, commissioned by Nicholas II. to quell these disorders. Now the people turned again; they would not see their Archbishop humbled in presence of a Legate. But Damiani faced them with supreme daring; he argued for the Roman claims, which they were not prepared to deny; and he compelled Guido as well as his clergy to take a solemn oath against simony and concubinage, which was equivalent in the circumstances to a general confession of guilt.

Nor was that all. In 1059 Nicholas II.—we must bear in mind that Hildebrand was his adviser—renewed the decrees which condemned these evils, and Guido signed them again. But neither he nor any Lombard Bishop ventured on publishing them. Anselm became Pope; the episode of Cadalus followed; Landulf died, and his brother Herlembald stepped into the office of agitator. He was a democrat to whom Alexander II. sent a sacred banner, Hildebrand urging this consecration of the popular cause which implied the triumph of celibacy. Pass a hundred years, and the Lombard League will vindicate his foreboding that the Free Cities would uphold the Church, even unto blood. Herlembald governed Milan; Ariald got the Archbishop deposed; but he was imprudent enough to substitute Roman uses for the Ambrosian, and it cost him his life. Guido had returned. Ariald escaped to Legnano; he was captured by the retainers of Oliva, the Archbishop's niece, taken to an island in the Lago Maggiore, tortured, mutilated, murdered (1066). Still Herlembald held the city; he kept Guido in prison, defied the Imperial Court, and was under the protection of Gregory VII. when a new insurrection struck him dead and trampled on his sacred banner.

Ariald and Herlembald were canonised; Milan yielded outwardly to the stringent discipline of reform; but in 1098 its clergy were handing down as of old their benefices to children born in the sanctuary; and Cremona, Piacenza, Pavia, Padua, exhibited the fiercest dissensions between the defenders of licence and the partisans of law.

This one sample may suffice. We need not dwell on the strife at Florence, the virtues of St. John Gualbert, the charges against Bishop Peter, the victorious ordeal of his opponent, Peter Igneus. Everywhere, law and piety, seconded by popular zeal, overcame the opposition of prelates who did not know what principles to rely upon when they ran counter to the ideas of the age. All owned monasticism to be the highest Christian aim; how, then, could bishops or clergy live as though merely ordained laymen? Celibacy was now sure of its triumph. Not so the war against simony, or the attempt to wrest from secular hands privileges and properties, a half or a third of whole kingdoms, which had been time out of mind at their disposal.

Neither of the parties to this quarrel can have dreamt that it would continue through vicissitudes of shame, triumph, and defeat, a long three hundred years, reckoning from Henry IV.'s accession to Charles IV.'s Golden Bull, which at last divided the Empire from the Papacy (1056–1356). Still less did they anticipate its consequences to themselves. Both institutions, it must be remarked, stood above or outside the nations of Europe considered in a tribal or territorial sense. If the Papacy controlled

a spiritual society, the Empire was often little
more than a political fiction. In both the ruling
power was influence, not the force of arms, but an
acknowledged yet always resisted law, and the
personal authority of the ruler. Both again were
elective monarchies, liable to revolution at every
demise of crown or tiara. They were not only
exposed to the intrigues, the corruption, the
sordid or ambitious views of possible candidates,
but, as we have seen in the French and American
systems which resemble them, were almost certain
to be wielded by average men chosen to keep out
the more daring spirits. By a singular coincidence, indeed, the Empire was now to become a
sort of family possession, the Papacy to move on
definite lines under its monastic Pontiffs, for a
hundred years and more. Nevertheless, no Emperor
succeeded in making the crown hereditary until the
brunt of this battle was over. And the immediate
successors of Gregory VII. inherited his policy
rather than his genius.

Gregory felt unbounded confidence in the " Divine
Idea " of Church and Hierarchy, of monks' vows and
religious profession, which from youth up he had
cherished. As legate in France, under Victor II., he
confronted the hostile multitude of prelates ; wrought
upon their conscience by miracle, as William of
Malmesbury tells us ; and saw forty-five bishops and
twenty-seven other dignitaries confess their guilt and
lay down the sacred trusts which they had bought.
In Damiani's language, he had been " Lord of the
Pope " ; or as Bishop Benzon, a Simonian, cried

aloud, he "kept Pope Nicholas like an ass in a stable," binding the wretched man by oath to do his will—a will, remarks Chavard, of marble and iron, which could not be broken. In all things, says the biographer of St. John Gualbert, he heard and defended the monks. Thus on one side stood the Pope, almost alone in the Hierarchy, relying upon the monastic orders and the popular enthusiasm ; on the other, bishops, nobles, courtiers, and married clergy looked to young Henry IV. as their champion. To him in exchange for freedom as against the Hildebrandine laws, they surrendered the Church estates, the right of election to benefices great and small, the immunities of cloister, fief, and Imperial city. In a contest so unequal it did not seem possible that Gregory should win.

Henry IV., as described by historians, was a Teuton, with the large limbs, blue eyes, flaxen hair, and truculent temper of his race ; bold, enterprising, and subject to fits of passion ; " a man," says Bonizo, "of deep counsel and remarkable sagacity." His bringing up had not been wise. The Empress Agnes spoilt him. Hanno, if a Saint, frightened and browbeat the lad whom he had kidnapped. Adalbert of Bremen, according to his enemies, suffered Henry to run wild at a critical period among evil companions, who gave to the Court at Goslar a scandalous name. These, however, were the " King's friends," to be rewarded with great bishoprics and the wealthiest abbeys in German lands. When the Saxons revolted they charged upon Henry crimes too enormous for belief ; yet he never broke loose from the religious

creed of his childhood. Among the strange
characteristics of this man we must reckon his moods
of repentance, his remorse after violent and outrageous behaviour, his tears and submission to those
whom he had been persecuting to the death. He is
called passionate, cunning, treacherous; the story
will prove either that he was unstable, or that in the
conditions of the time no basis of purely secular
independence could be discovered, on which to withstand the authority exercised by a Pope in God's
name.

June, 1073, the very day after Gregory had been
chosen, saw the Saxon chieftains revolt. Their cry
went, "For God's Church, Christian Faith, our own
Freedom!" Henry was asked to send away his
youthful counsellors, to quit his concubines, to take
back the wife whom he had repudiated, to dismantle
the forts by which he quelled these princes. Among
his friends were the Archbishop of Bremen, Liemar,
and the Bishops of Zeitz and Osnaburg. They were
driven into exile. Thuringia broke into open war.
Henry lost his treasures, fled into hiding; then with
the help of his prelates and the Rhine Princes he
gained a battle at Hohenburg (1075). In adversity,
when Gregory admonished him, the Emperor confessed to every charge—incontinence, simony, invasion
of Church property; he would repent and amend.
Messengers came from Rome demanding the fulfilment of his promise. Let him call a Council, degrade
the simoniacal prelates. He consented. There was
a frightful tumult at Cologne, perhaps in consequence;
Hanno just escaped with his life, the city underwent

horrible disorders. Germany was rent into factions. At Erfurt where Siegfried of Mayence presided, when he displayed the Roman enactments, the clergy, almost all married, rose against him, and threatened the legate in such terms that he fled, escorted by his own troop of soldiers. Hereupon followed a synod at Rome, and the Pope, in one peremptory decree, abolished the whole right of investiture ; to grant or to accept it was the sin of idolatry, its punishment was interdict (February, 1075).

This might be reform ; it was certainly revolution. While no one pretended that the sale of livings could be anything but a sin, investiture with ring and staff had been practised by the holiest laymen with the Church's consent or toleration. Gregory abrogated a long-standing usage ; he did not substitute any ceremony by which the Civil Power was recognised. Not only the person, but the property, of every cleric thus became exempt from secular burdens. While the Pope could dispose of bishoprics and their wealth, of parishes and their endowments, nay of abbeys and their treasures—as was shown by Stephen IX. in regard to Monte Cassino, by the crusading Pontiffs in regard to all Christendom—it might be asked in what manner King or Emperor could deal with contumacious prelates, or with ecclesiastical bodies which declined to share in the dangers and liabilities of the common government. This question, under various crude or debatable forms, was to give rise to Constitutions of Clarendon, Statutes of Mortmain, Premunire and Provisors, and to precipitate a crisis in the days of Philip the Fair and Boniface VIII., in the course of

which the Medieval Papacy, inaugurated by Gregory
at this moment, should complete one great cycle of
its development and a new era begin. It is not too
much to affirm that this double dispute, touching the
marriage of the clergy and the immunities of their
estate, which Henry IV. took up in defiance of the
monk Hildebrand, is the same as that which in 1517
was baptized with the name of the Reformation. At
Erfurt a yet unconscious Protestant Germany had
risen up against Rome. No sooner had Gregory
thrown down the gauntlet in his Lateran Synod, than
this entire party went over to the Emperor.

Had Gregory been no more than a politician,
he would have devised some way of hindering that
alliance. But he was what men of the world call
a fanatic, and his Church has declared him to be
a Saint. He struck at high and low, prince and
prelate, with undaunted resolution. The whole
German Church was leagued against him. In
December, 1075, Hanno of Cologne vanished from
the scene. The Saxon Bishops, his partisans, had
been conquered with their brother-nobles. Siegfried
of Mayence was a reed shaken by the wind. In his
Roman Council Gregory had suspended from office
a crowd of bishops, including Liemar of Bremen, and
the occupants of Strasburg, Spires, Bamberg, Pavia,
Turin, and Lausanne. When Altman of Passau read
from the pulpit Gregory's decree against clerical
marriage, he was almost torn in pieces by the furious
rabble. At Mayence the like tumults were renewed ;
neither Siegfried nor the Papal Legate could persuade
the clergy to obey. The law remained a dead letter.

Except very few—it is the Pope's lament—none of the Bishops exerted themselves to stamp out the evil of simony, or to insist on their priests leading a single life. Henry might assume that in defying the Roman authority he would have the world at his back.

And he was a victor in arms at twenty-three, while the Pope seemed defenceless, worn down with age and trouble. The Normans, for sins of their own, lay under interdict. Nor was Rome itself—the patrician, turbulent Rome, which never loved the clergy—favourable to the monk from the Aventine. Guibert, soon to be Antipope, may have stirred up old feuds, if they did not blaze out unprovoked. What we know is that on Christmas Eve, 1075, in wild weather, as the Pope was celebrating Mass in St. Mary Major's, Cenci, of the House of Tusculum, a pardoned traitor, seized Gregory, wounded him, and thrust him into the tower on the Via Sacra, bleeding and stripped of his sacred vestments. The mingling of sacrilege and murder was then, as long afterwards, peculiarly Italian. When day broke, the people assaulted Cenci's stronghold and rescued Gregory, who forgave this atrocious ruffian in mild terms. Such were the " weapons of lowliness " with which, as he told the Venetians, he meant to conquer.

But to Henry he turned a sharper edge ; his words were very swords. Within a few days he issued (January, 1076) a declaration of the Papal right to judge kings for their offences ; he rebuked the royal appointments to Milan and Spoleto ; he insisted on the discipline of celibacy, and he cited the Emperor, under threat of excommunication, to appear on February 22nd in Rome before a Church tribunal. Henry dared not risk his crown on the adventure. At once he summoned his Bishops to meet at Worms on the Sunday of Septuagesima. His intention was to depose Gregory before he should himself be deposed. The timorous Siegfried was president;

HENRY IV., EMPEROR A.D. 1076.
(*From a print in the British Museum.*)

Cardinal Hugo, a sycophant and simoniac, who had been the first to acclaim Hildebrand as Pope, now stepped forward and charged him with crimes of the deepest dye, but offered no evidence. A form of renunciation was drawn up, and every Bishop compelled to sign it. Henry sent the decree to Rome with a letter of studied insult, in which he maintained

that the Emperor could be unmade for no crime save apostasy. He did not perceive in his admission that the Pope alone could judge who was, or was not, an apostate. His letter concluded: " I, Henry, by the grace of God King, with all the Bishops of my kingdom, cry to thee, ' Down, down ! ' "

This message was carried to Gregory sitting among his ministers in the Lateran, by a priest of Parma, Roland. Tumult followed its delivery ; but the Pope read it aloud in his self-controlled way, pronounced a skilful defence of his action, and next morning launched the great anathema. In his audience sat the Empress Agnes, Henry's mother. He had already received letters of retractation from many who took part in the Synods of Worms and Piacenza. Now, by the authority of St. Peter, in the name of the Almighty, he proceeded to deprive Henry of the whole government over Germany and Italy. He released all Christians from the oaths they had sworn or might hereafter swear to him, and forbade them to yield him obedience henceforth. He bound the King in spiritual chains that all nations might know and acknowledge Peter to be the rock on which the Church was built by Christ, the Son of the living God.

It was a deed without example, but a masterstroke. Thirty years had passed since Henry's father at Sutri put down three Popes at once from their pride of place. Now the world looked on at a counter-revolution in which the spiritual power did as it chose with the temporal ; not only did the law of the Roman Pontiffs obtain wider sway than the law of ancient Emperors—which was Gregory's boast to the King of Denmark—but the successor of Charlemagne must become its humble minister, or his crown was forfeit. Henry heard the sentence and felt dismay. One of his chief advisers, William of Utrecht, perished miserably. Defection had begun among the bishops ; Suabia, Bavaria, could not be trusted ; some of the Saxon leaders had gained their freedom ; at Mayence opposition raised its voice ; Udo, Archbishop of Treves, broke away to Gregory ; and the King, losing himself in wild enterprises, failed in Saxony and retreated with disgrace to the Rhine. Six months had sufficed to ruin all his devices.

Meanwhile, Gregory exhorted him to repentance, but did not cease to remind the Germans that if he were contumacious, on them lay the burden of choosing an Emperor. At Tribur, near Darmstadt, a Diet, or as we now say, the Reichstag, was held. Three candidates appeared. Henry, with a handful of followers, lingered at Oppenheim across the river. During seven days the Diet took cognisance of his high crimes and misdemeanours, his private vices, his elevation of base-born men to responsible station, his distrust of the nobles, and his assaults upon churches and monasteries—these were counts of an indictment from which we gather that the feudal chiefs, lay or ecclesiastical, would have resisted a Patriot King as fiercely as they did a tyrannical Emperor. And he, quitting the semblance of dignity, flung himself on the ground before them. He offered any terms short of abdication. His offer was rejected. The wretched Siegfried now thought of crossing the Rhine, attacking Henry in person, and ending the war at a blow. But the Imperial bands confronted him, and this ignominy was spared the fallen Prince. Hard conditions, such as the Middle Ages had never heard before, were exacted from him. At next Candlemas Gregory intended to hold his court in Augsburg. Let him decide the whole affair, said these German oligarchs, who played off one authority against another, and were only not fickle because they looked always to their own advantage. Till then let the King disband his troops, send away his excommunicated Privy Council, withdraw to Spires, and live there with no state of royalty. To this extraordinary demand Henry submitted. Gregory was virtual sovereign of the Holy Roman Empire.

A terrible winter set in ; from November to April the Rhine was frozen ; his enemies, the Dukes of Bavaria and Carinthia, watched the passes of the Alps lest Henry should steal a march on them and make his own terms with the Pope, who was moving towards Mantua. With his wife and child, attended by one servant, the unhappy young man turned into Burgundy, bought from his kindred of Savoy the passage over Mont Cenis, and through ways cut by hatchets out of the frozen snow, not without accidents, he came down headlong into Lombardy. He was on the road to Canossa.

Among friends now of the Imperial cause he found himself ; a great army sprang up to meet him ; the deprived prelates, the married clergy asked, Would he not depose Hildebrand ? That undaunted yet wary pilgrim had turned back from Mantua on

16

hearing this news and taken up his quarters in
Canossa, twenty miles south-east of Parma, the
strong fortress where Adelaide, Queen of Italy, once
found shelter.   It belonged now to Matilda, the
saintly Amazon who ruled over Tuscany and was
the devoted friend of the Pope.   Thither came a
host of penitents, German bishops, German nobles,
barefoot, in mourning, to beg absolution.   It was
given with consummate kindness.   Matilda and
Hugh of Cluny interceded for the chief criminal.
Gregory referred him to the approaching Diet of
Augsburg.   They pleaded for a speedier reconciliation.   "Then," said the Pontiff, "let him put into
my hands his crown and sceptre, and confess himself
an unworthy King."   On January 25, 1076, Feast of
the Conversion of St. Paul, Henry was admitted
within the precincts of the Castle.   In deep snow he
stood there, the tall, fair German, stripped to his
shirt, fasting and barefoot.   That day passed, and a
second, in this ghostly silence, but Gregory from
within gave no sign that he knew of Henry's humiliation.   A third ended in like manner.   Was it the
severity of an Apostle or the arrogance of a tyrant
which the Pope displayed?   At length, in the chapel
of St. Nicholas, Henry fell down at Matilda's feet
and implored her intercession.   Then Gregory
suffered him to draw near.   They met—a strange
contrast, youth and age, the Emperor in his single
white garment trembling, the Pope with his red
mantle about him, slight, small, grey-haired, inflexible
as death.   The Emperor was conquered.

Terms as stringent as they could be made, with

compurgators to show that Henry was not to be trusted; and to crown all, the fearful adjuration which Gregory put upon him, holding the Host in his right hand, "May God strike me if I am guilty of the crimes alleged against me! Do thou, my son, do as I have done. Avouch thy innocence on the Lord's body." Conscious of many crimes, he shrank in terror; but the absolution had been given; Henry was Emperor again. His Lombards at the gates heard this announcement with angry contempt; they cried out that his son should be their King, that Gregory was a son of Belial. When the humbled Teuton quitted Canossa none would greet him or so much as look his way, and he passed on to Reggio in a cloud of grief, disowned by friends, a laughing-stock to enemies. Such a day as Canossa the world would never see a second time.

XV

NORMANS, CRUSADES, INVESTITURES

(1076–1123)

IT is the year 1083. From his snow-penance Henry had taken an undying hatred to Hildebrand. Though absolved, he had not been able to prevent the election of an Anti-emperor, Rudolph of Suabia, whom let not the careless reader confound with Rudolph of Hapsburg two centuries later. War was raging, with devastation on a grand scale and blood-shed less than we might imagine, but a horrible mixture of civil and religious broils. Rudolph was nearly finished, and Gregory's new thunderbolts against the Franconian Emperor did not help the Suabian, to whom he perhaps sent a crown from St. Peter. At Mayence and Brixen the Pope was deposed. Guibert, Italian Chancellor, Archbishop of Ravenna, usurped his place and for a long twenty years fought and wandered as Clement III. No serious historian believes the calumnies which were spread abroad against Gregory. That he was true

Pope every one knew. **But in the** battle of the Elster, while **Henry** suffered a reverse at the hands of the Saxons, Rudolph was killed. In the spring of 1081 Henry crossed the Alps, encamped under the walls of Rome, and began a siege that lasted amid fevers, alarms, and desultory fighting some three years off and on. Accident at length gave him the Leonine City, but Gregory was secure in St. Angelo. Negotiations led to no result. The Emperor pressed on **the siege** ; at Christmas, thanks to bribery, the Romans opened their gates. Henry held the Lateran as well as St. Peter's. His Antipope was consecrated, himself crowned on Easter Day, 1083, by Clement. Canossa might seem to be revenged.

Now came Desiderius, Abbot of Monte Cassino, like the messenger in a Greek tragedy, to announce that Robert Guiscard was approaching with six thousand knights and thirty thousand foot. Henry could not stay to meet him. Taking hostages and breaking down some of the walls, he fled towards Città Castellana. Three days afterwards, up marched the motley but formidable host, not only Normans but Saracens, all freebooters, on fire with lust of plunder and excitement. They carried the gate of San Lorenzo ; they released the Pope and conducted him to the Lateran. But in two days the Roman populace broke upon the barbarians as they were feasting, and attempted a massacre. Into these narrow streets the Normans urged their cavalry ; it was a fight from house to house, and the natives were getting the advantage, when Guiscard uttered the ominous word " Fire ! " Instantly, from Lateran to

Capitol, over the regions which Nero had once seen in conflagration, the flames rose up.   Houses of wood, churches and temples of marble, were consumed under a red cloud of night.   Inhabited Rome, Palatine, Esquiline, Quirinal took fire, blazed up, and was laid in ashes to an accompaniment of murder, rape, robbery, and all the unspeakable pollutions which heathen Saracen, and scarcely less heathen Norman, now brought on the Capital of the Christian World. From that day the region of Monti—the Hills— has been a desolation.   When the people began to build again they moved down into the Field of Mars. Modern Rome dates from Robert Guiscard and Gregory VII. and this great fire.

Thousands of Romans were sold in open market ; the city, however, was not safe ; and Gregory, broken-hearted, went in company of Robert to Monte Cassino, from which he retired to the stern seaside fortress of Salerno.   His last letter to Beatrice and Matilda breathes an unconquered spirit.   His last words have a proud yet sincere ring in them : " I have loved justice and hated iniquity, therefore I die in exile." Roman, with a Virgilian pathos, they were answered by one of his Cardinals in a more splendid strain : " In exile, Holy Father, thou canst not die ; behold I have given thee the heathen for thine inheritance and the uttermost parts of the earth for thy possession." Such was medieval Rome, a blending of Imperial haughtiness with the prophetic visions of the Hebrew Testament.   Then Hildebrand bowed his head and died.   He lies in a seldom-visited shrine, not far from the crypt of the Apostle Matthew, looking over the

TEMPLE OF ANTONINUS AND FAUSTINA IN THE FORUM (ROME),
SHOWING TRACES OF FIRE, A.D. 1083.

231

blue Tyrrhenian waves. In death as in life we admire his solitary grandeur, his devotion to an ideal which consumed him as it subdued the conscience of his century. But he perished while the battle was raging (May 25, 1085).

Four men he had pointed out among whom to choose a worthy successor ; they were all monks. The Abbot of Monte Cassino, after a year of flight and protest, became Victor III. Robert Guiscard had followed Gregory to the tomb in a few months. Desiderius was the friend of his son, and known already as an adherent of the Norman policy which would keep Emperors at a distance. " No German King," he said, " should institute another Pope." But his reluctance to wear the triple crown was unfeigned. With Jordan's aid Guibert had been chased from St. Peter's, Victor installed ; but the monk-Pope returned to Cassino, renewed at Beneventum the interdict on Henry, and died in 1087. After six months another Gregorian candidate, Odo, Bishop of Ostia, was chosen. A Benedictine, noble by birth, French by extraction, once a prisoner in the hands of Henry IV., he announced his election by declaring that he would walk in Gregory's footsteps. He was destined to an everlasting name as Urban II., the Pope who preached and consecrated the First Crusade (1088–1099).

The nations were grouping themselves afresh, and large domains were falling to the Roman See. On the day when Gregory died, Alfonso VI. of Castile captured Toledo from the Moors. Urban restored to it the Metropolitan dignity over Spain, which it had long lost. He was likewise called upon to

mediate between the heirs of Guiscard as suzerain ;
to Roger he gave Apulia, to Bohemond Tarentum.
A daughter of Robert's was married to Raymond,
Count of Barcelona ; in 1090 this Prince declared
himself and his possessions tributary of St. Peter,
which, as the diploma proves, had become a recognised style of independence from secular powers.
Tarragona was to be held as its peculiar property
by the Apostolic See. Yet, at this very hour, Guibert
occupied one half of Rome ; and while France
acknowledged Urban with joy, the Empire was
divided and England hesitating. Urban naturally
proposed to imitate the earlier Pontiffs who had
found in the Franks allies or champions when the
Germanic races pressed upon them. In proclaiming
a Crusade he was setting Rome free and holding up
Henry with his Antipope to the scorn of those
myriads who took the cross.

Before this came to pass fortune had favoured
only to abandon Henry. By way of helping the
Papal interest, Matilda, now past forty, consented
to marry Guelph of Bavaria, who was eighteen and a
husband only in name ; but this confederacy brought
down the Emperor into Tuscan parts. He captured
Mantua ; he was on the point of exacting an almost
dishonourable peace, when defeat and his son
Conrad's rebellion drove him home again. Conrad,
deeply religious, but a dreamer, believed or imagined
things too monstrous for recital which he charged
upon his father, and escaping to Matilda's partisans,
was crowned King of Italy in Monza and Milan.
The Pope, meanwhile, lived as a wanderer on the

face of the earth in the Norman dominions. When this intelligence reached him, he came back to Rome and kept Christmas there in 1093. Henry was shattered by his favourite son's defection. Guibert expressed his willingness to abdicate. At Piacenza in 1095 Urban gathered an assembly of thousands, eager to take the Cross; and before them all he gave ear to the frightful accusations which were brought against her husband by the Empress and declared them well-founded. These events broke the Imperial influence in Lombardy; and after some vicissitudes, during which Matilda separated from her foolish husband, a party of Crusaders took Rome on their way to Palestine. In 1097 Guibert was finally dislodged from St. Angelo.

But Urban had entered France in triumph. He acted with all the pomp and authority of a King. Philip I., weak and dissolute, not taking from his predecessors the severe warning administered to them by Nicholas I. and other Popes, had put away his Queen Bertha, and seized Beltrada, wife of the Count of Anjou. This pretended marriage was allowed by the Bishop of Senlis, denounced by Yvo of Chartres, who suffered imprisonment in consequence, and reluctantly condemned by Hugh of Lyons in a Council at Autun, which, however, excommunicated both the King of France and the German Emperor. Urban now arrived at Cluny, where another Hugh, forty-six years Abbot, welcomed him as an old disciple. The famous Council at Clermont followed (1095), and most remarkable it is that a French Pope should command all Europe to enter on a distant, a hazardous expedition, while his capital was in the hands of an Antipope, the Emperor lay under interdict, and the successor of Hugh Capet was excommunicate. In his own person Urban combined the temporal and spiritual sovereignty of the West; neither did this amazing double character of the Papacy provoke remonstrance on the part of nobles or kings, though it dated no farther back than Gregory VII. Philip apologized, shuffled, was absolved, and after a wretched comedy which lasted fifteen years, died in peace with the Church.

To complete our picture of times so unlike the present, we need only remember how Anselm of Canterbury was entering at the same period on his long quarrel with William Rufus and Henry Beauclerc, which fills a tumultuous chapter in our native history.

But the schismatic, the anti-clerical party as we should now term it, was no match for Saints or Crusaders. When Silvester II. conceived the daring idea of overcoming Islam in the Holy Land—a design taken up by Pope Gregory and carried out by Urban—he cannot have anticipated that the rights and privileges accruing thence to the Roman Church, would make it the mightiest of visible kingdoms, suzerain over Europe, rich with the tribute of clergy, laity, monks, and military orders, of which no account was asked or given. The Crusades dealt to Franconians and Hohenstauffen the deadliest blows, while investing the Papacy with a moral splendour as the defender of Christendom,

and awakening the consciousness, never afterwards
dormant, that in spite of local or national differences
Englishmen, Germans, Spaniards, and Italians were
members of one great Confederation.

This movement, so wide and deep, resembled the
outburst of new ideas which we call the French
Revolution in its immediate effects on lesser quarrels
and the internal dissensions of Europe. Where it
did not submerge, it tended to absorb them. Even
Henry IV. spoke of taking the Cross; if he drew
back it was because he could not join the orthodox
hosts without acknowledging Gregory's Ultramontane
successor. Yet the enthusiasm awakened at Clermont gave him four years' peace; and, in common
with other Princes, he proclaimed the Truce of God.
His Antipope Guibert died in 1100. Urban had
gone shortly before him; a year later Conrad, the
pious rebel, died at Florence. There was a fresh
Pope, Paschal II.; a new King of the Romans, or
heir-apparent to the Empire, in the person of young
Henry, whom his father saw crowned at Aix-la-
Chapelle in 1099. Reconciliation seemed in sight.
But the old Emperor would not sue even to a Pontiff
so mild and considerate as Paschal, who was forced
unwillingly to keep him outside the Church's pale.
In 1104 began the last act of an historical drama
which had gone on for fifty years. Prince Henry,
ambitious, subtle, seductive, quite innocent of a
conscience, revolted. With protestations of fervent
piety this bold youth took his father captive, imprisoned and deposed him—the Bishops and the
army applauding—while filial manifestoes in the

harshest language declared the Emperor unworthy to reign, not fit to live. Henry's cup was full; he died an outcast at Liège in 1206; his remains, in a stone sarcophagus, waited many years for the decencies of burial.

And now, says Montalembert, Churchmen were bitterly to atone for having accepted, even against a guilty father, the aid of an unnatural son. Henry V. was acknowledged by Paschal, the monk of Cluny, who had seen three Antipopes raised up and cast down in his presence at Rome. At once he claimed by his ambassadors the privilege conceded to Charlemagne of electing Bishops, and overawed the small number of Papal ecclesiastics in Germany. He strengthened his hands by an alliance with Maud, Henry Beauclerc's daughter. And the same year, August, 1110, the Emperor-elect, with thirty thousand horse, went down into the plains of Lombardy. As ever, the Italian cities were in deadly feud. Henry smote them into peace by the sack of Novara; received the homage of all, except the great Tuscan Countess, on the plain of Roncaglia; burnt Arezzo, and came to Sutri. The Roman Empire had suddenly revived in this active, formidable, keen-witted Prince, who was no less skilful in chicane than in war. Like his father he could be violent; but he understood, as Henry IV. never did, how to display his Imperial pretensions on a ground of law and custom.

He now reiterated his demands to Peter Leone, the Hebrew delegate who had been sent to him by Paschal. Investiture of the ring and the staff

did not exist in France. Thanks to Anselm of
Canterbury, it had just been surrendered by the
King of England. But Henry insisted on a practice
without which his German sovereignty was a mere
name—a practice, he argued, dating from Charles
the Great, and approved by sixty-three Popes.
Towns, castles, marches, tolls—perhaps two-thirds
of Germany—said the Archbishop of Treves before
Suger and the Pope at Châlons in 1107, went to
swell the regalia which clerics enjoyed, and how,
except by investiture, could the King maintain his
rights over them? But argument was not the
weapon of a lawless age. Paschal had beckoned to
the Norman knights of Apulia; they would not
stir. His Cardinals and the Romans themseves fell
into dire perplexity. Then the Pope made an offer
at which Europe stood aghast. Acting as supreme
administrator of Church property, Paschal consented
to give up the whole of the regalia—we must scan
it with the mind's eye: territories, cities, monasteries,
innumerable rights and revenues, the gifts of nearly
four hundred years—in exchange for freedom of
election to spiritual dignities. The Hierarchy was
to be disendowed, if Henry would suffer it to be
disestablished. On tithes and voluntary subscrip-
tions the clergy should subsist henceforth. By such
a measure the Church would pass out of the entire
feudal system; prelates would no longer yield
military service; the sceptre and the crozier would
be sundered; and the Emperor would find himself powerful enough to cope with his mightiest
peers, their sovereign not only in title but in fact.

Seven hundred years afterwards this dream of a Pope in extremity was fulfilled by the "mediatising" of all the German ecclesiastical princes, or their absorption into the secular dominions of Prussia, Austria, and Bavaria in 1815. When Paschal and Henry exchanged signatures, neither can have supposed that the compact would stand. Other parties to so momentous a transaction must be consulted. Henry, after hostages given on either side, and his guarantee of the Apostolic Patrimony, including all the South which he did not hold, entered Rome, took the customary oaths, and met Paschal in the portico of St. Peter's. He was declared Emperor; but now, when the terms of this astonishing compromise were read over, the Pope's followers broke out in tumult; the German himself would not ratify what he had signed. For a whole day Paschal sat a prisoner in front of the Apostle's shrine; the population rose, massacred stray Teutons, assailed St. Peter's, and wounded the Emperor. They paid for their temerity by a great slaughter. Yet Henry was compelled to withdraw uncrowned. He took with him Pope and Cardinals; wasted the Campagna for two whole months; and kept Paschal shut up in the fort of Treviso. At length, on the field of Sette Frati, the Pontiff gave in. He yielded up, without equivalent, the right of investiture. Henry was crowned and went back to Germany. The defeated Pope crept into the Lateran, and there hid his shame.

Paschal had sworn never to excommunicate Henry V. Bruno of Segni and the Cardinals argued that such a treaty was null and void ; they obliged their spiritual lord to renew the decrees of Gregory and Urban. In March, 1112, the Italian prelates held a Lateran Council, at which the Pope made full and ample amends for his concession to human weakness. He would not molest Henry; the Fathers might do as seemed right in their eyes. Without hesitation they cancelled the odious privilege. At Vienne, Guido, afterwards Calixtus II., cut off Henry from Catholic communion ; and though Yvo of Chartres stood up for moderate courses, opinion among Churchmen declared more and more violently against the Emperor. The German bishops, the monks of Hirschau, the people of Mayence with their Archbishop Albert, revolted. Matilda of Tuscany, dying in 1115, bequeathed her immense possessions, though fiefs depending on the Imperial crown, to Paschal and his successors. Again Henry must cross the Alps. In March, 1116, another Lateran Council, another confession from Paschal, "I am dust and ashes. Anathema to the unrighteous decree." His Cardinals treated him still with indignant contempt. The Romans, on their own account, were in rebellion. The Emperor took possession of Matilda's inheritance, and in 1117 he entered the city. Paschal fled south ; when Henry retired he came back, surprised and took the Vatican, but almost immediately after expired in St. Angelo (1118).

Straightway the Cardinals elected John of Gaeta, monk from Monte Cassino, friend and minister of Paschal, an erudite but not a strong person. Gelasius II. was hardly chosen when Frangipani

COUNTESS MATILDA IN THE VATICAN BASILICA.

(*Bernini.*)

(a Cencio) invaded the church, seized and struck
the Pope, and chained him up like a dog in his
citadel below the Palatine. These Tusculans were
Imperialist, that is to say, antipapal ; and their fierce
and brutal violence breaks in even on the rude
theatre of the Middle Ages like a thunderclap.
Other nobles took sides with the monks ; Gelasius
found the door open and escaped in a tempest,
during which he was borne on the shoulders of
Cardinal Hugo to Ardea. Henry lay outside the
Leonine walls. While the Pope in Gaeta bestowed on
William the Norman Naples and Sicily, the Emperor
had Maurice Burdin of Braga made Antipope.
Gelasius, after fresh perils in Rome, fled to Pisa, where
he consecrated the majestic cathedral, and thence to
Marseilles. He made a solemn progress through the
cities on the Rhone and died at Cluny (1119), after a
disastrous reign of one year.

Guido of Vienne, Calixtus II., succeeded ; and now
France, rising slowly to its great medieval honours,
held as a rule by the authentic Papacy, while the
Germans created or sustained Antipopes in the
Emperor's interest. Like Urban II., Calixtus, though
inflexible in defence of his order, showed no slight
diplomatic skill ; his French common sense enabled
him to bring this weary business of investitures to
a reasonable conclusion. Henry was not unwilling
to acknowledge a Pontiff allied with himself as with
the reigning houses of Europe, and already owned
by his German Bishops. At Rheims (November,
1119), in one of the most imposing Councils ever
held, Calixtus renewed the Truce of God ; listened

to the Kings of France and England pleading at his tribunal; and after fruitless negotiations, solemnly put to the ban Emperor and simoniacal prelates with Burdin the Antipope, calling himself Gregory VIII. He had boldly undertaken to meet Henry; now he went a triumphal progress through Southern France; he entered Italy, received the homage of Milan, was welcomed in Rome itself with transport, and ended his long pilgrimage at Benevento. In 1121 he captured Burdin at Sutri, exposed him to public derision in the streets of the city, and flung him into a forgotten dungeon, where he died.

No German had come to his rescue. Albert of Mayence and the Emperor stood up as to do battle with one another; but the Treaty of Würzburg and the Concordat of Worms proved that an agreement was desired by the whole Empire on terms which might leave the Bishops in possession of their fiefs, provided they were not absolutely independent of the secular over-lord. In 1122 the Bishop of Ostia relieved Henry and his partisans from the censures of the Church; the Lateran Council of 1123, with its six hundred abbots and three hundred Bishops, sealed up what had been accomplished at Worms. Something was yielded on both sides. The Emperor gave up his episcopal functions of the ring and the staff; he granted free election, and restored his conquests made during the war. And the Pope admitted that for the regalia there should be homage made by Bishops and Abbots chosen in the Imperial presence, who were to touch the golden sceptre and discharge all duties incident to their feudal tenures.

It was a fair **adjustment of** complex interests. Gregory VII. had gained the spiritual freedom for which he strove so manfully, and without which Bishops would have lost their sacred character, degraded into lieutenants of an earthly king. Henry V., though posterity does not admire him, gained the no less important admission that every kind of property carries with it social or political obligations, from which it can never be exempt. The Concordat of Worms respected in clergy and laity rights that are seldom violated without detriment to society as a whole.

SALERNO, WHERE GREGORY VII. DIED AND IS ENTOMBED.

XVI

ST. BERNARD OVERTHROWS ABELARD AND ARNOLD

(1123–1155)

To the great Burgundian Pope, Calixtus, a Burgundian Saint far more illustrious was destined to succeed, not in the Papal Chair, but in his influence over the hearts and actions of men, now awakening to chivalry, to culture, and to a romantic sense of the beauty and grace which Oriental lands had opened before the vision of Crusaders. It is a stirring, yet not altogether uncouth age, this first half of the twelfth century ; and its prophet, its king, is St. Bernard of Clairvaux. He reforms monasticism, nominates to the Papacy, preaches the Second Crusade, puts down Abelard, is more than a match for Arnold of Brescia. During well-nigh forty years he is the spiritual dictator of the West, and that in a period when men of strong character abounded, and genius was not wanting. The busy picturesque interval between Henry V.'s triumph at Worms and

the long troubles of Frederick Barbarossa, seems to
be filled with the person, the deeds, the sermons, the
miracles of this white-robed monk, whose pale and
refined features, consumptive in their fairness, leave
the impression of a detached, yet fiery soul. Far
more winning than Gregory VII. he is not a whit less
imperious. In spirit as in name he is the last of the
Fathers.

For with Abelard begins the strife of the Schools
which led up to Albert the Great and Thomas
Aquinas, and down to Luther and Calvin. With
the Republican Arnold, the national, Italian sentiment
springs to life which has created modern Italy. With
Barbarossa the German Empire emancipates itself
from the earlier conception familiar to Charlemagne
or Nicholas I., and sets up jurist against canonist,
the Civil against the Ecclesiastical Law, Cæsar against
the Pope as supreme in the secular sphere, and that
by right divine. Henry V. and Calixtus II. for a
moment held the balance even ; henceforth it swings
violently up and down, sometimes in the Pope's
favour, sometimes the reverse ; but it descends at last
laden with the *Pandects* of lawyers and the sword of
Julius. Individual Emperors might suffer defeat ; a
dynasty like the Hohenstauffen be sacrificed ; but
the movement which began blindly under Henry IV.
never was really arrested or thrown back until it had
bereft the Popes of their feudal overlordship, prepared the way for absolute monarchs, converted the
oligarchy of the Barons to a House of Peers, and by
an unconscious, yet irresistible, trend of events made
Parliamentary institutions possible, and gave the **Free**

Cities a share in government. To these far-off issues all parties contributed in turn. But we may trace their beginnings to the twelfth century.

Not Rome but Paris appears as the world's capital during this time. And Monasticism was entering on its last shining transformation, before it gave place to Francis and Dominic with their mendicant friars. Cluny had seen its best days. After St. Hugh's sixty years of stern Apostolic rule, came Pontius the feeble, came wealth and relaxation. The centralising government which brought dominion made a fresh start in fervour difficult, if not impossible. New forms of the higher life were demanded. Fontevraud had its singular story. Molesme was founded by two penitent brothers; Citeaux, yet more severe, by an Englishman, Stephen Harding, from Dorsetshire. This great man was Abbot when Bernard, the noble Burgundian youth, fled out of the world to Citeaux; and thus the Cistercian Order reached its high fame.

Once more monastic solitudes drew crowds of votaries; Bernard lived a life hard beyond description, but when he preached of its joys men, both single and married, left all things to follow him. This, too, was a form of crusading which attracted thousands. He was sent with a few companions to the Valley of Wormwood in Champagne; he called it Clairvaux, and it ceased to be a wilderness; but the simple fare and strict rule astonished those who came thither from Cluny. Bernard was not learned except in the Scriptures; he preached a figured and passionate mysticism with an eloquence as com-

manding as that of his later countryman Bossuet,
whose untroubled point of view, averse to subtleties,
dogmatic and decided, Bernard might seem to
anticipate. William of Champeaux, Bishop of
Châlons, gave him a commission to teach; his
colonies of white monks spread their Abbot's
reputation throughout Europe. A schism at Rome
made him the arbiter of the Papacy.

Henry V., last Franconian Cæsar, was gone.
Lothair the Saxon reigned in his stead. Honorius
II., after a contested election, had filled the Apostolic
throne six years, and dying in 1130 opened the way
to fresh Roman quarrels of the kind we have studied
so often. Sixteen Cardinals chose without delay
Innocent II. Thirty-two, after a pause, voted for
Peter Leone, of Jewish descent, vast wealth, and
undoubted popularity. On Peter's side were the
Frangipani, Roger the Sicilian Duke, and a majority
of the Sacred College. Innocent took flight to Pisa
and sought the protection of Louis, the French King,
who summoned a Council at Etampes. Many
Bishops attended, but the Abbot of Clairvaux was
called upon to direct them as another Samuel. He
pronounced for the fugitive. Innocent arrived at
Cluny, met King Louis at Orleans, and Henry I. of
England, whom Bernard had brought over to his
side, at Chartres. The Emperor followed suit.
Frederick of Hohenstauffen, and Conrad, King of
Italy, were included in the anathema hurled against
Peter Leone, called Anacletus II.

But when Pope and Emperor met at Liège it was
only Bernard's arguments that prevented the old

quarrel of investitures from being ripped up again.
Innocent passed a night at Clairvaux ; it was too
austere for his Roman Cardinals.   Still the Saint and
Prophet addressed vehement letters to Bishops, to
Genoa and Milan ; he went with the Pope to Italy ;
with him and Lothair he entered Rome.   "The
Jewish schismatic," supported by Normans, held
St. Angelo, even against the Germans ; and Bernard's
Pontiff spent four years at Pisa, until Lothair conquered all Italy down to Apulia (which he claimed)
and Anacletus died in his castle.   Victor II. became
the next Antipope.   Bernard persuaded him to
renounce his pretensions and the family of Peter
Leone to cease from troubling.   Not even the Roman
stubbornness could remain deaf to his persuasive
words.   He had brought the world round to
Innocent II.   The Lateran Council of 1139 sat under
his inspiration ; its decrees witness that Church
authority had attained almost all it demanded, but
that resistance to dogma as well as to discipline had
begun in the cities of Lombardy and the valleys of
the Alps.

If we assign the modern movement in politics,
philosophy, and letters to the twelfth century, it is to
Paris or France that we must look for its origin.
France was then a world in itself, with its rhymers in
Provence who fixed the measures of song and verse ;
its ardent, ascetic monks in Burgundy, destined ere a
hundred years had passed to lift the Cross in battle
against these amorous poets ; its thinkers from
Brittany, who found a voice in Peter Abelard, the
kinsman of Pelagius, the ancestor, not only of

CLOISTER OF ST. JOHN LATERAN, ROME.

251

Descartes, but of Chateaubriand. France was the brain, the eye, the armed right hand of medieval Europe. Its delicate genius invented the Gothic style, the troubadour minstrelsy, the romance of love and adventure; its clear thought strives in the technique of scholastic forms to arrive at a system which shall leave no question unanswered; its gay spirit, mingling with the Norman strength, the Celtic impetuosity, carried to all the coasts of Asia, to Euphrates and the Nile, a people so enamoured of fighting that to this day in the Moslem countries Frank and European are synonymous. In our time Paris calls itself the City of Light. During the latter twelfth century and all the thirteenth, it was even more the Capital of Intelligence than it is to-day.

From Abelard to St. Thomas Aquinas, the Doctor Angelical, such is the glorious ascent of its University. But it could reckon some earlier names, the promise of all that came afterwards. Charlemagne, no scholar himself, had founded seminaries in every bishop's house, and the Palatine School under his own roof. Thither he summoned Alcuin from Northumbria, whose training takes us back to Bede and Egbert; to the Greek Archbishop of Canterbury Theodore, sent to England by Pope Vitalian; to Bennet Biscop and John, precentor of the Vatican Basilica. It does not appear that Alcuin possessed an original mind; yet his talent for teaching entitles him to the dignity of first Rector over those institutions in Paris which later on developed into a genuine University. Paris, Pavia, Bologna were centres of learning associated henceforth with Charlemagne as their patron or founder. Thus on three distinct lines such culture as survived during the chaos of the tenth century may be traced out ; in the Benedictine monasteries, the Bishops' Courts or Seminaries, and the Palatine, that is to say, the royal schools. At Paris, when the University came to riper years, four nations were distinguished, the French, English, Picard, and Norman. At Bologna, Irnerius, the legal adviser of Henry IV., opened his school of Civil Law, which produced effects so momentous and lasting in European politics, towards the close of the eleventh century. And if, at the time we are now considering, Bologna might reckon its ten thousand students, Paris had at least its thirty thousand. The age of Greek speculation, with sophists, heretics, disputes of the market-place, sceptics and orthodox, pamphlets, Inquisitions, executions for condemned opinions, and universal unrest kept in order by the secular arm, was revived in the meadows of St. Germain, and drew to the Latin Quarter students from the four winds.

But the School philosophy did not begin its career on the banks of the Seine. At Bec in Normandy a converted soldier, Herluin, set up his abode under the rule of Benedict. He drew disciples from far and wide, among them Lanfranc, who opened a school of logic, wrote against Berengar, the rationalising Canon of Tours, and died in the See of Canterbury to which he had been called by William the Conqueror. Next came Anselm of Aosta, the Lombard, whose delight in learning and in friendship, whose trials under Rufus and Christian triumph over Beauclerc, adorn as romantic a page of history as the Middle

Age could illuminate. Anselm was a logician according to method ; but he was likewise a Saint and a contemplative ; in him the Benedictine quiet is not yet troubled by doubts or lost in wrangling, although at the Council of Bari he met the Greeks with their own weapons. He asked questions of which the solution was already given him by Revelation. But Roscelin took a farther step. His follower was Abelard ; and soon the world went mad over Being and Not-Being and the nature of universal ideas. About the year 1100 William of Champeaux was teaching in the Abbey of St. Victor. He disclosed the method of arguing on both sides in order to discover the truth. Thus he paved the way towards accepting Aristotle as a Christian philosopher. And he was the master of Abelard, an incipient sceptic, a man of letters, yet a foe to classic authority. If to Anselm we leave the honour of starting the orthodox system on its march, to Abelard we cannot but assign the beginnings of that rebellious movement which prompted one after another to fall out of the orthodox ranks, and to assail the Hierarchy that opposed them or the monasteries which they had quitted, with the arms of private judgment.

Peter Abelard (1079–1142) was born at Palais, in Brittany, of parents who both afterwards took the monastic vows. At sixteen he left home to study in the most famous schools ; at twenty-one he became the disciple of William of Champeaux. But he soon began to vex him with subtle arguments, and he left his master for Melun and Corbeil, where the enterprising youth set up on his own account. By and by, on his return after an illness, he found William had put on the religious habit in St. Victor's, and they were reconciled. But fresh combats ensued ; William, if not defeated, fell into discouragement. He took refuge in the See of Châlons ; and Abelard, brushing contemptuously aside another old master, Anselm of Laon, seized the vacant chair at Paris, began lecturing with an eloquence and acumen which dazzled the largest audiences, and soon attracted crowds from beyond the Rhine, the Alps, the English Channel.

He made a fortune by his lectures; he was handsome. winning, accomplished in music, an Alcibiades who reasoned like Plato, and a philosopher who was more than half a troubadour. Among those that listened to him were Peter Lombard, John of Salisbury, Arnold of Brescia, lights or guides to the next generation. But his chief scholar was a woman, of extraordinary spirit and equal beauty, Héloïse, niece of Canon Fulbert—the victim, the wife, the widow of unhappy Abelard. Their story cannot be told here. Enough that when the fallen Alcibiades hid his face in the monastery of St. Denis, Héloïse took the veil at Argenteuil. When we read her impassioned letters and his fragment of autobiography, so unlike St. Augustine's *Confessions* in its self-praise and sadness, we seem to have stepped from the twelfth to the eighteenth century, from St. Bernard to Rousseau, from the medieval cloister to a modern French drawing-room.

Hitherto Abelard had been a professor. Now he became a monk, and would have reformed St. Denis. The community thrust him out. He was accused of

heresy, and had to burn his book. Then he retired
to the Paraclete, a wild solitude in Champagne, and
once more scholars flocked round him. But they
obeyed no canonical rule; they discussed the mysteries of the Faith freely. St. Norbert, Archbishop
of Magdeburg, had reformed the Canons Regular,
and founded the widespread Order of Prémontré.
He joined with St. Bernard in denouncing Abelard.
Abelard retorted by calling them "the new Apostles."
But he could not fence with champions so well furnished. In 1125 he went home to Brittany; Héloïse
and her nuns took possession of the Paraclete. There
followed an interval of comparative peace. Then,
in 1140, when he was sixty years old, Abelard
appeared as a suspected heretic before the Council of
Sens. St. Bernard had stirred up the French prelates
against this unheard-of Gospel, these novel disputa-
tions. The modern writings penetrated everywhere;
but to overthrow them by syllogism could not be a
monk's business; and Bernard accused their authors,
while declining to argue in form against them. At
the Council mystic and rationalist came face to face.
Abelard appealed to Rome. The prelates, in a session
which has been grotesquely caricatured, condemned
his propositions. In like manner did Pope Innocent
II. The philosopher set out on his journey to the
Lateran; he was kindly entertained by Peter the
Venerable at Cluny; and he died at Châlons sur
Sâone, April 21, 1142. His remains were taken to
the Paraclete, where twenty-one years afterwards
Héloïse was laid by his side.

Peter Lombard, in his book called the *Sentences*

THE DUOMO OF PISA, CONSECRATED BY GELASIUS II., A.D. 1118.

257

of the Fathers, may be thought to have improved on the method of Abelard's treatise, *Sic et Non*—or " Yea and Nay "—which did suggest the recognised form of scholastic teaching. But in Arnold of Brescia he had trained not so much a philosopher as an agitator. This bold man appears to be the democratic soldier of Abelard, not less opposed to the Abbot of Clairvaux, nor in his opposition more fortunate. That his character was without blemish we learn from St. Bernard himself, who allows his captivating eloquence, while regarding him as little better than Antichrist. Brescia had revolted from the Empire ; it banished its tyrant-bishop, and under Arnold's direction reduced the clergy to their spiritual functions. Accused of schism at the Lateran Council (1139) he fled to Zurich. Five years after, the war of Rome against Tivoli and the revolt against Innocent II. of his intractable subjects, made Arnold for a brief space dictator on the Capitol. His patron at Zurich had become Cœlestine II. (1143). But in six months Cœlestine was gone ; and when Lucius II. took his place, the Roman Republic, by the lips of its Patrician Giordano, warned the Pope that he must exercise no temporal rule, but be content with tithes and oblations. Lucius called to the Emperor Conrad ; he armed his nobles, attempted to storm the Capitol, and perished in the assault. Giordano razed to the ground Cardinals' palaces and the forts of many high chieftains. It is clear that the whole movement, as directed by Arnold, was democratic. Friends of the Voluntary System, and all that uphold with Cavour 'a free Church in a free State," will recognise in this daring champion a spirit akin to their own. His hand was not dyed in the blood of Lucius; but his doctrine shaped the policy on which Romans were now prepared to act.

In their consternation the Cardinals turned their eyes upon St. Bernard. Would he accept the triple crown, or at least choose a Pope for them? He waved aside the glittering bait; and they nominated a poor, unlettered brother of his convent at Pisa, Eugenius III., in hopes that the Saint would persuade France or Germany to succour his late subject. Eugenius was crowned at Farfa. Rome saw Arnold with his Swiss mountaineers about him in company of Giordano the Patrician, who proclaimed the Republic, created new noble families and tribunes of the people, fortified St. Peter's, rebuilt the Capitol, and made pilgrims pay at the gates of the city. Bernard in a threatening letter commanded him to desist; in another he called on the Emperor Conrad to put down these rebels. Eugenius entered into a league with the neighbouring cities—he understood well the character of medieval Italians—and with the help of Tivoli he compelled Giordano to abdicate. He kept his Christmas in Rome (1146). But in March he was fleeing across the Alps to Dijon; for he would not betray Tivoli. The Abbot of Clairvaux governed the Church in his disciple's name. He deposed St. William of York on grounds which could not be sustained; he brought to his knees the Bishop of Poitiers, charged with a subtle heresy; and he roused Europe to the Second Crusade. Edessa had fallen; the Kingdom of Jerusalem was doomed

Eugenius published his Bull on the model of Urban's, and St. Bernard preached it in all the towns and monasteries, and along the highways of France, Flanders, and Germany (1146).

It is not easy to imagine this spiritual dictatorship; how the unarmed recluse gave their uniform to the Knights Templars; drew multitudes to Vézelay, where Louis VII., in spite of his sagacious counsellor, the Abbot Suger, took the Cross; compelled from the pulpit Conrad the Emperor to follow his example; and, more astonishing than all, put an end to the horrible massacre of Jews in the Rhine cities, where Rudolph of Mayence raised the cry against them. In the West, war could no longer be waged for lack of combatants; towns and castles were empty; the chivalry of Europe had gone to die at the fruitless siege of Damascus. Louis and Conrad returned in disgrace; a deep shadow fell on St. Bernard's last years; but when he died in 1153 he was instantly canonised by acclamation.

Eugenius died the same year. Twice he came back to Rome; his policy, Christian in its mildness, and successful because he made little or no pretence to temporal dominion, was to win his haughty people by generosity and magnificent display. He sent back the offerings of German archbishops, which was a new thing in Rome, wrote St. Bernard with more than a touch of sarcasm. Arnold was losing ground. In 1154 an Englishman, a priest, and a scholar, was elected, and Nicholas Breakspear became Hadrian IV. He had been brought up at St. Alban's, but was not a monk; he had served as legate in Norway; his experience taught him to strike hard ; and he pronounced sentence of exile against the Brescian reformer. Arnold denied his competence ; one of the Cardinals was murdered ; the sturdy Saxon laid Rome itself under an interdict. This was to quench the very lights at St. Peter's shrine. Towards Easter the clergy, reinforced by their people, insisted on obedience to Hadrian. Arnold had no choice but to disappear ; and the broken Senate laid down its arms.

But a fresh danger loomed on the Northern horizon. Frederick of Hohenstauffen had been called to succeed his kinsman in the Empire ; he was now coming over the Brenner to Roncaglia with a mighty host. Since Calixtus II. rebellions and disorders had weakened the Papacy ; while Henry V.'s judicious exchange of the crozier for the sceptre had united German prelates with German princes in a growing national sentiment. The Roman Law would speedily be pitted against the Roman Pontiff. Frederick felt himself every inch a Cæsar. Valiant, far-looking, ambitious, just in a barbaric and cruel fashion, strong in the conviction of his rights, and sure that he held his crown from God alone, he entered Italy as a victor who came to set the world straight. His prelate-vassals carried their standards before him. The Republics of Lombardy licked the dust. Tortona was made an example. From Viterbo Hadrian sent ambassadors to offer him the Imperial crown, and demand that Arnold of Brescia should be given up. Arnold must have seemed a mere rebel in Frederick's eyes ; he consented. The democratic leader was carried back to Rome, and delivered into the hands of Peter the Prefect at St. Angelo.

What followed has been variously told. But we may rely upon it that there was no trial of an excommunicated cleric; and all accounts agree that the execution was despatched with haste and secrecy. Was Arnold hanged and burnt like Savonarola, of whom we think as we read his melancholy fate? "The rope strangles him, fire and water carry him away," says the German story-teller—these precautions were taken lest the Romans should worship him as a martyr of their liberties. With his ashes the Republic was swept into the Tiber. Priesthood and Empire took up their never-ending quarrel. Frederick, from this hour, was not to enjoy a moment's peace for one and twenty years. The next century was to ring with the calamities of Hohenstauffen. "Look on my German nobles," cried Frederick to the cowering republicans, who came to meet him at Sutri; "these are my Patricians of Rome; this is the perpetual Senate; and I am your sovereign." By way of proof, when he received the diadem in St. Peter's shortly after, his soldiers massacred above a thousand of the citizens who were complaining that they had been excluded from every part in the election. They now got their share. Barbarossa would not hear of an independent Italy. Neither Hadrian nor his Romans would bend under the German yoke. It was a simple issue, to be decided by the fortune of war.

XVII

FREDERICK REDBEARD AND HIS TIME

(1155-1177)

GUELFS and Ghibellines—names cast up from the deeps of hell, cried honest Muratori—will now engage our attention during a hundred years of embittered strife. In such a contest religion had no direct interest; the Ghibelline was not a heretic, nor was the Guelf a saint; while, as regards the Papacy, its line of action was determined by the motives which long before had made it the enemy of a Lombard Kingdom at its doors. To escape from Astolf or Desiderius it was that the Popes had called in their Frankish allies, and created the Holy Roman Empire. But now the Empire had grown to be a peril. Frederick the Redbeard, taking homage, not only from the Northern cities, but from Capua, laying claim to distant Apulia, and grasping with a mailed hand the inheritance which Matilda had bequeathed to St. Peter, would do all, and more than all, that Arnold of Brescia had dreamed of doing against the Pope, confounding in one equal servitude Capitol and Vatican, Senate and Pontiff. "The imprudence of John XII., when he invited the Germans to Rome," observes an historical writer who was not exactly a Guelf—we mean Voltaire—"was the source of those calamities which weighed upon the city and the Peninsula for hundreds of years." Perhaps it would be fair to remark that Italy in the tenth century had fallen into barbarism, while in the twelfth its commercial Republics were evoking a new and glorious type of civilisation. The Othos had brought with them peace and prosperity ; the Hohenstauffen rained from their German clouds an iron hail that laid the land waste. Neither on medieval nor on modern principles could they benefit a race to which they were inevitably opposed. Absentee lords, who maintained their power by predatory incursions, have been the ruin of Italy ; and a Teutonic Hannibal— which is all that Frederick ever was in his five campaigns—had little right to judge the Pope or the Lombards severely, if they preferred independence to the Imperial chains.

Thus the Guelfs could march under a flag inscribed with religion and freedom, mighty names with which to conjure ; but to what standard did the Ghibellines appeal ? Otho, the Bishop of Freising, shall teach us. "Then you could behold," he exclaims, describing Frederick's coronation, "our men striking, slaying the Romans with huge strokes, as if they said, ' Take now, Rome, for the gold of Arabia German steel. With such coin our Prince buys his crown. Thus is the Empire purchased by us Franks.' " The appeal was to the strong hand, to an image of Cæsar fashioned by jurists out of their freshly opened law books, and, as Michelet truly observes, their "science most favourable to despotism."

Could there be a less even match? Yet when Hadrian IV., compelled to be Frederick's ostensible ally, went with him to Tivoli, and the Germans had caught their usual Roman fever, the Pope was looking for help towards Sicily and the Normans. This isle of Paradise became the key to all subsequent adventures in a war which depended as much on chicane as on armed battalions. If the Emperor might rule south and north of Rome at once, how was the Papacy not enclosed in his meshes? Hadrian had excommunicated King William of the Guiscard line. No sooner was Frederick gone, than at Benevento he invested William with Naples and the whole South, acting as suzerain, receiving tribute and fealty from the Norman.

Frederick retorted by prohibiting appeals and pilgrimages to Rome. At Besançon the Emperor was holding a Diet, and annexing Burgundy. The Papal legates, among them Cardinal Roland, afterwards Pope Alexander III., brought letters in which Hadrian echoed the language of Hildebrand, spoke of the Empire as a benefice, and himself as conferring it. Frederick's rage knew no bounds. Count Wittelsbach would have struck Roland dead with his sword. An Imperial manifesto came out, charging the Curia with venality and sacrilege; it was answered with no less warmth; but the Pope softened his Latin "benefice" to

" benefit," for Barbarossa was hurling upon Italy a host from all his dominions. The passes were choked. Milan dared to withstand him ; Milan was compelled to submit. A kind of Bearsark cruelty was natural in Frederick, and his legislation seemed not less passionate than his warfare. In 1158 the lawyers at Roncaglia recorded as for everlasting remembrance his claims over clergy and laity. He awarded the vast inheritance of Matilda to his uncle, the Bavarian Guelf. Negotiations went on with Hadrian, but they degenerated into personalities, or assumed that Constantine was lord of Silvester. The undeniable corruption, rapacity, and worldly pomp of Cardinals or Bishops furnished the Emperor with a stinging text. Hadrian threw off his guard ; demanded back the Eternal City, the Matildan legacy, and tribute even from Frederick for Ferrara. The reply was, " By God's grace I am Emperor of Rome." Prelates and princes, to say nothing of the Roman Senate, were leagued with this new Charlemagne. Then Hadrian from Anagni prepared to excommunicate and depose him ; the Lombard League answered the Imperial. But in 1159 the English Pope had done with fighting. He left it to his successor. Who now would step into the hottest front of this battle, and oppose in Barbarossa " the arts of a statesman, the valour of a soldier, and the cruelty of a tyrant " ?

An old situation brings familiar tactics into play. Hadrian had thought of deposing Frederick ; Frederick might acknowledge, if he did not create, an Antipope. Fourteen Cardinals chose the Guelf Roland, and invested him with the " mighty mantle," as Dante calls it. Octavian, the Ghibelline, plucked it from his shoulders, was acclaimed by two other Cardinals, and borne in state by a hired soldiery with drawn swords. He called himself Victor IV. The people appeared to welcome him, while Roland, Alexander III., lay in hiding. Both candidates soon left the city and were consecrated each as supreme Pontiff. Frederick summoned them to Pavia; but when Alexander would not come he acknowledged Victor. Excommunications were exchanged; the Emperor was posted up as a schismatic in every town of the Lombard League, now bent on securing its independence. Christendom fell in twain. While the Empire held to Octavian, the Western Kings naturally took their stand against him. Alexander might sing Mass in the Lateran. But precedent must be followed; a Pontiff in distress could find no better refuge than France. He arrived at Courcy on the Loire, was greeted by Louis and our Henry II., and stayed there three years.

Meanwhile, Frederick was once more on Italian soil, and his arms made an end of Milan (1162). "The buildings of that stately capital," says Gibbon, "were razed to the ground; three hundred hostages were sent into Germany; and the inhabitants were dispersed into four villages, under the yoke of the inflexible conqueror." Victor passed away, Guido of Crema clutched his falling mantle at which the Roman boys had mocked. The stars in their courses were now fighting for Alexander. For his Lombard allies were to restore Milan, and Thomas à Becket, Archbishop of Canterbury, was to win by martydom the cause of

Church immunities, which seemed to be at its last gasp all over Europe.

Of Saxon England we may affirm that it never had a quarrel with the Holy See, or with its clergy. Kings and queens ruled over monasteries, but as penitents, not by virtue of their sceptre. The Normans, however, a shrewd, litigious, and hardly devout race, were willing enough to draw their swords in defence of the Church, but resolute in keeping it subject to the Crown. Alexander II., no doubt by Hildebrand's advice, had sent William the Conqueror a consecrated banner and given him leave to invade England. But William paid no acknowledgment to Rome, and his intercourse with Gregory VII. was on the loftiest terms. He remodelled the Church; his successors despoiled or corrupted it. St. Anselm fled before the face of Rufus; in dealing with Henry I., he was no less tormented but something more fortunate. Henry II. accepted from Pope Hadrian the commission, which reads like a crusading Bull, to reduce Ireland beneath his own sway and that of the Christian religion. But Hadrian must have been aware that Henry, his Queen Eleanor, and his royal house, were tainted with every vice, passion, and crime. Henry's character is by no means doubtful— furious, cunning, unstable, a compound of lust and cruelty, he brought up children in his own image and likeness. His Normans had all the vices of the Greeks except cowardice, all the Teutonic rage without its intemperance. Not inferior to Barbarossa in resources or ability, by far the most powerful King of his time, Henry, like the Emperor, could not but

desire to make of the feudal system an absolute
monarchy ; and where one set up the Roman Law in
order to stand above it, the other founded himself on
our English Common Law, or the Customs of the
Realm. But liberty in any modern sense was unknown to the twelfth century ; and this memorable
contest had in view the privileges of an order, the
prerogatives of a King. In more specious language
Herbert of Bosham contrasts " the peace of our
sovereign lord " with the freedom which a clergy, not
always decent in behaviour, enjoyed to its own detriment. Acknowledged evils might demand a remedy ;
but the Plantagenets aimed at despotism.

To the virtues, energy, and accredited miracles of
such men as Hildebrand, Damiani, Anselm, Bernard,
the Church owed its victories in the century past.
These were Saints from their cradle. A converted
worldling was to be the instrument of Henry's defeat,
He had made his Chancellor an Archbishop, who
knows with what sinister design? The Archbishop,
on whom Canterbury monks had looked with no
favour, suddenly put them to the blush by his
austerities, prayers, and almsgiving ; he was perfect,
according to the pattern of medieval sanctity, in his
life and conversation. Yet there had been something
to reform. Thomas à Becket was of Norman descent,
singularly handsome, accomplished in chivalry and
courtesy, brought up in the house of Archbishop
Theobald, and thence despatched on errands of study
or diplomatic interest to Rome, Bologna, Auxerre.
He had gained legatine powers for his patron ; he
had induced Eugenius III. to reject King Stephen

as a usurper. Though in deacon's orders only, he was laden with preferments; as Chancellor his magnificence or prodigality, his pride and eagerness to be admired, are dwelt upon by John of Salisbury as blemishes in a man who still kept his clerical vows. Now he resigned the Great Seal. At Tours, in 1163, where Alexander welcomed him with distinction, he concurred in putting down the schism and in asserting the privileges of his order and the sacredness of its possessions. Next year he was excommunicating a royal vassal; he was in conflict with the high line of the De Clares; to feudal encroachments he would oppose the Church's censures; nor was he a whit less haughty and determined in his new office than he had been in the old. Compromise between two such antagonists as himself and the King might seem impossible. They could but win and lose alternately.

A Parliament was held at Westminster in October, 1163. Gross abuses were alleged as taking place in the archdeacons' courts, and Henry required that clerics charged with crime should be degraded from their office and given up to the secular arm. The Bishops refused. Would they, at least, observe the Customs of the kingdom? " Saving my order," replied the Archbishop. This amounted to defiance. Parliament was dissolved; severe measures followed. At the Bishops' entreaty Thomas relinquished the obnoxious word. But when, at Clarendon, he saw these Customs written down, he wavered. It was too late. He took the oath and his episcopal brethren did in like manner. Sixteen statutes reduced the clergy under the Common Law; forbade prelates to quit the realm without leave from the King ; carried all disputes touching benefices into his Courts ; allowed no excommunication of his officers or tenants

HENRY II., KING OF ENGLAND
(*From an engraving in the British Museum.*)

in chief till information had been laid before him ; and while encouraging appeals from the Archbishop to the Crown, allowed none to Rome without the

King's licence. If we compare with these enactments the famous law of Henry VIII., which transferred to him and his successors the supreme government of the English Church, we shall be startled at the resemblance. Thomas à Becket had surrendered almost as much as Thomas Cranmer surrendered afterwards, when the King became Pope in all his dominions (1164–1534).

He had sworn with no mental reservation—equally without reserve he did penance for his oath and sought the Pope's forgiveness. It was granted. Yet Alexander would not offend Henry, and he allowed Roger of York to exercise legatine powers in the province of Canterbury. The Pope, all through, is politic, never on the King's side, but tremulously afraid lest he should make common cause with Barbarossa. The English Bishops took part against their Metropolitan. On that bitter day of North-ampton when he redeemed his fault heroically, Becket was forsaken, reviled, condemned for perjury and treason; he sat alone in the open hall, and his Bishops urged him to resign if he would not be deposed. He appealed to Rome; passed through a storm of reproaches; fled over the fens of the east; and at length crossed to Flanders. He was received by Louis VII. at Compiègne. His messengers obtained an interview with the Pope at Sens before Henry's were admitted.

Alexander must, in any case, have annulled the Constitutions of Clarendon. He did so in public Consistory. The Archbishop tendered to him his resignation; it was not accepted. Henry banished his dependents and kinsmen; Thomas, in mortified retirement at Pontigny, drew the eyes of Europe on his sufferings. Barbarossa and the Plantagenet agreed at Würzburg (1165) to join their forces and set up Paschal III. in place of Alexander; but the traditional policy of England could not be changed; all this proved to be summer lightning. Becket in the same year cited the King's Ministers into his court, condemned the sixteen statutes, and put their defenders under interdict at Vézelay; his action provoked Henry to madness, and Pontigny could no longer serve as a refuge to the exile. He went to live at Sens. Alexander had now returned to Rome; and John of Oxford with letters from the Bishops, with vast sums for the Guelfs in Italian cities and for the Frangipani in the Forum, persuaded the Pope's advisers to curb this headlong Archbishop. That the Pope himself was bribed has never been asserted. But he suspended the acts of Becket by his direct authority, and appointed two Cardinals to decide the whole matter. Thomas exclaimed, " If this be true, the Pope has strangled the Church." His words, always strong, grew exceedingly bitter.

The issue was determined by great events now happening in Italy. Milan had been restored by the Lombards in 1165. Frederick, in his fatal year, 1167, came on with a powerful army towards Rome. The Romans imprudently chose this moment to attack their neighbours of Tusculum. They were defeated by the Archbishop of Mayence; and Barbarossa took St. Peter's after an obstinate defence. He was crowned by his Antipope in a

19

sanctuary reeking with blood; his troops had cut their
way to the very altar, slaying as they went. Alexander escaped in disguise. Yet a fearful vengeance
fell upon these sacrilegious invaders; their army
began to waste by some mysterious and rapid disease
which swept off the martial prelates and their men
between morning and evening. Barbarossa retreated;
Lombardy in all its towns except Pavia cast away his
yoke. He fled over the Alps, and what was left of his
army followed him.

It was an awe-striking catastrophe. "The angel
of the Lord," exclaimed Thomas, "had smitten
Sennacherib and all his host." With confidence the
Archbishop went forward to meet the Cardinals near
Gisors. Never had he been more contemptuous of
the "Customs," more disdainful towards those "slaves
in the old comedy," the Bishops of England. Henry,
in tears, besought the Legates to rid him of this thorn
in his side. And they, bribed or diplomatic, suspended
his action till next Martinmas, a legal year (1167–
1168). Even the Pope from Benevento approved.
Becket wrote to him in terms of extreme violence,
sparing neither the Curia nor Alexander himself.
The King of France added that such inhibitions were
a betrayal of the Church. Still, the Roman policy
persuaded to an attempt, fruitless and exasperating,
at reconciliation in the meeting of Montmirail. As
fortune favoured the Guelfs, whom Henry kept alive
with subsidies even in Rome, the Pope issued a new
legatine commission to Gratian, the stern Decretalist,
and Vivian, who was not so tainted with venality as
the average official. They discussed whole days with

Henry ; concerning whom said Vivian, " Never did
I know a man to be such a liar." The Interdict
threatened by Becket was telling on English public
opinion. In November, 1170, he published it
solemnly. The King met this tremendous charge
with proclamations of high treason, confiscation, forbidding of appeals outside the kingdom, all to little
purpose. And yet Alexander would still absolve the
Bishops whom their Metropolitan laid under censure ;
he did not forbid the coronation of Prince Henry by
Roger of York, who thus invaded the rights of the
Church of Canterbury. No one acquainted with the
facts can maintain that the Roman authorities supported their Archbishop. He was indeed to triumph,
but not by interdicts.

After much confused negotiation, it was whispered
to the King that Thomas in his See at Canterbury
would be less formidable than Thomas an exile
scattering censures from abroad. Henry was capable
of the utmost duplicity in word and conduct ; he
made an ambiguous treaty at Fretteville with his
enemy, in which neither pronounced the name of
Clarendon. To one pledge of honour the King could
not bring himself ; he never would give Becket the
kiss of peace. On December 1, 1170, six years from
his flight, the Archbishop landed at Sandwich. He
rode in splendid procession to Canterbury and made
a progress to London. The people had been all
along ardent in his support. Not so the holders of
Church property, whom he was now going to press for
restitution ; and, while he seemed more of a sovereign
in the Kingdom than his master, the excommunicated

prelates were at Bayeux, imploring Henry's protection. "While Thomas lives, you will have no peace," said one of them. He broke out into the words of doom, "Who will rid me of this insolent priest?" The four murderers, Fitzurse, Tracy, Moreville, Britto, set out on their never-to-be-forgotten errand, crossed

ARMS OF THE SEE OF CANTERBURY, SHOWING THE PALLIUM.

the Channel, rode to Canterbury, and arrived at the cathedral as Vespers were singing, on December 29, 1170.

The passion of Thomas à Becket, which scattered his brains on the floor of his own Cathedral, is perhaps the most dramatic episode in English history. After seven hundred and thirty years we can see it all with our eyes as it was enacted on that dark winter's evening. This champion of his order and the people, a saint in self-denial, an Athanasius against the world, who had overcome his King by sheer tenacity of principle, and conquered the venality, the waverings, of Cardinals in Rome and Bishops in England; at whose feet the country lay prostrate in a trance of worship and religious dread; shone forth in one moment with a martyr's crown. The vision filled every imagination, the tragedy melted all hearts. Within three days miracles of healing began to be reported from a distance. They multiplied as years went on; the pilgrimage to Canterbury did not yield in renown to Rome or Compostella; and Alexander canonised, not unwillingly, the defender of Church liberties who had poured out on himself rebukes the most scathing nor wholly undeserved. In his death Thomas had subdued friends as well as enemies. But it is only the historian who, looking back, can perceive that the great popular saint and churchman had delayed the Reformation in England by more than three hundred years.

On Henry the recoil was crushing and instantaneous. He fell under the weight of a universal execration; he was Herod or Julian; and Alexander would not suffer his name to be pronounced in his hearing. Interdict on all his dominions was averted only by abject surrender at Avranches of his Customs of Clarendon, and no less abject pretence of grief over Becket's martyrdom. His Queen stirred up revolt; his sons conspired against their father. As early as 1171 the proudest of Plantagenets was writing these words to Rome : " I and my eldest son, King Henry, swear that we will receive and hold the Kingdom of England from our Lord, Pope Alexander, and his Catholic successors." The land was to lie under the obligations of feudal law ; would not the Pope, cried this broken despot, come to the defence of England his fief ? Yet even that humiliation did not suffice. Henry had recourse to the Saint's intercession ; with bare and bleeding feet he

MEETING OF ALEXANDER III. AND ZIANI, DOGE OF VENICE, A.D. 1177. (*Bassano.*)

crept into Canterbury ; his back was scourged by the monks ; and St. Thomas appeared by the sudden deliverance which followed, to be his surest friend. Yet the conclusion of his reign was inglorious. Richard drove his father in headlong flight from Le Mans ; he sought mercy, and learned that his favourite son John was false like the rest of them. Henry cursed God and died. Doubtless the clergy exulted, " So let all Thine enemies perish, O Lord ;

but let them that love Thee shine as the sun at his
rising !"

Years before this catastrophe, the fierce and
terrible Barbarossa had been made to stoop, not in

ALEXANDER III. BESTOWS A SWORD ON THE DOGE.
(*Bassano.*)

a dead enemy's presence, but at the knees of the
living, the triumphant Alexander. Strong in his
alliances with Sicily, Byzantium, and above all with
the Lombard cities, now banded from Venice to the

Alps and the Apennines in a league of freedom, the Pope saw his rival Antipopes die or sink in disgrace. Though he dared not live in Rome, yet he was hailed as the saviour of Italy ; to this day the strong fortress of Alessandria which bears his name is a memorial of the federation between Papal claims and popular franchises. Frederick made overtures of peace ; they could not be entertained. Milan rose from its ashes. The Imperial squadrons were defeated at Cassano, repulsed before Ancona. At last, after an attempt upon Alessandria, came the fatal and glorious combat of Legnano in which the Lombards broke his chivalry and Frederick himself disappeared from the field in a cloud of fugitives (May 29, 1176). He had delivered his hardest blow and was beaten.

Early next March, after secret stipulations on both sides, Alexander sailed up the Adriatic in a Sicilian fleet, entered the Lagoon and was received at St. Mark's by Ziani, Doge of Venice. Legends hang about this voyage and the incidents that followed close upon it. In the Ducal Palace we may study the supposed expedition of Ziani to attack the Emperor's fleet at Salboro, the fight and the victory ; but of these things no chronicle near the time bears any record. Venice had the honour of ending this twenty years' struggle. Frederick arrived at Chioggia on July 23, 1177 ; he renounced the schism which he had kept so long alive, and took his absolution from Alexander's three Bishops sent to meet him. The next morning he passed up to St. Mark's where, in the splendid vestibule, Alexander himself sat in state : around him stood the envoys of England, France, Sicily, and the Free Cities, with a crowd of nobles and dignified churchmen. The Emperor drew near, flung aside his cloak, and bent his knee to the porphyry slab which testifies yet to this great act of homage. With tears and the kiss of peace Alexander raised him. The legend puts a muttered phrase on the lips of both. "Not to thee, but to Peter!" said Frederick. And the Pope, "To me as to Peter!" An idle tale, not without significance. Te Deum was chanted ; Frederick held the Pope's stirrup ; truce, converted six years later to an abiding peace, crowned the meeting. In 1183 at Constance twenty-four Lombard cities had won their freedom.

XVIII

ENTER INNOCENT III. AND FREDERICK OF SICILY

(1177–1214)

VICTORIOUS but worn out with exile, battles, and marches, Alexander inscribed the results of his long day in the Third Lateran Council, 1179. Hohenstauffen was down; the Papacy had got back its capital and its Patrimony. But the Guelfs had not annihilated the Ghibellines who swarmed in Italian cities; and fresh denunciations of Cathari, Paterines, usurers; of Christians wicked enough to furnish Saracens with arms; and of proud prelates living in secular pomp, warn us that if Feudalism had lost its purchase on ecclesiastical rights, there was a yet more fearful enemy in front who would not want for auxiliaries. After an interval of barbarism the human mind was stirring once more. And in contrast or opposition to Bishops that reigned like princes with hosts of retainers, with hawks and hounds—to say nothing of worse extravagance—simple men, weavers or merchants, began to preach Apostolic poverty, to ask whether a dissolute minister could give true Sacraments, or the Mass of a bad priest should be attended by the Lord's faithful; whether all good men and women were not priests; and whether Rome was not the Babylon of Revelations. Tanchelin of Antwerp had been quelled by St. Norbert at Utrecht. Eudes from Bretagne had been cast into prison by Suger, the Abbot-Chancellor of Louis VII. At Vézelay men called Publicans were condemned, and seven of them burnt for denying the Sacraments and the priesthood. Along the Rhone a movement was spreading which combined austerity of life with study of the Bible; its preachers were disciples or forerunners of Peter Waldo, and as the Poor Men of Lyons must not be confounded with the Manichees, or Paulicians, who passed like a cloud of locusts from the mountains of Armenia by the way of Thrace and Bulgaria into Italy, and onwards to Languedoc, which they had made their Judea.

When Alexander III. ended his course, Europe was trembling under these spiritual convulsions, which could not be quieted until measures of unexampled severity had been taken. Lucius III. repeated the Lateran censures at Verona, but neither Manichees nor Waldensians were daunted. Medieval Protestantism was now born. The Poor Men of Lyons anticipated Wyclif. But for the moment all eyes were turned to Palestine, divided among quarrelsome feudal barons, menaced by the rising power of a Kurdish Knight, Saladin. He, after putting down the Fatimite heretics in Egypt, had slain or captured almost all the Christian peers of the Holy Land with

their King at Tiberias and entered Jerusalem (1187).
The shameful event was ascribed, not without cause,
to Henry II. and Louis VII., who had taken the cross
but stayed at home to fight their own wretched
battles. A fresh Crusade was proclaimed. Richard,
the least English of heroes, was Angevin and Gascon.
He plundered, sold, and borrowed for this tempting
enterprise. He made an effort to get hold of Sicily
on the way; he possessed himself of Cyprus; and
at Acre he behaved with all the fury of an Orlando
and the insolence of a Norman Achilles. His rival
and comrade, the mean-spirited Philip Augustus, did
nothing and went home again. Hundreds of thousands
from every European nation flocked to the siege of
Acre, which has been well termed the medieval siege
of Troy. But not all these hosts with all their cruelty
and chivalry could tear Jerusalem from the grasp of
Saladin. He saw them quarrel in their tents, die of
the plague, or disappear into the West again. This
was the last genuine Crusade. It accomplished no
part of its design. Frederick Barbarossa, who had
set out before these Kings, displayed his ancient
courage when he met the Greeks, and still more the
Turks, whom he vanquished with Homeric slaughter
at Iconium. But in crossing a torrent of Pisidia, the
Emperor was drowned; and his people, who could
never believe it, translated him in their mythology to
the subterranean vaults of Kyfhäuser. There the
Redbeard slumbers with his Paladins until the
Armageddon battle, which they call the Day of the
Birch Tree, shall awaken him and his mail-clad
knights, to save the Fatherland.

Frederick had pacified Germany, but not given up his claim to be lord of the Italians. He was on terms of extreme tension with Urban III., a Milanese, who held the Papacy without resigning the See of Milan. But Barbarossa had taken a step which brought in its train a war of seventy years, and entailed ruin upon his house and dynasty. In a sixth expedition over the Alps, he had his son Henry married to Constance, the heiress of the Sicilian throne, whom he tore from a convent and compelled to break her vows. This meant nothing less than to make the Pope his ever-lasting vassal. Urban protested in vain. He would not crown Henry at Monza; violent disputes were the consequence. Then Pope and Emperor died. Clement III. made a precarious treaty with his always turbulent Romans, and after a couple of years was followed by Cœlestine III. In the neighbourhood of Rome appeared Henry VI., with Queen Constance and an army. The Pope consented to crown him, on con-dition, added the Roman populace, that Tusculum should be destroyed and its inhabitants massacred. Henry let them work their will; Tusculum was no more. It is only in such merciless feuds between city and city, nay, between one quarter of a city and another, that the Italian genius of the Middle Age can be adequately studied. The Popes had conceived a certain world-policy on a scale which was becoming ever more magnificent. But the vision of Popular Rome did not reach beyond Tusculum.

All accounts picture Henry VI. as a man of blood and iron. Clement III. had dared to invest the illegitimate Tancred with Queen Constance's do-

minions.   This Norman chief overran Sicily, invaded
Naples, took Constance at Salerno, but when
Cœlestine interceded he sent her with gifts to her
husband.   The Pope might with as good ground
have written to the Emperor on behalf of Richard
Cœur de Lion whom he held a captive, bought from
Leopold of Austria; but he never did so.   When
Richard was set free, excommunication struck
Leopold at length and he did penance; it was the
fashion of the time to plunge into deepest guilt with
the hope of repenting on the death-bed.   Meanwhile,
Henry VI. traversed Italy with an invincible host.
He passed by Rome, went on to Messina, entered
Palermo, and took the homage of young William,
whose father, Tancred the Conqueror, was now dead.
On some pretext, true or false, Henry began a
terrible proscription at Christmas, 1194.   The loftiest
heads in the Island were struck down.   Prelates and
nobles were hanged, burnt, mutilated.   Queen
Sibylla and her daughters were thrown into prison;
William underwent dishonours worse than death.
It was remarked with shuddering horror that on the
day when Henry opened this sanguinary campaign,
his Queen gave birth at Jesi to a child, who should
be known as Frederick II.

We learn with rejoicing that Pope Cœlestine, feeble
old man as he felt himself, at once excommunicated
the Bearsark Emperor.   He did not seem to mind.
Moving back through Italy, he gave to one of his
ruffians, Markwald, Ancona and Romagna ;   on
Diephold he bestowed Apulia.   He dragged Roger
the Norman through the streets of Capua at a horse's

tail. To his brother Philip he made a present of Tuscany. He proposed to the German Princes that they should hold their fiefs by hereditary right, and that the Imperial crown should be settled on the House of Hohenstauffen. It was almost agreed upon when he returned to Sicily and set up the siege of Castro Giovanni. There all his plans came to an end. The Emperor went out hunting, caught a fever and expired at Messina September 28, 1197. In January Cœlestine died, and Innocent III. was elected by a unanimous vote.

It was now the turn of the Papacy. Cardinal Lothair, a Roman with Northern blood in his veins, was thirty-seven when he assumed the tiara. He had studied law in Bologna, theology in Paris ; during the reign of Cœlestine, being put on one side, he had written a book on the *Contempt of the World*. His morals were beyond suspicion ; in character he displayed that strange mingling of severity and sweetness, of resolute determination and humble self-abasement, which we have remarked in Gregory VII. His reign of eighteen years filled Europe with the fame of his deeds, and has been called an autocracy ; it was the rule of a strong man, not without blemishes in word and conduct, on which partisans or enemies will pronounce more decidedly than those who look from an historical perspective over the time. When we remember that the thirteenth century, at which we have now arrived, produced in one age and in the same Church Innocent III. and Frederick II., King John of England and St. Francis of Assisi, Simon de Montfort and Stephen Langton, we shall acknowledge that a Pope whose duty it was to steer over these troubled waters might easily turn the helm a few points out of the direct course.

Though sprung of a popular Roman house, the Conti, Innocent was unable to suppress the violence or avert the bloodshed which furnished daily occupation to the Orsini, his enemies from of old, and the Scotti, his mother's kindred. He undertook the reform—always needed—of the spiritual courts, insisting that they should not sell or barter justice. He drew up the Canonical decrees himself. But he suffered the Romans to humble Viterbo; and after demanding their allegiance was insulted, of course at the altar, compelled to quit the Lateran and to spend a winter in Anagni. No wonder he fell into a dangerous illness. He came back and a democratic Senate was appointed. In Rome the Pope could but look on while the nobles built or demolished the nine hundred towers from which they made war upon one another. He had no means of keeping the peace except persuasion, or by playing off one set of miscreants against an equally infamous set, their born adversaries. On this sombre background Innocent's qualities as a world-ruler shine out with redoubled splendour.

Some great advantages he possessed. Not even Gregory VII. could enjoy a clearer view of the prerogatives which, as Supreme Judge, he attributed to the Papacy; nor was there any Barbarossa to question them. Constance, in her widow's weeds, had thrown herself and the infant Frederick under his protection, declared Sicily a Papal fief, and accepted a Bull which asserted these claims with the utmost energy. The Queen got back her son and had him crowned in Palermo. But this had not been accomplished until an uprising, almost universal throughout Italy, had overthrown the German tyrants

POPE INNOCENT III., A.D. 1198.

who ravaged land and people. Innocent demanded Romagna from Markwald. The Guelfs everywhere sided with the Pope ; and now, at least, their cause, observes a modern writer, was the cause of freedom and humanity. The whole Exarchate was up ; Markwald, after wasting it to the gates of Ravenna

20

had to retreat. Conrad, Duke of Spoleto, submitted, when fighting became impossible, and Innocent received in person the homage of the liberated cities and renewed the alliance with Lombardy. The Tuscan domain he vindicated to the Holy See.

Soon after this happy moment in Italian history, Queen Constance died. Her little son became the Pope's ward ; Innocent might almost be termed Regent of the Peninsula. But Markwald, the excommunicate, raised his banner as Seneschal ; he was defeated by Papal troops at Monte Cassino, and later on near Palermo. In 1202 he also died ; but his confederate Diephold pursued the same policy, in which the Pope was forced to acquiesce. Charges of duplicity were made on all sides ; and in such an atmosphere of deceit and intrigue was Frederick II. brought up.

His uncle Philip saw and seized the opportunity. Philip had retired across the Alps, followed by Italian maledictions, leaving Tuscany to be recovered by and by from Innocent, but himself bent on wearing the Iron and Imperial crown. He was elected at Mühlhausen. But could the Pope accept a man who was usurping his nephew's inheritance? Could he look on approvingly while the House of Suabia passed on the Empire from kinsman to kinsman, establishing a prescription which would make it independent of the Church? No question of a spiritual nature was this in the modern sense; but concerned the Pope's immunity from political thraldom, and Innocent must have been delighted when Adolphus of Cologne raised a party, the object of which was to break the Hohenstauffen. This Archbishop and his fellows set up Otho, son of Henry the Lion, Guelf of the Guelfs, who came forward as a champion in Church defence, with English gold in his purse, the nobles of Flanders at his back, May, 1198. Innocent did not immediately declare his mind. A Legate arrived from Rome, demanding the release of Sibylla, Tancred's widow, and her daughters, but above all, that of the Archbishop of Salerno, imprisoned by Henry VI. The penalty threatened was an Interdict over all Germany. But, besides this, Philip, even now excommunicate, must surrender the lands which belonged to the Holy See. Philip made vague promises, and bribed the Legate, who gave him absolution. He was at once disowned by his indignant master. Nevertheless, the absolution had been pronounced, and the Empire seemed to have chosen Philip.

Both candidates were crowned—by no means an empty ceremony in ages when symbols convey the virtue they express—but Otho appealed to Rome. France and England were taking opposite sides. Still the Pope kept silence, and war broke out. After a year, when Otho began to lose, Innocent required of the Electors that they should remit the cause to himself. Philip would not formally appeal; yet he sent up a great list of his supporters, including the King of France and a host of prelates. The address which accompanied this manifesto threatened an invasion of Rome. Innocent replied with firmness. Again the war broke out; horrible deeds were done; and in 1200 the famous " Deliberation " was carried to

Germany by Pierleon, Bishop of Palestrina, in which, after comparing the merits and claims of Frederick, Philip, and Otho, Innocent declared that the Apostolic See had the right of passing judgment on an election to the Empire.   He went on to say that the House of Suabia, as far back as Henry V., had ever been hostile to the Popes, and in Henry VI. had been guilty of repeated sacrilege ; that Philip himself was a persecutor ; and that Otho, chosen by a minority, was yet a good son of the Church, and came of a loyal Catholic stock, wherefore he, and not Philip, should be Emperor.

Otho came before the Papal Legates ; made every concession ; and was proclaimed by Cardinal Guido. But, in the Diet of Bamberg and elsewhere, almost all the great prelates stood by Philip ; and ten years of war ensued which might be fittingly compared for the murders, pillagings, and havoc perpetrated in them, to the Thirty Years' War itself.   Whose was the fault ?   Many, then and since, have laid it to the charge of Innocent, careless what befel the German lands while no strong Emperor menaced him at Rome.   Others will not allow that Guelfs and Ghibellines could be subdued into peace by Papal Encyclicals ;   Otho represented one powerful party, Philip another ; they must have fought their battle to the end, though Innocent had taken no side.   However, Adolphus of Cologne was paid to desert Otho, whom he had himself proposed ; in 1207 Philip and the Pope came to terms ; and the Papal Legates kept Christmas Day at Metz with the Hohenstauffen, now absolved again.   Ere the July of 1208 had run out,

Philip, the best of his dynasty, was stabbed to death by another Otho, Count of Wittelsbach, and the Guelf became Emperor a second time.

If, as the facts lead us to conclude, Innocent had broken his pledges to Otho IV., he was doomed in a brief space to undergo the severest penance. They met at Viterbo with rejoicings. The Pope crowned his elect son in St. Peter's. And, as always, the Roman crowd fell on a German bishop; the German soldiers fell on the sons of Romulus; horses and men were slaughtered; and Otho drew away from the field of blood—but only to resume the Tuscan cities from Florence to Pisa. He gave away Spoleto; he made Diephold Prince of Salerno; he defied the Pope and his interdict; and then set forth to subdue Naples. There remained no enemy behind him except Innocent, who uttered over the renegade his most solemn censures on Maundy Thursday, 1211. But in an hour the tide of victory turned. Siegfried of Mayence published the excommunication from his cathedral. Innocent, by force of events, had become a Ghibelline. For if Otho should be put down—and his avarice, insolence, falsehood, richly deserved it—who could succeed but young Frederick of Sicily? Here then was to begin a most romantic episode in the life of one whose adventures, like his genius and his character, exhausted the capacities of good and evil.

The King of Sicily was no more than seventeen, but already married to Constance of Arragon, and the father of a son destined to bear the name of Henry VII. In Frederick himself all manner of graces were combined with an intellect which his

friends called philosophic, a courage that would
shortly be put to the test, a vivacity and versatility
which astonish us at so great a distance from his
time, and a genius the true epithet for which is
" modern," not " medieval." In his exquisite youth,
amid the golden groves and the shining seas of
Palermo, poetry was the language he took pleasure
in ; and the quests of a knighthood, not crusading but
early Greek or contemporary Provençal, drew him on
towards the unknown.   Anselm of Justingen and
Henry of Niffen were now charged by the Suabians
to bring him up from the South. In Rome they had
an interview with Pope Innocent ; he yielded to the
logic of circumstances ; and in his Sicilian garden
Frederick was offered the crown which Otho had not
yet surrendered. He accepted it without hesitation.

But Otho, in November, 1211, rushed from Apulia
to Frankfort, summoned a Diet, began to war upon
certain of the nobles, and, by way of enticing others,
married Beatrice, daughter of the Emperor Philip.
In four days she was dead. Her cousin from Sicily
had set out in March, 1212, with only a handful of
soldiers. He made his entrance into Rome, received
the welcome of Pope and Senate, was conveyed by
sea to Genoa, and by side marches came to Trent,
where a squadron of Guelfs held the pass. Escaping
over mountain roads he arrived at Chur, and the
great monastery of St. Gall. Otho was advancing to
Constance ; Frederick with his few knights and some
retainers of the abbey ran swiftly forward, reached
Constance three hours before Otho, and persuaded
the Bishop to shut his gates. The Empire was taken.

At Basle other Bishops and a crowd of noble horsemen saluted Frederick. The Primate Siegfried lent
him all his strength ; at Frankfort he was named
Emperor ; and Otho retired into Saxony. There
was not much fighting. England and Flanders
leagued with the Guelf as in previous campaigns ;
Philip Augustus with the Ghibelline. A battle of no
heroic dimensions, but which marked an epoch, the
battle of Bouvines, decided that France should exist
henceforth as a great European Power ; and that
Frederick should win his wild enterprise (May 27,
1214). Otho went back to his own land ; built
monasteries ; lived three years in retreat and repentance ; and died in 1217 forgotten. Frederick at Aix-
la-Chapelle put on the crown of Charlemagne. One
Pope had made him Emperor ; that Pope's successors
were to spend their lives, treasures, and reputation, in
unmaking him.

XIX

CRUSADES AGAINST GREEKS AND ALBIGENSES

(1201-1233)

By a singular good or evil fortune, Innocent III., who was to subdue the Western Empire, began his reign by conquering the Eastern in his own despite. Henry VI. may have dreamt of stretching his iron sceptre over Constantinople ; but the honour and shame which this new voyage of the Argonauts brought with it were reserved for Venice and the pirates of the Fourth Crusade. Saladin was no more. Fulk of Neuilly preached the Cross from Brittany to Flanders, a penitent, saint, and humourist, whom crowds followed and princes obeyed. Immense offerings flowed in, not always expended on the Holy War, though Fulk appears to have dealt honestly with them. Baldwin of Flanders took the Cross; so did a host of nobles, including Simon de Montfort, who had lately made truce with the Saracens in Palestine on behalf of his fellow-Christians. And this was to be a great French expedition, of which Villehardouin, Marshal of

Champagne, would write the story in his picturesque and soldierly prose.

But the divisions could not march across an Empire now one huge battlefield, nor attempt the land journey to Byzantium. It was resolved to convey them by sea. And the carrying trade of Europe had long been in the hands of Genoa, Pisa, Venice. To Venice on this errand came Villehardouin. Terms were arranged ; the old half-blind Duke Dandolo required eighty-five thousand silver marks as the price of transport ; the Republic would furnish fifty galleys in addition, commanded by the Doge, and would be entitled to half the conquests made by its more enthusiastic allies. Boniface of Montferrat, a pious condottiere, was captain-in-chief. The crusaders swarmed to Venice in 1201, but on the eve of departure they could not raise the pile of silver marks to the height stipulated. What was to be done ? Dandolo suggested an equivalent for the thirty · thousand marks wanting. Zara, on the Dalmatian coast, had fallen off from Venice and sworn allegiance to Hungary. Let the crusaders take Zara. True, the Hungarian King had himself assumed the sacred emblem, and to make war on him meant excommunication. True, also, that Cardinal Peter forbade the plundering of a Christian city in the Pope's name. Nevertheless, Dandolo led the fleet, a glittering show, across the Adriatic. Zara was taken and spoilt, its wealth divided (November, 1202). Istria yielded to Venice. And now, says Villehardouin, there came to pass a great wonder, the strangest and most unlooked for adventure in the world.

Alexius Comnenus had dethroned and blinded his brother, Isaac Angelus, and this man's son, Alexius the Younger, had in vain traversed Italy, beseeching now the Pope and now his own brother-in-law, the Emperor Philip, for assistance to overturn the usurper. His messengers had already appeared in Venice, not without hope; for between the Republic and Byzantium a long-standing quarrel existed on the subject of commerce injured by the Greeks, and moneys due from them. Dandolo had his private grievance; it was in handling these Easterns that his sight had been nearly destroyed. Now in the camp at Zara, fresh proposals were made. The Pope would not hear of such a thing. He interdicted the Crusaders, excommunicated the Venetians; Simon de Montfort went over with his followers to the King of Hungary. All to no purpose. It seems not unlikely that Dandolo from the first intended to revenge himself and the Republic on a State which supported Genoa, while harassing the Venetian Colony at the Golden Horn. And so, while Rome put forth one protest after another, the galleys sailed down to Corfu; they went on to Constantinople. When the towers, walls, and domes of that incomparable city broke on their view, the Crusaders, astonished, felt like men in a dream. On the shores appeared sixty thousand Greeks in arms. But before the charge they vanished. Dandolo, whose friends had concerted with him already, seized twenty-five towers; the banner of St. Mark waved over the city of Constantine. During hundreds of years Venice was to hold the gorgeous East in fee and to share with the Franks in Morea and the

Greek Archipelago such dominion as their united arms and wealth could secure.

But the self-styled army of the Lord pillaged, murdered, desecrated, broke the monuments, plucked up the bones of dead Emperors, set Isaac and Alexius on the throne, hurled them down again, offered the crown to Dandolo, carved the city and the Empire into slices, and gave what was left to Baldwin of Flanders. There was a King of Macedonia, the Marquis of Montferrat; a Duke of Nicæa, the Count of Blois. Shakespeare's Duke of Athens dates from this period. Villehardouin was Marshal of Roumania; Guillaume de Champlitte was Prince of Morea, and built his castle, as did Templars and Teutonic Knights their churches, at Andravida in Elis, by which the tourist passes now on his railway journey to Olympia. As late as 1300 French was spoken at Athens, where Otho de la Roche had founded a dynasty, which Walter de Brienne, with the help of Catalonian mercenaries, overthrew.

Innocent, who had done his utmost to prevent a catastrophe which he felt could never bring about the union of the Churches, took some dubious pride in having let down the net. But his indignant language holds up the Crusaders to reprobation as "worse than dogs," stained with lust, avarice, cruelty, steeped in Christian blood. The Venetians appointed their own Patriarch; Innocent unwillingly approved of him. He took the Latin Empire under his especial protection. Yet feuds of the Western type between clergy and nobles, Pope and Patriarch, could not be kept down. The Latin Church at Constantinople added, if addition were possible, to the deadly hatred of the Greeks whose Emperor, Lascaris, had withdrawn into Asia, while their Archbishop, Camaterus, set up his throne at Nicæa. Ancient history repeated itself; the King of Bulgaria took Baldwin captive at Adrianople, though Bulgaria had submitted, both kingdom and Church, to Rome. Yet Baldwin died in the grasp of Johannes, whose submission was little more than a pretence. From 1204 to 1261, the Latin Empire lingered out its agony. Between East and West the greatest and most calamitous of schisms had become irremediable. In taking Constantinople, the Crusaders prepared the way for Mohammed II. and his Turkish hordes; they gave an example which was immediately followed, of beating the Cross into a sword against Christian countries and peoples; they may even be said to have created some of the circumstances which made the Reformation plausible and popular. Such were the results of that marvellous undertaking so vividly described by Villehardouin, alternately cursed and blessed by Innocent III.

After this we hear no more of a universal Crusade. Venice, the gate of the East, poured into Italy treasures of art and learning; decorated St. Mark's with brilliant mosaics in which the whole Bible seems to glow upon its walls and cupolas; and held the golden chain that binds the Renaissance of the thirteenth century to that of the fifteenth. We have left the Dark Ages behind. A revolution was approaching in the West. England, thanks to King John, had lost Normandy. France, under its able, mean, unscrupulous Philip Augustus, had united to

SAN MARCO, VENICE.

the crown those Northern dukedoms, and would, by and by, annex the Southern, wrenched from the trembling hands of Raymund of Provence. In 1212, an innumerable Moorish host was to be cut in pieces at Navas de Tolosa, and Spain would become once for all the Catholic land we know. But in Europe at large a revolt, due to many causes, mingled of most confused ingredients, mystic, dogmatic, economic, had long been preparing. It burst forth while Innocent was receiving ambassadors from Armenia, Bohemia, Iceland, from both Empires, and from all the Kings of the West.

This widespread insurrection has been celebrated in undying literature. It is regarded with sympathy by all such as consider it the first though unsuccessful effort towards a true Reformation. Catholic historians, on the other side, paint it in the darkest colours and hold that it would have brought down in a common ruin Church and State. In the mysterious anarchy which was ever shaking the pillars of the world as with subterranean earthquake, Michelet perceives an influence, Oriental, Jewish, and Arabian, but above all, Manichæan, propagated Westwards from the Crusades themselves. We can follow the movement across Northern Italy and upwards from Southern Spain, until its streams meet in Languedoc, a country which resembled Judea in physical features and of which Toulouse was to be the Mount Zion.

Hebrew scholars taught at Narbonne and Montpellier. Moorish science, philosophy, and even theology, penetrated into the Universities of Christendom by way of the Pyrenees. The exaltation of love and chivalry was a chord never silent in Provençal verse. And a tremendous word had been uttered in secret, yet was repeated by many, " Nothing is true, everything is lawful." Did multitudes believe in the two principles, Ormuzd and Ahriman ? How, then, could the standard of morals be saved ? Was there a design to level the Hierarchy ? But in a crowd of wrangling sectaries what would be the fortune of truth? Toleration as a general axiom would have been scouted and called blasphemy by all the parties concerned in this frightful crisis. Jews, indeed, might be tolerated ; but they were aliens, soon to wear the badge of the yellow quoit. Heretics, who wore no badge, who lived everywhere, and might be found in all stations, how were they to be dealt with? These immoral mystics, it was said, deserved to fare worse than Saracens ; they must be run upon like mad dogs. If a Crusade were holy which aimed at delivering the Lord's Sepulchre from infidels, was it not as holy when it took up arms in defence of priesthood, Sacraments, the Commandments themselves, and the social order? But in truth no one questioned its lawfulness. To the powers that were in the year 1208 heretics appeared precisely such as anarchists appear to us now—insane revolutionaries that cannot be reasoned with, but must be cut off by the strong arm of the law.

So thought Innocent III., and on this principle he acted. As Captain-General of Christendom, he received from every quarter bulletins which announced that the enemy was growing in force through all the towns of Italy, and even in Rome.

But the centre of the storm was Languedoc, with its Moorish culture and its Asiatic creed.

Toulouse was a republic under Raymund VI., the richest prince in Europe, dissolute but accomplished, the friend of Saracens and patron of heretics, lord of seven wealthy provinces, seemingly a match for the unarmed Pope, who could not reckon on a street in Rome as loyal. But the Pope could summon a Crusade. Not against Raymund, whose orthodoxy, if suspected, had not been disproved ; yet against his subjects, should he persist in declining to coerce them. For his indulgence was more perilous than open heresy. If Macaulay is justified—and our documents bear him out — "the Papacy had lost," in Provence and Languedoc, "all authority with all classes, from the great feudal princes down to the cultivators of the soil." Let this plague spread, as it threatened, from the Rhone to the Meuse and the Rhine, there would come an end of the Catholic Hierarchy, which in those lands governed not only in the holy place, but in the university, the army, the market, and the State at large.

Innocent was not the founder of the Inquisition, any more than St. Dominic, whose name has been associated with a tribunal which did not exist till after his death. But the Bishops' Courts had taken cognisance of heretical pravity from of old—and their jurisdiction received fresh strength under Lucius III., in 1184, when the Paterines were active in demanding a reform of the Church. No sooner had Innocent been elected than he gave most extensive powers to the Cistercian Order, naming as his legates in the

South of France Arnold d'Amouri, the Abbot of Abbots, Raoul, and Pierre de Castelnau. They were to preach repentance, but also to insist on the local authorities putting in force the ban, or outlawry, equivalent to civil death, which Innocent judged to be the portion of apostates.

Citeaux, indeed, was rich, corrupt, fallen from its first fervour. The Abbot displayed a magnificence unbecoming his vows, a hardness of heart which he mistook for Gospel charity. On his travels he fell in with the Spanish Bishop of Osma and St. Dominic, returning from Rome. He complained that his preaching bore no fruit. Dominic reminded him that the Lord's disciples were sent to preach barefoot, without scrip, without staff, and set him an example which he unwillingly followed. But still the conferences proved barren, or showed that the Paulician dogmas had admirers, if not adherents, in every town where a public discussion took place. The only means likely to avail with these stiff-necked dissenters were such as Raymund would not employ. After eight years of preaching, Pierre de Castelnau declared a general peace among the feudal chieftains and a campaign against the heretics, under threat of interdict. His strong measures were enforced by the Pope in a vehement letter to the unfortunate or guilty Raymund, charging him with heinous crimes, and concluding with a menace to deprive him of his territory. This was followed up by the proclamation of a Crusade in November, 1207, to be undertaken by the King of France and the Duke of Burgundy. Two months afterwards, Pierre de Castelnau was murdered by one of Raymund's esquires on the banks of the Rhone.

That any prince not out of his mind should have instigated this crime is highly improbable. No fair judge will lay it at Raymund's door. It was, indeed, the prelude to calamities which did not finish with his life, and which proved the ruin of his dynasty. But the Pope assumed, and rumour asserted, his share in the murder. Cowed, as Henry II. had been on the death of Thomas à Becket, like Henry the Count submitted to a public scourging at the martyr's tomb. But his presence, his protestation, was of no avail. The eagles were gathering to their prey. Innocent called on Philip Augustus to be up and doing as a Christian soldier; the two swords were to smite Languedoc; and though Philip would not move, being apprehensive of King John, now allied with the Emperor Otho, thousands were ready and willing to enter on the Promised Land. Citeaux, proud of its warlike Abbot, was the mother-house of the Templars, the Teutonic Knights, the Orders of Calatrava and Avila. With its royal Duke and its white Cistercians all Burgundy seemed on the march; behind came Germans, Lorrainers, the chevaliers of the Rhine. But the most famous leader was Simon de Montfort, in whose story the tragic Muse finds volumes — Montfort, a saint, a hero, fierce, gentle, fascinating to his enemies, but one whose sword never turned back from blood. Twenty thousand knights, two hundred thousand of the commoner sort, sings the Epic historian, flung themselves on the land of olives, roses, serenades, and love songs. Innocent had precipitated the North on the South. Raymund knew that there was no turning these battalions home without conquest and booty. Captive in their hands he was dragged along to the destruction of his people. The judicial process became a war, at the remembrance of which mankind has shuddered ever since, and apologists themselves have fallen silent.

Led on by their Abbot of Citeaux, the Crusaders besieged, massacred, and burnt all before them. The sack of Béziers is the St. Bartholomew of the thirteenth century. Not a living soul was left in its ruins. Carcassonne was taken and ravaged. Five hundred castles or towns opened their gates at the tremendous summons of warriors who burnt women and children "with an extreme joy," and whose delight it was to treat these doubtful Christians more vilely than if they had been Turks or Saracens. Raymund, excommunicated—was it a third or a fifth time?—fled after Carcassonne to Rome. He met with Italian courtesy from the Pope and his great prelates; but could not hinder the burning of Minerva and Termes with their garrisons. In the Council of Arles (February, 1212) fourteen stipulations were submitted to him by the Legates which amounted to his virtual abdication. He refused and fell back on Toulouse, which became immediately the scene of havoc between himself and its Bishop. Ferocity was not confined to the orthodox; but they gained on him continually; before the year was out he had lost every inch of land except Toulouse and Montauban. The miserable Count now took refuge with his brother-in-law, Pedro of Arragon, who had just won a battle of giants at Navas de Tolosa. Montfort had secured the attainted estates of Béziers; he was becoming lord of Languedoc. Pedro argued that this could no longer be deemed a Crusade but a mere campaign of robbery; yet, though he startled, he could not convince the Pope, who may have felt some remorse, but dared not intervene. The King of Arragon moved forward with a large army. Montfort, with less than fifteen hundred men, encountered him at Muret (September 13, 1213). Pedro was defeated and slain. Raymund, with his son, took to flight. It seemed that all was over.

But the end was not yet. At Montpellier in 1215, the Legate, by advice and consent of a great meeting, bestowed on Montfort the whole dominions which these two Counts had forfeited. The same year, Innocent in the Lateran Council declared Raymund VI. fallen from every tittle of sovereignty: condemned him to exile, but was willing to leave Provence to his son under conditions. War was resumed. In 1216 Toulouse underwent a siege that lasted nine months; Simon de Montfort was killed; his son Amaury made over no less than four hundred and thirty fiefs to the Crown of France. Young Raymund, as we might expect, fell under the same suspicions which had ruined his father. Louis VIII. overflowed the land with an army; threw down the walls of Toulouse and Narbonne; but died in Auvergne on his way home to Paris. Three years later, when the infant St. Louis was on the throne, Blanche of Castile gathered in this magnificent spoil, which made the French Monarchy stronger than it had been since Charlemagne. Raymund VII., in 1229, became a vassal instead of a sovereign prince. The sternest Inquisition was established by a Council at Toulouse. If any Manichæans survived, they could be handled without a Crusade. Between the years 1230 and 1233 the Dominican friars superseded the Bishops' tribunals, and for a while the Albigenses gave no further sign of life.

I happen to be writing this page of history in the garden at Lausanne where Gibbon added the last stroke to his immense and as yet unrivalled panorama of the Roman Empire in decline. Out of those ruins a second Empire had grown ; and Innocent III., the Catholic Augustus, wielding both swords, temporal no less than spiritual, reigned when the New Rome stood at its highest point above Kings and peoples. Yet as we survey the prospect on which Gibbon's eyes so often rested, other names rise into the memory, as well known and as enduring as the mountain peaks which are reflected in Leman's blue waters,—names of men whose heralds or forerunners Innocent opposed even to the death. This quiet garden calls to them, as if in all one spirit lived and wrought. There is Calvin at Geneva; but over against him there stands Voltaire. From the Bohemian Huss, committed to the flames at Constance, Farel and Beza seem to point on to Zwingli perishing in battle with the Forest Cantons ; while they and their disciples forebode the crimson-dyed preacher of Social Democracy, Jean Jacques, out of whose volcanic heart and moonstruck brain the French Revolution burst. Gibbon himself, the mocking not unkindly sceptic, from this little Paradise saw his own world shattered by the Rights of Man, guillotined by Robespierre, blown to atoms by Dumourier's artillery. To hinder consummations such as these it was that Innocent smote Kingdoms with interdict, hewed down the Albigenses, sent forth Dominic and Francis to announce a Gospel rich in mercy yet terrible in vengeance. He would hear of no liberty, no learning, no sanctity of life or beauty of holiness, which had not been consecrated by his Papal hands. Unconsciously, yet with all his might, he aimed at making the Calvins, Voltaires, Gibbons, and Rousseaus impossible. But they arrived in their hour, and the light of Innocent III was darkened at their coming. Yet, as sitting here we muse upon the whole story, it may occur to us that not Dante alone, the medieval seer, but Shakespeare too, sovereign among mortal minds, and Goethe, one of the wisest, would have preferred Innocent himself to Calvin, St. Bernard of Clairvaux to Jean Jacques, and St. Francis of Assisi to Voltaire.

XX

ST. FRANCIS—THE FRIARS—THE LATERAN COUNCIL

(1182-1215-1226)

PROVENCE had been tamed in the fire. But Italy was overrun with Waldensian reformers; the Cathari abounded in its cities; and a succession of bloody crusades might have ended in revolt everywhere, when the most wonderful scene of a time rich in contrasts was enacted in Central Italy. There is a white stone village, perched midway on Monte Subasio, called Assisi, which looks towards Spoleto and Perugia over a land of vines and olives. In 1198 Conrad of Suabia held the castle; down below, nobles quarrelled with villeins, as in every medieval township; luxury and leprosy flourished side by side; our vilest modern alleys show nothing equal to the disease, filth, and beggary, which were at home in these fever-dens. The people could not read; seldom heard a preacher; died young. Feudalism plundered them; prelates neglected them; the religious orders behind their

high walls no longer, on the whole, fulfilled a civilising mission. Prophets, like Joachim the Cistercian
Abbot of Flora (1132–1202), announced revolutions
which would end the reign of Bishops, and bring in
the Kingdom of the Holy Ghost. Others, such as
the Humiliati, the Poor Men of Lyons, and their
nameless followers, sighed after Gospel simplicity,

ASSISI.

but were by design or prejudice confounded with
Manichæans and liable to cord and stake. Innocent
III. might subdue the Ghibelline chiefs, and among
them Conrad of Suabia ; but there is no evidence that
he meditated an evangelical crusade among the
people. Never had the Church seemed so near
destruction as at the moment when Francis, the
Poverello of Assisi, came to her succour. It has

ST. FRANCIS WEDS POVERTY. (*Giotto.*)

313

been said of him, with pardonable warmth, that he added a page to the New Testament and put off the Reformation for three centuries. He is the one Saint whom all succeeding generations have canonised.

Francis, at first called John, was born in 1182, son of Bernardone the merchant, who changed his name and taught him to speak the charming French language. Slightly educated, gay and impetuous, he was fired with enthusiasm by the wandering minstrels who sang of Charlemagne and the Table Round in their lofty lays. At sixteen he took a lad's part in the uprising against Conrad. He scorned the merchant's trade, fell into dissipation, went out with his townsmen to fight the Perugians, was wounded and taken prisoner; but he fed on his visions of chivalry, and at two and twenty he underwent the great spiritual crisis that we call conversion. Disowned by his father, the young man stripped himself bare in the presence of the Bishop of Assisi, and was wedded to his bride Poverty, in which name he comprehended the utter renunciation of goods, honours, and privileges. It was an inspiring word. He had learned it from the Gospel, and put it to the touch in attending on the lepers out of whose loathly dish he brought himself to eat. Then he went forth preaching peace, the herald of the Great King; and Assisi, Umbria, Italy, were stirred as though never before had Christ been announced to them. Umbria became the Italian Galilee; Francis the beneficent shadow of the Son of Man.

His detachment from the secular greatness of noble and bishop was perfect. But he built no cloister and went straight to the people. His rule, he said, was the life of Christ. Men and women came about him asking for guidance, and this was his one reply. Ordained deacon, he never would become a priest; he remained entirely a stranger to the learning, classic or theological, of his time; with Canon Law he was unacquainted; but his reverence for the clergy, his devotion to the Eucharist, saved him from the perilous conflicts in which Waldo and the Paterines had gone down. With a few companions he drew near Innocent at the Lateran only to be repulsed. His aims were judged by those high rulers of the Church impossible; but to resist the sweetness and joy of which he held the secret was not in men still enthusiastic, violent, and youthful. The new Order, tolerated or approved, made converts, especially among the middle class, or the " Minores," after whose name it was called. It drew to itself votaries whom an austere heretical movement would else have swept away beyond the Catholic pale. Among his friends was the brilliant, passionate, severe Cardinal Ugolino, afterwards Gregory IX., a kinsman of the reigning Pope, attached undoubtedly to Francis, whom he venerated as a Saint but managed as an enthusiast. To bring these lofty ideals within rule and compass Ugolino did not shrink from a policy in which Francis himself had little share, nor could witness its execution without suffering.

This figure that took all hearts was not moulded on lawyers' traditions; we must seek him in the idyls of the *Fioretti;* in the legends of his tender dealing with bird and beast; in his *Canticle of the Sun;* in his journeyings to convert the Soldan of Cairo; in his fraternity with the poor; and at last in his ecstatic visions on Monte Alvernia which stamped him with the living sign of Christ. He died at forty-four, amid scenes of touching simplicity; worshipped as already a Saint; but leaving to his disciples the task of reconciling inspirations so unstudied and free with an order of things which they had outgrown. That was the long tragedy of the Franciscan brotherhood. Medieval in its colouring, yet a fresh type of religious development, orthodox and progressive, it accepted from Gregory IX. an interpretation of its idea that to the Fraticelli, or the Spirituals, seemed a betrayal. These mystic disputes, lasting over a hundred years, were marked by revolt on the one hand, by repression on the other,—both accompanied with harshness and even cruelty. We shall hear of them again. But when Brother Elias built the splendid Basilica of Assisi and Gregory IX. canonised Francis, in 1228, the Moderates had overcome. From this time forward, the Papacy could reckon on the Friars; and a new chapter of Catholic achievements was beginning.

No such poetic legend flings its light over the simple but earnest commencements of St. Dominic (1170–1221). A grave Spanish hidalgo, a learned Canon of Osma, he was always well seen in Rome. The idea of poverty with him was not original; he took it from St. Francis; and while the Umbrian wanderer would have no stately houses built, and forbade his companions to teach in the Universities or accept graces of any kind soever from the Roman Court, Dominic followed older precedents, encouraged the study of the sciences—kindled thereto by the glories of Moslem Spain—and adapted to his own St. Augustine's Rule. His brethren have been happily termed the Jesuits of the thirteenth century. They were preaching Friars, like their friends or rivals the Franciscans, bringing the Gospel into streets and market-places, not always to the delight of the silent secular clergy or the gentlemanly and often indolent monks. But religion revived; a wave of mystic enthusiasm swept over Europe; and gifts began to pour in which it would have been well for these reformers had they declined. Their palmy days lasted till near the end of the century. Perhaps the chief works they accomplished were to furnish the Holy See with its own spiritual militia; to put down heresy by means of the Inquisition; to create a synthesis of ideas in which Aristotle's philosophy became a prelude to Christian dogma; and to knit up the middle and working classes, over which the Catholic Hierarchy had lost its hold, into a strong confederation of orthodox believers. In this many-sided enterprise it is difficult to say which may claim the larger influence, Francis or Dominic. But we cannot imagine the later Middle Age without its friars; the schools of philosophy without St. Thomas Aquinas; or religion itself without the Poor Man of Assisi.

From these heights we come down by a very rapid descent to kings and princes. Philip Augustus of France had married Ingeburga of Denmark with a

view to prosecuting over England some shadowy
claims derived from the famous Knut.   The lady did
not please him: on the score of affinity (in the Middle
Ages disastrously extended) Philip divorced her, with
the assent of the courtly Cardinal of Rheims.   Ingeburga made appeal to Pope Cœlestine III.; but she
was shut up in the castle of Beaurepaire and the
King married Agnes of Meran.   At this point in
1198 Innocent took up the Danish quarrel.   He sent
Cardinal Peter of Capua to demand that the French
should make peace with England, undertake a new
crusade, and acknowledge Ingeburga's rights.   With
his subjects Philip was not popular.   He granted a
truce; was willing to take the cross; but would never
give up Agnes.   The usual consequences followed.
At Dijon Cardinal Peter suspended religious services
all over France; the nation was awed and irritated;
Philip's nobles insisted on his submission; and at
Soissons in 1201 he consented to admit Ingeburga as
his lawful wife.   His partner in this great scandal,
Agnes, had passed away; but during the troubled
years down to 1212 Ingeburga was queen merely in
name.   Innocent had protected the law of marriage;
nor did he deal harshly with the King or even with
Agnes of Meran.   It was France that suffered,
according to the Horatian maxim here and afterwards fulfilled to the letter, *Delirant reges ; plectuntur
Achivi :* "Kings play mad tricks, the people pay for
them."

But interdict was growing dangerously common.
Similar disagreements arose from causes matrimonial
south of the Pyrenees.   Innocent annulled the

marriage between Alfonso of Leon and Berengaria of Castile, as Cœlestine III. had done before him, and with like penalties in case of disobedience; the ban lasted nearly five years, after which Berengaria retired to a convent. Again, the King of Navarre, having made a treaty with the Moors, was deposed : his realm would have been annexed to Arragon but for a seasonable composition of terms which he made with his rivals. Yet Pedro the Arragonese, eight years before he won the battle of Navas de Tolosa, had entered on a more than doubtful marriage, against which Innocent did not utter one syllable of protest. Neither did he open his lips when John, King of England, sent away his wife, daughter of the Earl of Gloucester, and took from his own vassal the Count de la Marche Isabella, his betrothed consort. This shameful deed cost England the sovereignty of Maine, Touraine, and Anjou ; but the Pope had need of allies against the Emperor Philip, and counting on the dissolute John he let it pass. For the moment John was gained over.

John had lost at Château Gaillard the Continental dominions of his house. He was destined to make up for one crime by committing another and thereby to secure to the English people their chartered rights, coming down from old Teuton customs and precedents. The Pope himself unwittingly and unwillingly led the way. A quarrel, by no means singular, between the monks of Canterbury when the See had fallen vacant threw the choice upon Innocent, who appointed Stephen Langton, Cardinal of San Crisogono (1207). Langton was a " scholar of

European fame, star of the University of Paris,"
and in morals unimpeachable. But John, who had
named De Grey of Norwich to the Primacy, would
not suffer this Roman Englishman to set foot in his
kingdom. Once more the tremendous machinery of
the interdict was brought into play (March, 1208).
Public festivals, ceremonies, and sacraments were
abolished ; only baptism of infants and the Eucharist
for the dying were permitted ; the daily life of the
nation came to a standstill, as if plague and famine
ruled in the land. John had his prelates and his
ministers who took no heed of interdicts ; he could
seize the revenues of bishoprics, abbeys, and parishes.
and put the clergy outside the law. Himself furious,
wanton, disbelieving, but as energetic as ruthless.
guilty of enormous and unspeakable sins, he laughed
to scorn the spiritual censures of Innocent. Excommunicate, he held out still ; but after four years of
confusion and misery, in 1212, he was deposed ; his
crown and kingdom might be seized by any Christian
soldier ; and Philip Augustus, though not a pattern
Christian, flattered himself that he was the man.

What followed is written in all our historians. The
crusade was announced at Soissons in presence of
Langton and other Bishops—traitors according to
modern law, patriots and good Christians in the
opinion of medieval Europe. John gathered sixty
thousand men on Barham Down ; he put forward, or
hinted at, a treaty with the Spanish Mohammedans ;
yet he negotiated with Innocent in spite of all ; and
he yielded to the diplomacy, the menaces, and the
imposing person of Pandulph, the legate, a man of

JOHN, KING OF ENGLAND.
(From a Print in the British Museum.

consummate ability, who held a conference with him at Dover. The King gave up everything. On Ascension Eve, 1213, in the Temple Church, he made the great surrender; England and Ireland were to be fiefs of the Holy See, paying annual tribute of a thousand marks; the deed was subscribed by John, his bishops and nobles, and he took the vassal's oath of fealty. There was now no kingdom in the West which, directly or indirectly, did not hold of Innocent III., except France.

Acts of feudal homage were so familiar to the time that John's submission called forth no protest; England was hardly yet a nation. Pandulph now bade Philip Augustus put back his sword into its sheath; but France stood behind the King, eager to attempt a new Norman Conquest of Britain. Yet the league which had threatened Lackland melted away. He himself invaded Poitou; stirred up the Count of Flanders and the Emperor Otho to attack Philip at Bouvines; but, in their persons, was defeated at this small yet epoch-making battle which delivered France for ever from the German yoke. When he returned across the sea, barons and people were confederate against him. Innocent, by his Legate, would have shielded this incomparable tyrant; on the other side rose Stephen Langton who, says a modern writer, "from the moment of his landing in England had assumed the constitutional position of the Primate as champion of the old English customs and law, against the personal despotism of the kings." He had compelled John to swear that he would observe the laws of Edward the Confessor. Now in a meeting of the Barons at St. Paul's he produced Henry I.'s neglected Charter. Bouvines assured the popular triumph. The Legate was recalled; but Innocent menaced with anathema the Barons' alliance; he rebuked the Archbishop, and sent back Pandulph. War broke out. The "Army of God and Holy Church," led by Fitz Walter, consecrated by Langton, though acting as a genuine peace-maker throughout, appeared before Northampton. John lost his tyrant's sway without a battle. At Runnymede, in presence of Pandulph, he signed Magna Charta. It was the birthday of English freedom (1215).

How Innocent took these famous proceedings is too well known. An accomplished and imperious statesman, he was no prophet; and with his legal Southern mind he failed to understand the North. John was his man by public acknowledgment; as overlord he annulled the Great Charter, calling it "vile and base," suspended Langton from his office, and renewed the interdict. The City of London answered boldly that "the ordering of secular matters appertaineth not to the Pope." Simon Langton, brother of the Primate, bade his countrymen disregard these censures. And Louis the Dauphin, setting at naught Innocent's prohibition, landed in Kent, called thither by the people. Langton was in Rome, attending on the Lateran Council, frowned upon by the Pope, and held in a sort of imprisonment. From this confusion two events cleared the air. Innocent died; John within a few months followed him, though not perhaps to the same place.

Henry III. was crowned ; Prince Louis, after the Fair of Lincoln and some other fighting, retired across the Channel ; and William Earl Marshal, in conjunction with the Papal Legate. issued Magna Charta once more.

Innocent's last enterprise, and the crowning, in truth, of that immense edifice which he had so largely built up, was the Fourth Council of the Lateran, held in November, 1215. It was attended by 412 bishops, eight hundred abbots and priors, the Masters of the Orders of Chivalry, and a host of secular representatives. " With desire have I desired to eat this Pasch with you," quoted the greatest of medieval Popes, and tears streamed down his cheeks as he welcomed united Christendom in his opening discourse. The three thousand four hundred Briefs which in these seventeen years he had issued were to be wrought by Conciliar decree into a legislation binding from Servia to Iceland, covering the whole of human existence from the cradle to the grave, and upheld by penalties that neither haughtiest monarch nor meanest peasant could escape. But the immediate occasion was to settle the succession of Languedoc. to put down the Cathari, and to enable the Pope, as Captain-General of Christians, to raise men and money for a fresh Crusade.

This all-embracing Code was no free compact between rulers and subjects ; it rested on a Divine Right, and was enforced by rigorous sanctions. It took for granted that all except the Jews, now compelled to put on a yellow badge, who claimed the protection of the laws, must be practising orthodox

Christians. They were to confess and receive the Eucharist once a year; to pay tithes and other church dues; and not to touch the freedom of the clergy, who enjoyed large immunities and were an independent, self-taxing corporation, subject in every land to the Pope alone as to their spiritual sovereign. By a species of eminent domain he could appoint to livings, canonries, and bishoprics whenever he so decided; from all the clergy he might exact contributions, as he judged fit, for the general good of the Church; his power of dispensation was limited only by the strict terms of the New Testament; and he owed no account to any earthly tribunal for his actions.

But, on the other hand, rulers were liable, in their quality of baptized Christians, to be admonished, censured, and deposed by the Pope if, in his eyes, they had broken the laws which he enacted. The Lateran Council of 1179 had released from their oath of allegiance all subjects of a prince fallen into heresy, so long as he did not repent. This Council of 1215 directed, says Cardinal Hergenröther, who gives the decree, "that temporal sovereigns if they neglected to cleanse their kingdoms of heresy should be excommunicated by the Metropolitan; in case they made no satisfaction within a year, the Pope was to be informed, in order that he might declare the vassals free from their allegiance, and give over the land to Catholic rulers." To this engagement every man that entered upon office, temporal as well as spiritual, was bound to subscribe by oath. Hence, if he did not fulfil its conditions, the law held that he had forfeited his dignity ; and, as in illustration, Raymund of Toulouse had been deprived of his vast dominions and even condemned to exile.

" As a general rule," says Hergenröther once more, " excommunicated persons who were not reconciled within a given time forfeited their civil rights and incurred political proscription." In this Lateran Council, and in 1220 by the laws of Frederick II., it was laid down that such as made no satisfaction within a year should be deemed " infamous," incapable of pleading though liable to action at law, and deprived of dignity and office. The excommunicate were imprisoned, and fined heavily at short intervals ; their property was confiscated, and themselves by many Councils were judged, if persistent, as suspect of heresy, which led to examination under torture and the extreme penalty of the law.

What then was heresy? The Canonists, like the Civilians, did not shrink from constructive reasoning which tended to make heresy rather a moral temper than a mental attitude ; it was " contempt of the power of the Keys," disloyal neglect of the Church's jurisdiction, and might be inferred from silence, or a secluded way of life, or consorting with others already under the ban. Besides the " greater " excommunication, which struck the guilty, there was the " lesser " inflicted on all who held intercourse with them. Gregory VII. in 1078 had relaxed these terms so far as to permit a man's wife, children, and domestics, not to forsake him—a regulation which Innocent III. acknowledged, while insisting that none, except these few, should eat, drink, or do

TOMB OF ST. DOMINIC—BOLOGNA, A.D. 1221.

327

business with the excommunicate. It was not forbidden to supply them with the bare necessaries of
life. But again the lawyers felt disposed to merge
the lesser anathema in the greater, as is shown by the
mild protest of the Council of Lyons in 1245, which
enacts that canonical warning shall first be given
and complicity proved before this be done. On the
whole, travellers, pilgrims, merchants, were to refrain
like their fellow-citizens from intercourse with these
spiritual outlaws ; and no obedience of any sort was
due to them.

Neither the Bishops nor the Pope undertook to
pronounce on purely secular causes ; " I judge the
sin, not the fief," said Innocent ; and in like manner
the Holy See did not itself depose Kings or burn
heretics. The Canons repeatedly forbade clerics to
be partakers in a judgment of blood. Hence we see
two Courts, the spiritual, presided over by ecclesiastics, and the lay by secular magistrates, which must
combine to make the outlawry effective and to bring
persons condemned for heresy or other religious
offences to punishment. This is the doctrine of the
two swords, always supposed, often expressed, in
Canon Law, summed up at length in an aphorism by
Boniface VIII. When the Church delivered a culprit
to the secular arm, it was the duty of magistrates to
inflict the prescribed penalties ; but, except by using
the spiritual weapons of anathema and interdict, clerics
had no means of coercing the lay authorities. Thus
Canon Law rested ultimately on public opinion, or
religious belief, or inherited custom. While Europe
was Catholic as a whole, it prevailed, though with

frequent and ever-strengthening protests not only against its abuses, which were often extreme, but against the conception out of which it arose. When the crown overtopped the mitre, that mixed jurisdiction, called spiritual but in fact dealing largely with temporalities and immunities, was annexed by the sovereign. It has now been so strangely transformed that many will suppose it no longer to exist. Yet the last shadow of the deposing power can be traced in the explicit or silent compact, according to which a Catholic King may not occupy the throne of England, nor a Protestant that of Hungary. In either case the sentence would be carried out by a democratic Parliament; but the principle of exclusion founded on religious motives, is the same in both.

And so the dream of Gregory VII. was fulfilled. Innocent III., "a man of commanding genius and extraordinary force of character," as one English historian reckons him; gentle, wise, blameless in private life, according to another; might have said in his Lateran Council, "Here is my throne, bid Kings come bow to it." IIis aims wcrc lofty, as high indeed as "the eternal principles of justice, righteousness, and humanity"; never personal or self-regarding; in a certain sense, even those who do not bend before the Papal power have admitted that he carried on "the noblest and most religious contest for ascendency over the world of man." That he, unarmed, without a single soldier at his beck or call, should have brought to their knees German Kaisers, and French, English, or Spanish Kings; reigning like some being from a higher realm over their nations, which he smote as with thunderbolts ; is a witness to the faith that was yet in them, and to his peremptory greatness. He is calm, majestic, invincible ; he rules by edicts and lieutenants from Byzantium to the borders of the West ; and he dies at fifty-four, worn out by seventeen years of crowded and incessant undertakings, which all seemed to end in victory.

PERUGIA.

Yet we pause over the verdict and dare not call him saint. Of this astonishing age the hero is Francis rather than Innocent. The mighty Pontiff strikes with mailed warriors upon heretics, and exterminates without converting the unhappy thousands of Provence. He yields to subtleties and dissimulation ; he plays off one Christian ruler against another, and is answerable for wars in Germany, the Netherlands, Italy, England ; he cannot keep within bounds the rapacity of his Court ; personally just-minded, he lets a system of exactions flourish that was to undermine the Papal grandeur and almost bury the Church in its ruins. Never, perhaps, did any Pope illustrate more decisively the strength and weakness of Canon Law, which appealed to men's fears while taking too little account of their affections. Long spaces of interdict tempted them to view with growing indifference the services of religion, granted or withheld for reasons, too often not so much spiritual as worldly and diplomatic. If Mass and Sacraments could thus be taken away, were not pious minds thrown back upon themselves, and might not the clergy be dispensed with ? Neither Innocent nor his advisers could have prevented the outbreak of what was already Protestantism, had the friars been wanting whom Francis called up in their preaching hosts and sent through Christendom. Most opportune was the alliance of Law and Gospel, bearing witness to the amazing genius, as men speak, of that Catholic Church wherein both could flourish side by side, and a period of expansion grow as by magic out of a period of repression hitherto unequalled in Europe.

But Innocent on his judgment-seat is less winning, and to our later age far less comprehensible, than the lowly friar, who improvises popular chants instead of solemn decrees ; who begins Italian literature ; inspires Giotto and Dante ; preaches universal brotherhood ; looks beyond the schools to Nature and its everlasting beauty ; is tender to all forms of disease ; and converts from vice by the simple joy of loving. Sinai with its thunders may be grand; Galilee is sweet. That Innocent, by measures of awful severity, preserved European civilisation has been asserted, and on grounds not easily shaken. Francis did more. His vision of faith and charity; of a Christian life in the world without vows, yet in accordance with the Gospel; pure, compassionate, laborious, cheerful; at peace with God and man; is one that can never grow old. It is higher, by all the grace of the New Testament, than any society which we have yet realised; and to say that Innocent III., while allowing it, still deemed it impossible, is to mark the limit beyond which he could not pass.

On July 16, 1216, this tamer of kings died at Perugia. He was succeeded two days after by Honorius III.

XXI

EXCOMMUNICATION—WARS—FATE OF FREDERICK II

(1216–1250)

EIGHTY-SEVEN years, in round numbers, are left of the story which we have undertaken to tell. From now onward it becomes a drama in four acts, of almost Greek simplicity, though with many a stirring episode, and the background is ever that Sicilian Paradise over which the Popes claimed to be feudal lords. The first act, down to 1250, is filled with the exploits, sufferings, triumphs, and death of Frederick II. It is followed by a sequel lasting till the execution at Naples of young Conradin, heir of the Hohenstauffen, in 1268. Act the third brings on Charles of Anjou and the French domineering in Norman Italy, but suddenly blasted to pieces by the Sicilian Vespers of 1282. The closing, unexpected, but decisive fourth act shows on our stage Philip the Fair at death-grips with Pope Boniface VIII. When Colonna and Nogaret, ministers of the French King's vengeance, seize the Father of Christians in his palace at Anagni, pull him from his throne, and kill him with their shameful handling, the Papal Monarchy is no more. Never again does the Pontifex Maximus bestow crowns, or depose Kings, or exercise to any effective purpose the over-lordship hitherto granted him in Europe, which had made him supreme from Russia to the Western Sea. His spiritual dominion remains; and he will in time be absolute master of Rome and its territories; but with Boniface VIII. comes to an end medieval Christendom.

In this mighty struggle the Holy Roman Empire lost its meaning and melted to a shadow; Pope and Emperor between them ruined the system of which Charlemagne had drawn out the lines and Dante sang the exceeding glory. A new idea, that of independent nations, with no Cæsar above them, was coming to the birth. The great Roman unity—a Theocratic King seated beside a Feudal Pontiff—broke up when the Hohenstauffen defied the Papacy and Clement IV. saw the blood of Frederick's grandson staining the scaffold at Naples. While the combatants imagined that one of them must be victor, both were surprised by the growing power of France; the firm and haughty legislation of Edward I. of England; the end of the Crusades; and the anarchic fourteenth century. The Hohenstauffen sank; the Popes went into a Babylonish captivity at Avignon. Such is the spectacle to which we invite our readers' attention, who will find that these far-off events have had on their own story an influence no less direct than decisive.

It was now a recognised duty of the Pope to pro-

claim the Crusade, binding it on Kings whether they
would or no, and raising contributions all over
Christendom to carry it out. Honorius, mild and
feeble in health, a contrast to his adamantine predecessor, had stirred up Andrew of Hungary, and seen
with joy the capture of Damietta in 1219 from the
Egyptians, whose offer to restore Jerusalem was
treated with scorn. Christians still dreamt of
conquering Islam on Mount Zion ; and Frederick II.
aspired to lead the armies of the Cross, if he might
be Emperor in fact, and his son Henry King of
the Romans. His enemy, Otho, was dead in
1218 ; his counsellor was Hermann of Salza, the
Teutonic Master ; at Fulda the German Princes
gathered joyfully about Frederick ; would Honorius
yield to him and his the Imperial Crown? There
had always been a party in Rome hostile to the
Suabians ; they charged Frederick himself with
designs which he does not seem yet to have entertained ; but the Pope would, under no circumstances,
grant him the joint investiture of Sicily and the
Empire. As Voltaire observes with justice, the
Italians did not want a foreigner to lord it over them ;
the Pope considered that his freedom would be lost if
he were shut in by German territories on all sides ;
but he had consented to certain terms when, at the
Diet of Frankfort, young Henry was elected without
his leave as Frederick's successor. Still no quarrel
broke out. The Hohenstauffen Prince descended
upon Italy ; he was crowned in St. Peter's ; he
solemnly took the Cross from Cardinal Ugolino. He
swore to set out in August, 1221 ; and meanwhile

surrendered to Honorius the great and constantly
disputed inheritance of Matilda. His concessions of
Church immunity were so large that we can scarcely
believe them sincere. His laws against heretics repeated and enforced the decrees of Lateran. But he
had gained the double investiture; he soon showed
that rebellious clerics in Apulia would appeal in vain
to their surplice and shaven crown; nor did he,
though Damietta fell in 1221, press on the expedition
to which he had pledged himself. These are the
facts; that Frederick apologized for them could
never set him free from the first duties of an
orthodox King.

After two years spent in Sicilian troubles and
delights, a new agreement was made. Frederick, in
August, 1227, would sail for Palestine with a thousand
cavaliers; he would pledge a hundred thousand
ounces of gold as a forfeit if he did not embark; his
successors were to be bound like himself, and all
under interdict. He wedded Iolanthe, daughter of
King John, and immediately took the style of King
of Jerusalem. In these actions we perceive a chivalrous, unsteady, medieval Byron, passionate, sensuous,
not so much crafty as fired with the spirit of adventure,
drawn many ways by the calls of a situation to which
no genius was equal. Engelbert of Cologne had been
murdered; Italy was in flames; the Emperor struck
hard at his rebels like a Ghibelline; an immense Lombard League was forming against him. Honorius
began to remonstrate in the language of Innocent,
and upheld the Lombards as though they owed no
allegiance to the Empire. At this critical moment

ROGER, KING OF SICILY, RECEIVES HIS CROWN FROM CHRIST.
(*Mosaic in la Martorana, Palermo.*)

he died, leaving the succession to Cardinal Ugolino, henceforth to be known as Gregory IX. (March, 1227).

Of this extraordinary man the tale is told that he was elected Pope at eighty-six and lived to be a hundred. Handsome, grave, devout, impetuous, learned, and resolute, he had been the attached friend of St. Francis and St. Clare, deep in the counsels of his cousin Innocent III., and on affectionate terms with Frederick. But the old Pontiff deemed his Canon Law, which he was now digesting into the Decretals, to be supreme without appeal or adversary. The youthful Emperor did not take that view. He sat on the throne of Justinian; he was himself the embodiment of Roman Law; he held authority over the world by Right Divine. To the clerics of the Curia he opposed his lawyers; his Pietro della Vigna would be a match for any Cardinal; nor did he hesitate to claim a power at the Capitol to which the Lateran never yet had willingly submitted. He was a strangely mingled character, reminding us of the Moorish Sultans, his contemporaries, rather than of the unpolished Northern chiefs from whom he descended. In outward looks he was Norman, fair, slender, ruddy-haired, with blue eyes, and a winning tongue; but his gift of gay improvisation, his softness of living, his metaphysical talk, his polygamies, and what else may not be named but was currently reported of him, bring before us a light Epicurean, to whom the repressive doctrines of Gregory IX. must have been intolerable. That he believed in no religion at all was the rumour of the day; but, in the contest now approaching, had he been as orthodox as

St. Louis, there were elements of dissension which could not be reconciled. Gregory struck the first blow.

The moment he was crowned, his word went out for the Crusade, and he fastened an instant obligation upon the Emperor. He was equally severe with the Lombard cities, delaying to keep their engagement; they must obey Cæsar and despatch their own soldiers to Palestine. From Anagni he addressed a vehement rebuke, which was undoubtedly deserved, to the Court of Palermo, where Jews and Mohammedans held great sway and a heathen licence flourished. Sicily was becoming a second Provence; the Pope may well have dreaded lest Christian faith should hardly survive Christian morals; and he despatched his Friar Gualo to prophesy against the dissolute Prince who had bound on himself the cross of his dying Lord. Frederick began to negotiate with the Sultan of Egypt, Kameel. Yet his preparations for the voyage were extensive; he sailed round to Otranto; met the German expedition of which thousands perished in the amazing Southern heats; himself embarked; but after three days hastily returned to port. Then he broke up the armament, and giving out that he was ill, retired to Pozzuoli (summer 1227).

At Michaelmas the Pope excommunicated this recreant crusader in language at once passionate and scornful. He made out a strong case, if not altogether convincing; twice he repeated the censure, of which its subject seemed to take but little heed; yet Frederick did answer, by appealing to all his fellow-sovereigns against the monstrous regiment of clerics. He made friends in Rome. Gregory during Holy Week had menaced him with deposition: a few days afterwards the Frangipani raised a tumult while the Pontiff was saying Mass and drove him out of the City. He took up his residence on the heights of Perugia. It was soon announced that the pilgrims to the Holy Sepulchre had turned back on hearing of Frederick's defection ; but news came that Moeddin of Damascus, who had been a scourge to Christians, was dead, and the Emperor set sail in April, 1228. Gregory had forbidden him to stir till the interdict was raised ; he drew into revolt the churches and monasteries of the Sicilian Kingdom by ordering them not to pay their taxes ; he called Frederick a pirate and other bad names—all on grounds which, at this distance of time, do not appear to warrant such high-handed proceedings. Attempts at reconciliation came from the Emperor ; they were rejected by the Pope.

But Frederick, who now lost his wife Iolanthe, sailed to Cyprus and thence to Acre, with about six hundred knights. Two friars had gone swiftly before him ; they warned the clergy, the Templars, the Hospitallers—by no means friendly to his Sicilian laws which put them under civil jurisdiction—that they must not receive the excommunicate. He was opposed on landing ; he could gather no sufficient army; and, making terms with the Sultan of Cairo, he entered Jerusalem, March 17, 1228. At once the Archbishop placed the city under a ban, interdicting the Holy Sepulchre itself. These frightful dissensions, carried to the utmost pitch in the presence of Islam, strike us with horror. Had Frederick been more of a Christian, he would now have shrunk from any further acts. Yet he proceeded to crown himself in the desecrated Church of the Sepulchre, where Hermann of Salza read his master's defence, which was a loud indictment of Gregory. Idle tales, exaggerated or wholly false, depicted the Emperor as a mere infidel; his presence irritated the Moslems and was a scandal to the orthodox. He wrote in glowing terms to Europe of all he had accomplished; but on the third day he left Jerusalem; and his treaty, denounced by Pope and Patriarch, came to nothing. He must hasten home; John of Brienne was invading Apulia; Albert of Austria had been tempted to throw off his allegiance; while Gregory was proclaiming a crusade, for which he demanded benevolences even in the British Islands (and obtained them) to put down the sacrilegious Emperor. A Crusade against Cæsar! It was the strangest perversion of medieval laws. It shocked Christendom. But the Pontiff did not heed remonstrance. He joined in one sweeping anathema Frederick with all possible heretics; condemned his adherents; and set his subjects free from their oaths.

But the man himself was in Southern Italy once more. He drove back the Papal forces which had poured over into Naples; he relieved Capua; he settled his Saracens at Nocera. With his squadrons bearing the Cross on their armour he met and slew Gregory's retainers, who held aloft St. Peter's Keys.

No sadder moment is on record through all the
sanguinary and confused chronicle of that century.
The friars stood by the Pope; but clergy and laity
were in high dudgeon with him; on neither side of
the Alps could insurrection be stirred up; and when
the Romans, terrified by a fearful rising of the Tiber,
had called back their Pontiff to the Lateran, he made
peace at San Germano (June, 1230) with this infidel
whom he had lately drawn in the blackest colours.
Frederick forgave all his rebels and restored clerical
immunities to the full.   He gave up confiscated
estates; in general terms he submitted; but regarding
the Crusade or the Holy Land not a word was uttered
on either side.   The enemies met at Anagni, embraced, and, as Frederick tells us, were charmed with
one another.   It is difficult to understand these
sudden, dramatic changes which are so frequent in
medieval history.   Acts and speech were equally
violent; enthusiasm, liable to such hot fits of love
and hate, takes on the air of deep dissimulation; yet
we must suppose it genuine.   The nine years' peace
which followed seems to confirm our better thoughts
of men who to rare qualities added passions not less
beyond the common.   Frederick went on to complete
his Code of Laws; Gregory, aided by Raymund of
Pennafort, the Dominican, gathered up into his
Decretals whatever was extant, or gave itself out as
such, of his predecessors' enactments from the first ages.
Yet legislation, however sound, which did not seek
approval of the Holy See, was looked upon with
distrust.   This new and growing conception of a
purely secular Code pointed back to heathen, not

Christian Rome, and forward to a condition of things when the Pope would be no more the supreme law-giver. A fresh struggle on this larger battlefield was at hand.

Like Solomon or Mohammed, the Sicilian had many wives and concubines. We must distinguish

CLOISTERS OF THE CHURCH OF MONREALE.

four sons of his,—Henry the eldest, now ruling Germany; Enzio, the golden-haired offspring of Bianca Lancia, and his brother Manfred, who displayed all the genius of the Hohenstauffen; lastly, Conrad, son of Iolanthe and heir to Jerusalem. Of these Henry, now grown up to manhood, was fractious and feeble; his Teutonic counsellors tempted him into rebellion against a distant power; and in May, 1235, Frederick, as in olden days, crossed the Alps to save the Empire. It is certain that Gregory did not encourage the foolish youth. Henry was soon made to submit; he was banished to Naples and died a prisoner.

But these troubles had involved the Lombard League; moreover, the popular party in Rome, never quite extinguished, was secretly Imperial; in 1234 Savelli the Senator had pulled down some of the Lateran, defied Cardinal Ranieri, taken tribute and allegiance from Tuscan towns. The everlasting quarrel between camp and sacristy was on foot again. Frederick, called in to mediate, restored peace. He was now getting ready to break the Lombards on the singular plea, which Gregory himself had put forward, that they dealt too easily with heretics, compounding for their offences and giving back their fines. Heretics, in these Northern parts, were not only weavers or small tradesmen but well-to-do merchants; the middle class, when not under guidance of Franciscan Saints, often fell away from Church and clergy. Thus the Pope found his chief allies discredited, himself in danger. He proposed arbitration. Before it could be done, Frederick had taken Verona, stormed Vicenza, beaten the Duke of Austria to his knees. On November 27, 1237, he won the fight of Corte Nuova, in which the Lombard legions were ruthlessly slaughtered; the Caroccio of Milan fell into his hands; young Tiepolo, the Podestà, son of the Venetian Doge, was bound a prisoner to its chariot wheels. From Cremona he published an Imperial Encyclical,

vying in strength of language and pride of power
with those of the Roman Chancery. The Caroccio
he sent to the Capitol; Tiepolo was put to death
at Naples. Who could withstand Frederick now?
Surely, this world was made for Cæsar.

Gregory rose to the occasion, not as Pope—for how
did Frederick impeach his spiritual prerogatives?—
but as an Italian patriot. He leagued together Venice,
Lombardy, Romagna, Genoa; bound in one all the
charges to which forty years' perplexed litigation had
made the Emperor amenable; and especially urged
that he had fomented rebellion in Rome; had usurped
Sardinia, which was an estate of the Holy See; had
cherished Saracens; had hindered the recovery of
Palestine; and had oppressed the clergy. On these
grounds Pope Gregory, in the Palm Sunday Mass
of 1239, excommunicated, interdicted, and deposed
Frederick II., and delivered him bodily over to
Satan for the saving of his soul.

Pietro della Vigna harangued against the sentence
at Padua; his master condescended to justify himself
in an assembly of Bishops; again he appealed to his
fellow princes; and he called on the Romans to avenge
his insulted honour. "Fierce, indecent invectives,"
as Matthew Paris terms the Pope's rejoinders, were
bandied to and fro. The Barons of England refused
every contribution towards this fresh Crusade; the
clergy did in like manner. Then Gregory took a fatal
step. He offered the Empire, now considered vacant,
to Robert of Artois. France was to take the place of
apostate Germany. But on the French throne sat
Louis IX., whom all Christians looked upon as an angel

of God ; and he not only forbade Robert to seize the
tempting bauble, but addressed a severe remonstrance
to the Pope, while his nobles sent Frederick an
embassy which touched him even to tears.   Among
Germans the cry went that if Gregory had not helped
Milanese rebels, peace would never have been broken.
It seemed as if the only sure partisans of the Pope
were Lombards in Italy and the friars everywhere.   He
had canonised St. Francis and St. Dominic—to whom
indeed St. Louis cherished an equal devotion.   But
even the friars were rent by factions—Moderates for
the Holy See, Spirituals for the Eternal Gospel.
Elias, their crafty, versatile General, joined the
Emperor and fell under the same excommunication.   We have come to the middle years of that
thirteenth century in which Catholicism brought forth
its most mystic saints, built its unrivalled sanctuaries,
squared the stones of its Canon Law, soared into
Heaven on the wings of its transcendent philosophy,
—yet heretics are in every land, dissensions rife between
universities and religious Orders, the friars themselves
persecuting and persecuted ; the Emperor is an out-
law, the Pope menaced in his own house ; the clergy
burdened, the nations restless ; and from the Far
East is heard the tramp of innumerable barbarians,
for in 1241 the Mongols pour down on Europe,
advancing to the Danube and the Alps.   We can
neither conceive nor imagine such a time ; therefore
we shall do well to refrain from judging it.   But
surely Pope and Emperor must have been alike
unhappy.

Milan burnt her heretics ; Enzio, the beautiful

youth, began to conquer his father's enemies; Frederick swept towards Rome. He showed no mercy to the so-called crusaders; but it was a confused indecisive war. Enzio, at Meloria, broke the Genoese fleet and took many Bishops, with all the treasure which Cardinal Otho was bringing from England. The hordes of Genghis Khan moved forward. The Pope was in Sant' Angelo, undaunted but nearly alone. He meant to call a General Council; Frederick and St. Louis would have welcomed it. Under this awful cloud, charged with red lightning, Gregory died (August 21, 1241). All his efforts had come to an untimely end; but his courage was never less than his convictions; and he stands forth, a commanding figure, in the Papal dynasty.

It is to the everlasting honour of Frederick that, while chaos ruled, his sons, Enzio and Conrad, reinforced from Italy, drove back the Mongol hordes on the Delphos and saved Europe. Acting almost as Regent of the Church, he suspended his armaments, allowed the Conclave to meet, and would have made peace with Cœlestine IV., had not the newly-elected passed away immediately. For two years the small body of Cardinals wrangled over a successor. St. Louis threatened to appoint one; Frederick insisted; they chose Sinibaldo Fieschi, a Genoese, and the policy of Gregory IX. was resumed. To speak of Innocent IV. with respect for his person would be in defiance of the multiplied proofs which exhibit him as grasping, cold-hearted, insincere, and a nepotist. He has been held up, not for reverence, to posterity in the terrible but unquestioned indictment which Robert Grossetête, Bishop of Lincoln, delivered to his Court and Cardinals. But where the headlong Gregory failed, Innocent succeeded. Hitherto, he had affected kindness towards the Emperor ; but, as Frederick observed, " No Pope can be a Ghibelline," and so the event proved. Innocent, however, began by proposing terms. A treaty, thanks to Adelaise of Sardinia, was drawn in 1244, but never executed. Next year the Pontiff escaped by sea to Genoa where he was welcomed " with loud applause and aves vehement " ; he took up his quarters in the Imperial free city of Lyons ; and called a General Council in 1245.

St. Louis, throughout, was calm and neutral ; Arragon was hostile ; the English people murmured against Martin the collector and all collectors ; barons, bishops, middle class felt no tenderness for the Pope ; but though historians like Matthew Paris are themselves evidence of widespread discontent, the great system stood foursquare against revolution, stained as it was with age-long scandals. At Lyons the 140 Bishops and numerous abbots were protected by a vile freebooter, Philip of Savoy, who was named Archbishop of that See but never took orders, and who died a Duke and a married man, ancestor of the present King of Italy. Thaddeus of Suessa, that politic civilian, appeared on Frederick's behalf ; he charged Innocent with double-dealing and appealed to a future Council. But the prelates sided with the Pope. Innocent, by the power of the Keys, deposed the Emperor in a vehement speech ; reserved Naples to himself ; declared the Empire a feud ; and by and by gave it to Henry Raspe, " the priests' king."

PALERMO CATHEDRAL, IN WHICH IS THE TOMB OF FREDERICK II.

There was civil war in Germany. St. Louis tried
in vain to soften Innocent. Plots and counterplots ;
frightful cruelties, of which Frederick can never be
absolved ; Henry Raspe's defeat at Ulm, death at
the Wartburg ; triumph of the Guelfs at Parma ; and
Thaddeus of Suessa captured and hacked in pieces,
—such are the gloomy incidents of those miserable
days, down to 1249. The Empire was collapsing to
anarchy. Frederick, not old but worn and savage,
felt the blows of outrageous fortune and struck
fiercely again. His beloved Enzio was taken at
Bologna, spending in captivity the twenty-three years
that remained of a tragic story. His bosom friend,
Pietro della Vigna, turned traitor—why or under what
provocation has never been known ; he "held the
keys of Frederick's heart," said Dante, and now he
became false and being taken in the manner dashed
out his brains against his prison walls. Guelfs,
Ghibellines, Free Companies, laid Italy waste. It was
time the Alcibiades of the century left it to work out
its own confusions. In 1250, at Ferentino, not far
from Lucera, the Emperor breathed his last in
Manfred's arms. He sleeps with his royal robes
about him, in the Cathedral at Palermo. But we
cannot look upon the great porphyry urn, which
holds all that is left of Frederick II., without feeling
that he was truly a spirit misunderstood, never wisely
handled, full of mysterious charm and powers wasted,
the most captivating, enigmatic, and unhappy of
Christian Emperors.

XXII

CONRADIN DIES—THE SICILIAN VESPERS

(1250–1299)

WITH Frederick expired the Holy Roman Empire. William of Holland, the anti-Emperor raised up by Innocent, a lad of twenty, held on till 1256, then perished fighting with the Frisians. An interregnum of seventeen years followed; but, if we look at realities and pierce through the forms of things, the new dynasty inaugurated by Rudolph of Hapsburg, poor, proud, and pious, in 1273, took over little but an empty name and was merely German, never Roman. There will be in time a crimson-clad Sigismund at Constance; a lord of many lands, Charles V.; but even these do not fulfil the idea which was dreamt of by Charlemagne or Frederick; and the rest are shadows.

Innocent IV. had yet to deal with the remnant of Hohenstauffen. He excommunicated the able though somewhat stern Conrad, who should have succeeded his father, but was now charged with heresy and made the object of a crusade. From Lyons the

Pope went down to Italy in triumph, everywhere rooting out Ghibellines and Nonconformists; at Perugia he stayed a year and a half. Manfred, who kept a grip on the South, found rebellion springing up at the Pope's instigation, and it is curious to note the Count of Aquino, brother of the great St. Thomas, among its leaders. Capua, Naples, fell away from the Imperial party, when Conrad, crossing the Alps and sailing from Venice, arrived at Siponto, chastised the revolting cities with storm and slaughter, and restored the balance. Factions broke out among the Pope's own partisans. He turned to the feeble though exquisite Henry III. of England, made his second son, Edmund, King of Sicily, and swept into his coffers an infinite tribute. This became the cause of civil war between Henry and his people, out of which rose Simon de Montfort, who laid the foundations of a free English Parliament. So wide-reaching were the effects of that quarrel between Papacy and Empire! But Edmund did not get his Kingdom of Sicily; as we shall see, it was the golden hook wherewith to catch princes; for Innocent never scrupled at breaking his pledge. He sold bishoprics as he trafficked in crowns, always to fill his own purse or to dower his kinsfolk, for he practised nepotism on a lordly scale. As Pope he had built, in the energetic words of Robert Grossetête, for hell-fire; as a ruler of this world he showed himself crafty and invincible. He foreshadows at once Innocent VIII. and Julius II., neither of whom do we reckon in the list of edifying Pontiffs.

Rome, the city, has fallen into the background

during these tempests of "blood and flame, rage and despair." It now possessed a Senator, Brancaleone, called in from Bologna to appease its everlasting tumults. He hanged culprits, established quiet for a while, and sent the Pope a peremptory message to return to his long-abandoned See. Innocent appeared, withdrew, was compelled a second time to come back. We may conjecture that his pleasant hours in the free city of Lyons had given him a foretaste of Avignon; but with his antique Senator and a murmuring people he did not dare to trifle. From the Lateran he continued to make war upon the children of Frederick. Conrad was too strong for him; accused, as we said, of heretical sentiments—an unlikely charge—he defended himself in the Papal Court. His juvenile brother Henry died on a visit to him at Naples: Innocent gave out that the lad was poisoned. In 1254 Conrad, by some mysterious stroke, lay on his death-bed; rumour babbled of the wise Manfred's guilt, but he would not even accept the Regency.

One legitimate descendant of Frederick II. was left, Conradin, a boy of three years, on whose behalf Berthold of Homburg wrote in suppliant terms to Pope Innocent. The answer was that Conradin should be King of Jerusalem—a kingdom in the air—but by no means of Naples. William, Cardinal of Sant' Eustachio, Innocent's nephew, was to be Regent, to seize, confiscate, interdict, levy taxes, and govern the South as a Roman province. To this Manfred's reply was the assumption of sovereign power in the name of Conradin. But, in the midst

24

of treachery on all sides, he submitted ostensibly to the Pope and invited him to enter the kingdom. Innocent came to Ceperano with a splendid retinue ; Manfred fell at his feet, was raised up and appointed Papal Vicar. Still more gloriously did the Pontiff triumph in the city of Naples ; his nephew took the homages absolutely in his name. Then Manfred escaped to Lucera ; beat the recreant Marquis of Homburg and the Pope's squadrons at Foggia ; and swore to maintain the rights of King Conradin. The game was now to be simplified ; its last pieces were on the board. Innocent, from his palace at Naples, utterly disregarding English Edmund, offered Sicily to Charles of Anjou. We may remember that Gregory IX. had set the example of tempting on this expedition the younger Princes of France. Not many days after, in December, 1254, " he that sold the Church was dead," writes Matthew Paris of the Pope. Almost his last act had been to pave the way for the Sicilian Vespers.

Alexander IV., of the house of Segni, who succeeded without an interval, was a good Pope, embarrassed by the rapacious Curia which Innocent had bequeathed to him, and still more by the *damnosa hæreditas* of a suzerainty over Naples. He could not put down Manfred, in possession of the whole kingdom ; he stumbled between Charles of Anjou and Edmund of England ; his dealings with Boniface, the Savoyard Archbishop of Canterbury, a worldling and a reprobate, as with Sewal, Archbishop of York, threw a lurid gleam on the least defensible of Curial practices — the intrusion of foreigners into Sees which they administered like proconsuls, and the exaction of subsidies in aid of wars which had become purely secular, though disguised under the title of crusades. In Rome, Brancaleone was acting as temporal sovereign.

POPE INNOCENT IV., A.D. 1254.

Flung into prison but delivered thence, he broke the proudest nobles; pulled down their robber-dens to the number of a hundred and forty; stood out against the Pope himself, who had taken part with the Patricians; made alliance with Manfred; and was Senator till his death.

The year 1258 saw **this** highly-gifted son of Frederick, hitherto Regent, crowned King at the request of the Sicilian Estates which he alone could protect. He had no lawful sons; and he promised that Conradin, now Duke of Suabia, should succeed him. The interminable war of Guelfs and Ghibellines went on. Florence had banished its "white" or Imperial citizens; they united with Pisa and Siena, overthrew the Guelfs at Monte Aperto, and would have razed their native city to the ground, had not Farinata persuaded them to spare it. Michelet, the French historian, considers that the Guelfs were, on principle, democratic and revolutionary; they drove out their feudal masters; levelled the ranks of their fellow townsmen to one class which we should now call industrial or artisan; were loyal to the Church as long as the Church was loyal to them; and, like other Jacobins, while jealous of superior men, fell under military sway, the victims of hired cut-throats. But they never ceased to be genuine Italian patriots; thus we comprehend why **they** looked on the Pope as their anointed chief.

Of the Ghibellines it may be said that in origin they were feudal lords who would not relinquish the fierce rights they had so long enjoyed. They fell back, when assailed, on the Emperor; but they relished his impartial centralising law as little as they welcomed the people's uprising. The old Greek tyrant in a small city like Corinth or Athens, on his guard night and day against assassination, might seem to live once more in the portentous Ezzelino or the subtle Visconti. Every vice, every horror, that

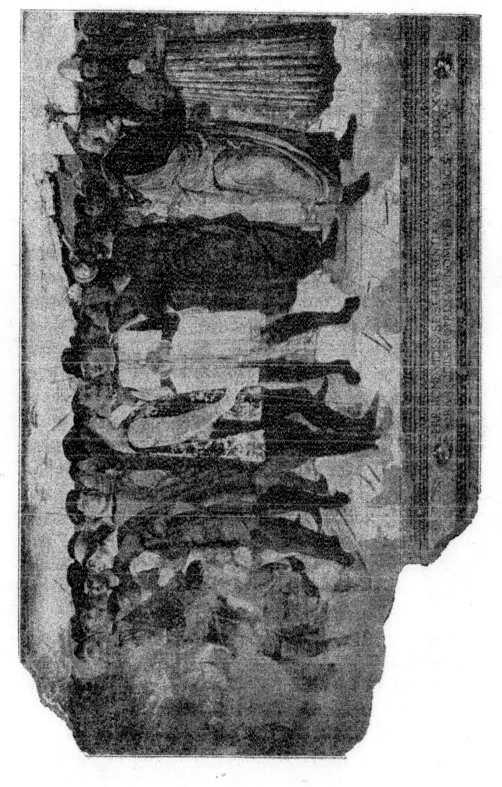

ESPOUSALS OF THE VIRGIN. (*Fresco at Viterbo*)

357

legend ascribes to the Greek was renewed in the Italian despots. But the age did not condemn their crimes so loudly as it admired their good fortune. True, they often came to a bad end. Ezzelino himself, whose father had been a monstrous compound of sins and superstitions, ruled Padua with a rod of iron ; yet was he regretted when his Ghibelline confederates, finding he meant to betray them, turned round, wounded and imprisoned him. The half-crazy tyrant tore away his bandages and died blaspheming. Such were the miscreants with whom Manfred, gay, subtle, courageous, but certainly not much of a Christian, had to make alliance. He won over Venice and Genoa ; when Alexander IV. died at Viterbo in 1261 the Papacy had no friend except St. Louis ; and its always precarious dominion over Rome was hardly even a name. Eight Cardinals were left of the Sacred College. They chose a Frenchman, born at Troyes, son of a shoemaker, and raised by his own merits to be Patriarch of Jerusalem. It was a hundred and forty years since the last French Pope, Calixtus II., had mounted St. Peter's Chair. Pantaleon called himself Urban IV. He proceeded at once to name fourteen Cardinals, of whom seven were French. And he offered the crown of Naples to St. Louis.

Certainly the spectacle is an imposing one ; this cobbler's son, meanest of his subjects by birth, makes a present to the Most Christian King of Southern Italy ; he holds the balance between Richard of Cornwall and Alfonso of Castile, candidates for the Empire ; and he successfully withstands the Ghibel-

ESPOUSALS OF THE VIRGIN. (*Fresco at Viterbo.*)

359

lines at large, who were pressing Conradin's claims.
But he could not cope with Manfred. The Italian
cities had lost or overturned their Guelf administration. St. Louis argued that if Conradin were not
heir of Sicily, Edmund was; and the King of
Arragon took a decisive step, hotly condemned from
Rome, when he allowed his son to marry the daughter
of Manfred. This alliance was fated, in the end, to
bring with it the Sicilian dowry; for the moment it
exasperated Urban, who procured Edmund's renunciation and bestowed the title, with all it implied, on
Charles of Anjou. The Romans made him their
Senator; and the last, bloodiest, and most hateful
chapter in this deplorable conflict began.

Personally, the combatants were not ill-matched.
Manfred, whom his rival termed the "Sultan of
Nocera," had inherited his mother's fair face, his
father's versatile and dangerous charm; adored,
detested, a knight-errant with his Saracen Mamelukes about him, no friend to priests, he calls up
an image of Napoleon by this mixture of logic,
violence, and adventurous fancy which, for a time,
no power could resist. Charles of Anjou, Count
of Provence, in his wife's name, had nothing of
the gay troubadour; this tall, thin man, with the
olive complexion and eagle countenance, never
laughed, spoke little, hardly slept. Regular as a
monk, says Villani, who gives us his picture, Charles
professed to be a zealous Catholic; he took no
pleasure in mimes or courtly feastings; he was
prodigal of arms to his followers; but was himself
greedy after lands, lordships, and money. His high,

severe thoughts made him, as years went on, dreadfully cruel. But where, except in the heart of St. Louis, shall we look for mercy during that wild age? Manfred was cruel too; yet history, when it speaks of Charles, never has a kind word for him, and on the tomb of the Sicilian hero the tears of generations have fallen. Friendship was the jewel of these Hohenstauffen Kings.

We pass over the troubles of England in which Urban played no successful part. Scarcely had he called to the Angevin when he died on the way to Orvieto (1265), and an anxious interregnum of five months ensued. Hugo Falcodi was Legate at Boulogne—for he dared not cross the Channel to daunt with anathemas the English barons. A Southern Frank, from the Rhone, Archdeacon of Narbonne, Cardinal of Santa Sabina, in early days wedded, he was that formidable character, a Churchman who is likewise a man of the world. His French colleagues elected him. Clement IV. at once made his way over the Alps to Perugia; he proclaimed a Crusade, pledged the Roman basilicas, excepting St. Peter's and the Lateran, and to raise supplies, sent out his begging Friars with ample authority, who stirred revolt on the borders of Naples.

Meanwhile, Charles of Anjou, having gained his terms, embarked at Marseilles with a few galleys, reached the Tiber, was in Rome at Whitsuntide, 1265, and—evil omen!—took up his quarters in the Lateran. He meant, Pope or no Pope, to be master. As summer ended, the French army passed Mont Cenis; most of the great families sent sons or representatives; the Crusade was fed with French money; and these thirty thousand invaders joined Charles under the crumbling walls of Rome. The Pope saw them go by; he did not join them. At once Anjou drove forward to Ceperano. Manfred drew out his motley forces in front of Benevento (February 6, 1266). The shock was fierce; French, Germans,

RUINS OF THE ARCHBISHOP'S PALACE, VITERBO.

Saracens, Guelfs of Florence, fought with desperate rage. But never have Italians resisted the Gallic outset victoriously. Manfred lost the battle. He fell by an unknown hand. His body was recognized, set on an ass, and brought to Charles. It was buried under a great cairn, for in holy ground it must not lie; then torn up again, and cast out of the Kingdom, as Dante sings with severe pathos, to repose by the stream called Verde. The French sacked Benevento. Apulia, Calabria, and even Sicily submitted. Clement invested Charles with the conquered South. Florence took back her Guelfs ; Pisa was humbled ; Milan was treated despitefully. From that day to this Italians have feared and hated the French dominion. Clement might tax distant nations, excommunicate Simon de Montfort, and set his Legate above the King of England ; at home he was the humble servant of Charles, who held all Italy in his grasp and " made horrible exactions under the Royal Seal," as the Pope, not without indignation, writes to him.

Two years were enough to provoke the counter-revolution. Frederick Lancia made his way to Germany and persuaded Conradin, the boy not yet sixteen, to assert his rights, cross the Alps, and march on Rome. With four thousand troops and his insepar-able friend, young Frederick of Austria, the last Hohenstauffen came to Verona. Clement at Viterbo launched his thunder at this serpent sprung from a poisonous brood. He appointed Charles, "peace-maker" in Tuscany and throughout the Empire. But Sicily was in revolt. Another Lancia had seized the Lateran ; his ally, Henry of Castile, occupied St. Peter's. Down rushed Conradin, while Charles lingered about Florence ; when he went to besiege Lucera the bold lad and young Frederick rode in sight of Clement, under the Viterbo battlements ; "victims to the slaughter," said he, looking down on them with a kind of melancholy, which did not hinder his subsequent acts. Rome opened its gates with joy to the Suabian, whom it soon expected to crown Emperor. Some churches were plundered. The small army marched on behind Sabine peaks to fatal Tagliacozzo. There, a first success ended in utter ruin, August 26, 1268. Conradin and Frederick were taken, sold by the Frangipani to the Angevin; their followers dispersed. Charles had now his desire; the two Lancias were caught—all the hopes of Hohenstauffen might be struck dead at a blow. But even he could not murder his prisoners. By an extraordinary device, to be long argued over, execrated, wondered at, he brought them to a mock trial in Naples. They were condemned as rebels to their liege lord. Germany has never forgotten, pity will always tell with shuddering, how Conradin knelt on the scaffold in presence of a numberless throng, cast his glove among them defiantly, cried, "O my mother, what news will they bring thee this day!" and on that word was smitten by the headsman. His comrade, Frederick, died in like manner; then the Lancias; then two Pisan nobles who had cleaved to his cause. "Life of Conradin, death of Charles," the Pope was fabled to have written; all we know is that he did not stay the fall of the axe. We think with gladness that Anjou was never to hold Sicily fast; that if the Hohenstauffen were gone, the seed of Manfred should yet enjoy his kingdom. There is a logic in events which the wise call Providence; it cannot be mistaken even in so dark a tragedy.

Young Conradin was beheaded on October 29, 1268. Within a month, on November 29, Clement IV.

died. Charles of Anjou, irresistible, kept—or permitted his French Cardinals to keep—the Holy See vacant for two years. At length, on March 22, 1272, a Visconti, Archdeacon of Liège, then away in the Holy Land, was chosen. He is known as Gregory X.

This admirable man united the simplicity of a saint with the wisdom of a lawgiver. His journey from Brindisi to Rome was a peaceful triumph. He made a treaty between Venice and Genoa, hoping they might combine in a naval expedition to the East. At Florence he attempted the impossible, to persuade the Guelfs and Ghibellines that they should dwell together in unity. He ordered a new election to the Empire, which would henceforth be Teutonic, for all its short or sudden irruptions into Italy; he confirmed Rudolph of Hapsburg when chosen. He had seen the Latin usurpation at Constantinople end in 1261 ; nay, though he knew it not, he had taken part in the last of the Crusades. Instinct and policy bade him recognise Michael Paleologus, whose name and succession were to continue until Mohammed II. should desecrate Sancta Sophia into a mosque. Gregory, advancing north as he fulfilled these deeds of reconciliation, opened the great Council of Lyons in 1274.

Round about him sat five hundred Bishops, seventy Abbots, a thousand of the clergy. The King of Arragon was there ; all the West had sent representatives ; in June the Greek ambassadors came. No anathema was pronounced ; the Churches of East and West uttered a common creed, acknowledged one Pope, and bowed to the orthodox Emperors, Rudolph and Michael. Gregory issued stern regulations which might hinder Conclaves in the future from paltering with their duty. On his way home, when the Council was happily concluded, he met the Hapsburg Emperor at Lausanne and dedicated that august and now desolate cathedral. But he never reached the Eternal City. At Arezzo, January 1276, he expired. The ancient strife began again, though under circumstances which were substituting French for German actors, and reversing the part of the King and the Pontiff.

In three years three Popes; Innocent V. lasted till June, 1276; Hadrian V., a Genoese, not ordained, suspended the imperative rules made by Gregory for election to St. Peter's Chair, and died in August; John XXI., chosen amid tumults, was killed in May, 1277, by the falling in of his palace-roof. Nicholas III., an Orsini, followed. He built the Vatican; got from Rudolph the magnificent, empty cession, not only of all the Papal States, but of the Italian Islands; showed little friendship to Charles of Anjou; enriched his own nephews; gave one the Castle of St. Angelo, made another his Vice-Senator in Rome; filled the Sacred College with his kinsfolk; died at Soriano, which he had confiscated; and for his avarice, nepotism, and Guelfic pretensions was seen by Dante burning in hell. Yet he is described as no less irreproachable in character than aspiring and energetic. Charles of Anjou would not endure a second like him. By sheer compulsion he forced on the Conclave, after six months' stubborn fight, his nominee, the Cardinal of Santa Cecilia, formerly Canon of Tours, a born Frenchman

(1281). Martin IV. kept his court in Orvieto. He had but one principle of conduct, to register the decrees which his creator Charles might dictate.

When this sour, truculent conqueror had seized Naples, where he exercised a grinding tyranny, the Greek possessions of Manfred also fell to him. Sicily, once the lady of kingdoms, he trampled upon like a slave; his lieutenants at Palermo kept a list of marriageable heiresses, whom he bestowed on his Provençal adventurers, and, though himself decorous, he let this unbridled soldiery insult the honour of a people as jealous and reserved as the Mohammedans, whose blood they often shared. We must fancy these things and worse going on year after year, while Pedro the Arragonese watched his opportunity to strike, in his wife Constanza's name, for the Sicilian crown and freedom. Charles was effectively chief of the House of France. St. Louis had perished in Africa on the foolish noble quest into which he was betrayed by this designing brother. Philip the Hardy did not deserve his bold addition. But Anjou looked to be lord of Italy despite the Hapsburg, who, indeed, was never able to hinder these distant thunderclaps. More, he dreamt of an Empire on the Ægean, of Byzantium and the Golden Horn. Paleologus could neither subdue his own clergy nor fulfil the promises made to Gregory X. at Lyons. He was excommunicated and would have been left to the tender mercies of Charles by Martin IV., but his own subjects made an end of him and renounced the Papacy.

Looking thus East and West the Angevin was caught between two fires. Arragon joined hands with the Greeks ; it is even possible that Nicholas III. was no stranger to plots or combinations which might reduce an enemy who had come as the Church's deliverer and now held so much more than had been granted him.   This was ever the risk of appealing to the secular arm.   Romance, taking up its parable, here weaves in the travels, disguises, hair-breadth escapes of the physician, perhaps alchemist, John of Procida, who arranges everything beforehand like a stage conspirator.   The story will always be told with a sigh or a smile that it should be too strange to be true.   We will grant Procida's negotiations ; it is known that Martin IV. did his utmost to bring the Ghibellines under, and he must have felt the storm advancing from Arragon.   But the real stage villain was Charles, whose soldiers exasperated to madness a proud and sullen people.   "Hate and wait," says the Corsican proverb ; the Sicilians never ceased to hate, but during fourteen years they waited.

On Easter Tuesday, 1282, as the crowds were pouring out of church after Vespers, a French soldier named Drouet insulted the daughter of Roger Mastrangelo.   The assailant was instantly stabbed with his own sword, snatched (as legend says) by the girl's bridegroom.   "Death to the French !" resounded on all sides ; the bells of San Giovanni degli Eremiti rang out the tocsin, and two thousand strangers were massacred on the spot.   Into a common pit their carcases were flung.   Then King Roger's palace was invaded ; the Justiciar fled ; foreign priests, monks, residents—every one that could not frame his mouth to pronounce the shibboleth "Ciceri," says

SAN GIOVANNI DEGLI EREMITI, PALERMO ("SICILIAN VESPERS," A.D. 1282).

369

the legend—fell under an indiscriminate vengeance.
It was a day of rebuke and blasphemy, when churches
and convents were themselves polluted with slaughter,
as in frantic revolutions before and since. Mastrangelo. with his friends, improvised a Government ;
thirty miles off the Justiciar was caught and killed.
The Island rose in fury ; from Corleone to Messina
was nothing but murder, insurrection, a medieval
Feast of Pikes. Heribert the Viceroy, pledged to
return to Provence, escaped into Calabria. Whatever
French he left behind were done to death ; and by
the end of April Sicily was free. But everywhere
the Church's banner, the cross-keys, floated on the
wind. With Rome the liberated cities sought no
quarrel.

Charles's prayer, when this Job's news was brought
him, is on record : " O God, if I must fall, be it by
slow degrees." He sat gnawing his sceptre, by
turns raging and silent. His French Pope, Martin,
laid Palermo under an interdict which these sanguinary Vespers had well deserved ; he confiscated
the property of rebels, from the Archbishop to the
meanest layman, and he uttered once more the
detestable word Crusade. To him the Sicilians gave
reply by calling in Pedro of Arragon, who was making
war on Tunis. He came to Trapani, not far from
ancient Eryx, with Roger Loria, his great admiral,
most adventurous of medieval sailors ; with Conrad
Lancia and other exiles. He was at once hailed
King of Sicily. Meanwhile, Anjou with Cardinal
Gerard was thundering at Messina, vomiting destruction like Ætna upon the stubborn town. His assault

was beaten back. Roger Loria came sailing into the Straits ; compelled him to desert his tents ; took forty-five galleys and six thousand prisoners ; the Catalan King and army triumphed. Charles, a little out of his mind, challenged Pedro to single combat ; the absurd proposal was eluded. Again Roger Loria drew out his fleet in array before Naples. The Angevin was on the march, but his son, Charles the Lame, went forth to battle, was defeated and taken. "Would to God he were dead !" exclaimed the angry father. Had his enemies retaliated on the crippled young man that which Conradin had suffered, who would have called it unjust? They spared him, and he lived to be King of Naples.

But the melancholy Charles sank under his misfortunes ; he died at Foggia, January 7, 1285. It was a year of illustrious deaths. Pope Martin, in 1283, had deposed Don Pedro of Arragon ; the Kingdom he presented to Charles of Valois (yet another Charles !), second son of France. A Crusade once more ; this time led by Philip the Hardy, with a light-minded, numerous host. Italian fleets ravaged the shores of Catalonia ; Don Pedro lost all but a few strong places. Then the tide turned. Roger Loria, pirate or freebooter at sea, broke the French ships, tortured the French captives ; Philip had to raise the siege of Gerona, to leave his dying soldiers in the passes of the Pyrenees, himself to die at Perpignan this same year, October, 1285. One month later Don Pedro joined him in the shades. Martin was gone already in March. Some handfuls of white dust were left of them all—Kings, warriors,

Churchmen. As for Sicily, never more did it obey its Papal overlord. The war of twenty-one years, which we need not follow through its twists and turnings, issued in a compromise (1299). Frederick, brother of Don Pedro, was to keep the Island for life ; he bequeathed it to his descendants and founded a dynasty. Charles the Lame succeeded to the other Sicily, which Italians call " Il Regno," on the mainland. Over Conradin and his slaughtered friends this Charles built, in the busiest part of Naples, the Church of Mount Carmel, even yet a place of pilgrimage to the hurrying traveller.

Honorius IV., who passed across the stage one moment on Martin's death, annulled the compact which divided the two Sicilies. But he could not hinder that division. From the investiture of the Normans by Nicholas II. in 1059 with the splendid South two hundred and forty years may be reckoned (to 1299) during which the Holy See exercised or insisted on those feudal rights which were judged necessary at Rome to its independence. They were now brought down to parchment decrees and ceremonial services. Even the strange, and in modern eyes unjust, absolution from sealed engagements which Nicholas IV. in 1289 gave to Charles the Lame, thereby hoping to keep a hand upon Sicily, availed not for one instant to delay the inevitable. Feudalism had done its work, it was going the way of men's devices ; the Pope, conservative by nature, tenacious of what had once been his on whatever conditions, felt the approaching change ; not he alone, but all feudal sovereigns must suffer or be transformed.

VITERBO—PALAZZO ALESSANDRINI.

The absolute monarch was to absorb in himself powers of the clergy, powers of the nobles ; to be protector of the free cities and the whole nation, a Cæsar who would take no orders from Pope or Parliament. In this long-threatened revolution France led the way. France, at the end of the thirteenth century, broke up the system of Europe, as she did on a larger scale at the end of the eighteenth. We are now to trace the steps of this most memorable transaction.

XXIII

ROMAN LAW VERSUS ROMAN PONTIFF

(1226–1287)

GIBBON has told us that the Kingdom of France
was made by the French Bishops as bees make their
honeycomb. Clovis, Charles Martel, Pepin, Charlemagne, were all champions of the Church. And even
the " bad seed " of Hugh Capet, the wicked excommunicated Kings, did not shoot up into rebellion
against Rome, despite their scandalous living.
Rheims and Tours, famous for their shrines, were
minor capitals in which the " Abbot of St. Martin's "
was always at home. He was brought up in the
cloister of Notre Dame or St. Denis ; he had Suger
for his Prime Minister, St. Bernard at his right hand
in council ; Pope after Pope took refuge with him
from the fury of Roman mobs or German lanzknechts ;
he was their man, though never a feudatory. His little
kingdom, hemmed round about by the wide provinces
of insolent Norman England ; by industrious, hard-
fisted Flanders ; by Burgundian Dukes and Counts

of Provence; was yet compact, defensible, and in a manner sacred. When the Godfreys of Bouillon rushed off to Crusades, he stayed behind to pick up the inheritances which they left in pledge. Seldom a man of genius, he was singularly debonair, a father to his people, and in their hard fights with iron barons a Patriot King. Until the twelfth century was out he did not count for much in Europe. But John Lackland dropped his French provinces like silver plates from his pocket, and Philip Augustus rounded his dominions with them. Normandy, Picardy, fell to his share. Bouvines set him free from the German Empire. The Albigenses by their Counts of Toulouse, of Foix, of the whole South, were forfeit to Rome. But it was Amaury de Montfort, son of their conqueror, who threw himself into the arms of France. Louis VIII. subdued Nismes, Albi, Carcassonne, but died of this hot campaign, leaving a Spanish wife, Blanche of Castile, to cope with unruly nobles, and a child who became St. Louis (1226).

The Salic kingdom had, in legal phrase, fallen to the distaff. But Queen Blanche managed the spindle like a sword. We figure this valiant woman as a haughty, severe, not amiable Madame de Maintenon, gifted with more will and resolution; hard upon her gentle son, whom she carried with her as a relique in its shrine when she attacked the feudal chiefs; pure as an angel, but always Spanish—that is to say, looking on her enemies as Moors and her friends as knights bound to follow her in the Holy War. She proved a match for Mauclerc, the bandit Count of Brittany. From Thibaut of Navarre she got by purchase Chartres, Blois, Chateaudun. In 1236 Louis came of age. He reigned until 1270. The Hohenstauffen at this very time were going down to their grave, and with them the Empire. Heresies were rife. It cannot be said that the Popes, though men of consummate ability, gave edification to thoughtful Christians. If St. Francis of Assisi, by his exquisite goodness, lights up the beginning of that troubled thirteenth century, St. Louis sheds lustre on its middle period. We may define him as the Catholic Marcus Aurelius, or as St. Francis on the throne. In every situation he is charming, brave, just, tender, unaffected. Who has yet written of him without a smile and a tear? He is Marcus Aurelius, stoical towards himself, considerate of all the world, but never melancholy as he that on the Pannonian frontier wrote those beautiful, sad pages we know so well. The Middle Ages, it has been too graphically said, came to an end in a Saint-King and an Emperor-Pope.

St. Louis kept no diary of his thoughts; but a precious inheritance from the Middle Ages, more authentic than the *Fioretti* which describe the Umbrian Saint, and hardly less picturesque, is the Life in Old French by the Sieur de Joinville, candid as a child's story, and as touching. His slight frame, long thin fingers, delicate health give an impression that Louis was not meant for active life. He never showed a general's sagacity, but was simply a knight in armour. Yet he won the battle of Taillebourg in 1242 over Henry III. of England, which utterly smote feudalism; he kept Provence and Languedoc against the younger Raymund of Toulouse, whom, on his submission, he treated kindly ; and, in 1235, he took the Cross to drive back that immense Mongol or Kharismian invasion, before which Jerusalem had yielded and all the Western States, Mohammedan equally as Christian, were paralysed. For once, Blanche of Castile dissuaded her son from the heroic course, and for once he would not obey.

From the Danube, as we saw, Frederick's gallant sons had turned back the Tartar myriads ; but even the Moslems entreated Louis, as did the unhappy Emperor of Byzantium, to lead his Franks against these wild shepherds. At Citeaux, not without repugnance, he met Pope Innocent IV., who had vainly striven to draw Louis into his quarrels and now did not favour a distant Crusade. Many of the Albigenses, despoiled of their lands by De Montfort, the King took on this sacred expedition. He had it in mind to colonise the coasts of Egypt ; there was a great gathering, but eight months' delay at Cyprus, whence he sailed for Alexandria in June, 1249.

But a tempest drove him towards Damietta ; he landed, captured the town, and should have marched to Cairo. His soldiers plundered ; lagged on the road ; fought well ; but knew no discipline. Louis, taller than most by a head and shoulders, in his golden helmet, a German sword in his hand, was the picture of a perfect knight. They told him that his brother, Robert of Artois, had been killed. " God be praised for the grace He has given him ! " cried Louis, and dashed away the big tears ; " I know he is in Paradise." He won the battle of Mansurah ; but the sick, the wounded, the plague, Greek fire, and an enemy in pursuit on the Nile, as on its shores, brought the inevitable disaster. The Crusaders were slain in heaps or compelled to deny Christ. Louis was taken with his chief nobles and ten thousand of his men. If he would consent to give up Jerusalem, he might

KING LOUIS IX. (ST. LOUIS) OF FRANCE.

be free. He offered Damietta and four hundred thousand bezants of gold. But when the Soldan was for accepting these terms, his Mamelukes murdered him. The story ran that they thought of setting up Louis in his stead. Just as likely is it that they would have murdered the French King too, but for his mild intrepidity and unruffled cheerfulness, which none that saw him could ever resist. On conditions deemed moderate he was held to ransom. He lingered a whole year in Palestine ; built again the walls of Acre, Jaffa, and Cæsarea ; and returned to Europe in November, 1252, with the glory of a saint and martyr. Queen Blanche was dead ; his country cried out for him.

It was the destiny of Louis, in a quaint but apt phrase, to be justice of the peace to all nations. England, which under John had been made the fief, seemed under his vacillating successor to be the farm, of the Papacy. Henry III. squandered and plundered ; his Queen's uncle, Boniface of Savoy, little better than a bandit, was thrust into the See of Canterbury. Innocent IV. treated English riches as an inexhaustible mine. He once demanded for his absentee favourites no fewer than three hundred livings ; the clergy, as he argued, were his vassals ; they must render suit and service, or its equivalent in hard cash, while he carried on his war against Frederick the Antichrist. Langton had all along upheld the Great Charter ; Edmund, who succeeded him, a lesser but very winning Thomas à Becket, did what in him lay to reform abuses, and died in exile at Pontigny. The manly Grossetête rose up at Lyons to denounce iniquities that he had fought against at home, and withstood Innocent to his face. The undergraduates at Oxford assailed Otho, the Papal Legate, and drove him out of the city.

To supply Prince Edmund with funds for his mad Sicilian expedition which never came off, Henry pawned the kingdom to the Pope, and asked his barons to redeem the pledge. They answered by the voice of Simon de Montfort, a saint like his father, in the Oxford Parliament (1258). Its provisions made the King a lay figure, managed by fifteen nobles. Alexander IV. dispensed him from his oath, which Edward the Prince insisted on keeping. Civil war followed. St. Louis was called in to arbitrate. He annulled the Provisions, gave back the royal power to Henry, but left the English Charters in force (1264). A second campaign was the result, ending in the battle and the " Mise " of Lewes. Then came the first real Parliament, and the King's abeyance, which led up to the Fight at Evesham and De Montfort's heroic death (1265). His Parliament had been " partisan, revolutionary, transient." Ottobuoni, the Legate, appeared in St. Paul's, did away with Henry's oaths, and declared all that Simon had striven for utterly abolished. It was in vain. Edward I., who is called the " English Justinian," would complete hereafter that which the great Earl of Leicester had begun.

That St. Louis when he annulled the Provisions of Oxford acted according to his lights, no man may doubt. Conscience had already urged him into surrendering large lands in Aquitaine to England which any but he would have held against all comers. Read his spirited words in Joinville. But as the Popes, in these Charters and Parliaments, could see nothing but rebellion demanding unheard of privileges, so Louis felt that the royal authority must be maintained in spite of barons whose fellows

in France were men like Thibaut, the Robber-Count
of Champagne. Thibaut was a Crusader, therefore
inviolable, and under the Pope's emphatic protection;
yet Louis had smitten him down. But at Westminster
the Commons' House, with its knights of the shire
and burgesses from the towns, was destined to the
long trials and decisive triumphs which have made it
supreme; at Paris the so-called Parliament was to
become a lawyers' assembly, the instrument of an
absolute monarch whose decrees it gloried in carrying
out to the utmost. England never lost its Magna
Charta. But of the French legists it is said that the
Pandects were their Bible; they would allow no
check upon the King; he was their Cæsar, to whom
they rendered the things that were God's, as well as
his own.

We have watched this movement at its beginning
under Frederick Barbarossa; since his day, it had
embraced Church and State; the turbulent, half-mad
thirteenth century strove yet with all its powers to
establish the reign of law. From Innocent III. to
St. Thomas Aquinas; from Frederick II. to Philip
the Fair and Edward I., it goes on, an immense
and partly successful attempt to bring confusion out
of chaos, to restore the supremacy of Roman Law in
its twofold form, Canon and Civil. But here, almost
of necessity, layman and priest came into conflict.
When Frederick II. codified the Norman statutes in
Sicily, he trenched on immunities which the clergy
would not give up. All over Europe the quarrel that
in Henry II.'s time raged round the Constitutions of
Clarendon was now, or soon would be, the question of

Photo]   [Neurdein Frères.

ST. LOUIS ADMINISTERS JUSTICE.

(*Fresco in the Pantheon, Paris.*)

the day. It was at once home and foreign; were
clerics prepared to submit their temporal causes to
the Common Law? Would the Pope cease to tax
them and the Kingdom without regard to the duties,
rights, and charges of the Crown? The dispute was
concerned with lands and money; it never directly
touched doctrine. As the law became centralised,
taxation followed it. The Pope, in his quality of
Commander of the Faithful, had long raised a
revenue from the whole of Christendom. But the
Crusades were ending; these subsidies had often
been misused and turned aside from their legitimate
object, never more so than under Innocent IV. and
Clement IV. Kings built up Codes by way of
consolidating their jurisdiction. Alfonso the Wise in
Spain, Frederick in the Empire, set an example; but
it was probably St. Louis to whom Edward I. owed
his lawgiving; and beyond peradventure from him
the French legislation is derived which set the royal
Court of Appeal above all others. In this sense the
Pragmatic Sanction, though not his work, may be
attributed to his age and advisers, among whom the
chief, Pierre de Fontaines, had embodied no little of
the Roman Law in his *Counsel to a Friend.*

When, beneath the oaks of Vincennes, he did
justice, "fair and round," as Joinville says; when he
declared to Enguerrand de Coucy that he would not
admit him to wager of battle lest in such cases the
Church and the poor should never find champions
against lordly barons; when he took counsel with
St. Thomas Aquinas, and yet gave judgment adverse
to haughty prelates like the Bishop of Beauvais; in

all this he was bringing the idea of law, impartial
and without regard for privilege, into a world which
confounded right with station and sacrificed modern
society to its ancient defenders. " Fair son," he said
in his illness at Fontainebleau, to Philip the Hardy,
" win the love of your people; for I had rather a
Scot came from Scotland and governed them well
and loyally, than that you governed them ill in men's
sight." Such was a saint's conception of law. But a
kingdom could not be ruled by open-air courts in the
Forest of Vincennes ; from the middle class had
begun to spring up an aristocracy of the robe, men
who were neither nobles nor clerics, and who discovered in the Crown an authority which they soon
learned to manipulate. They were " knights of the
law," masters in chicanery, hard as iron ; these were
the new order that " with texts and quotations " from
Old Rome transformed the Middle Age to the
despotism of the sixteenth and later centuries.

Old Rome meant the city of the Cæsars. Papal
Rome had long been falling into ruin, its ways
desolate, a thousand towers looking down on the
Seven Hills, inhabited by robber-chiefs who preyed
on every sort of pilgrim, cleric or lay, and lifted their
banners against the Pope, though enraged when he
fled from them. But Paris was the capital of civilisation. Philip Augustus had done great things for it ;
he may be said to have founded the city that has
ever since included the Palace, the People, and
the University, as in a ring fence. Thanks to Robert
de Curzon in 1215, to Gregory IX. in 1231, the
University was self-governing ; and with its four

26

nations, its twenty or thirty thousand scholars, offered to later times a picture of that fierce intellectual democracy which has made Athens immortal. Seven Popes, in the thirteenth century, were among its students. Thither came the most brilliant of the Schoolmen, Peter Lombard, who died Bishop of Paris, Alexander Hales, Albert the Great, St. Bonaventure, St. Thomas Aquinas, Duns Scotus,—all Mendicant Friars, devoted to the Papacy, as the lawyers, clergy, and doctors were to the Crown. What did their coming portend?

At first, if we believe the pious Tillemont, they were received with joy. St. Dominic had never forbidden his friars to cultivate learning and take degrees. But St. Francis had other thoughts ; he would not have one of his disciples seated in a teacher's chair ; they were to be humble saints rather than Canonists or divines. The torrent swept them on ; it was a century of ambition to know, to read Aristotle, to lecture on the *Sentences* of the Lombard. In 1228, when the wild young scholars rebelled and fled from Paris, the Dominicans set up their first chair ; in 1244 Innocent IV. commanded that the Begging Friars should be admitted to academic honours. They carried all before them. Genius and success were theirs ; opposition broke out ; the Dominicans were expelled, reinstated by Innocent, but put under episcopal authority (1254). Alexander IV. revoked this unusual clause. Then William de St. Amour attacked the friars in a pamphlet which is the medieval equivalent of Pascal's *Provincial Letters*. He published his *Perils of the*

THE GLORY OF OBEDIENCE. *(Fresco by Giotto—Assisi.)*

Last Times, an invective in which all alike, Dominicans, Spiritual Franciscans, and Moderates, were denounced as false prophets, believers in the "Eternal Gospel" of Abbot Joachim, Beghards and heretics, shameless in their rapacity, sworn enemies of the clerical order. His book was condemned by a Papal commission. St. Amour appealed. At Anagni, in presence of Alexander IV., the case was debated, Albert the Dominican acting on behalf of the friars. Pope Alexander would not convict St. Amour of heresy ; but he censured the writing as a libel, having already deposed John of Parma, the mystic General of the Franciscans. St. Thomas Aquinas, with his prodigious memory, reduced the discussion to order and answered St. Amour. But in popular estimation the University had won. During the latter years of the thirteenth century, trials, dissensions, and discredit clouded over the great hopes which, at its beginning, had dawned on the Mendicants. Their eclipse darkened the Papacy, which could no longer rely upon them in the crisis that was rapidly approaching.

Amid these never-ending disputes between the old order and the new, symptoms at once of death and birth, came the horrid intelligence that the Egyptians were seizing in Palestine whatever had escaped the Mongol ravages. Cæsarea, Jaffa, Antioch had fallen ; seventeen thousand Christians were slain, a hundred thousand sold. King Louis resolved on taking the cross ; he did his utmost to draw in the neighbouring States ; he led with him a great company of barons ; but he could not persuade his people. Clement IV., though willing to raise subsidies for the Holy War, neither approved nor encouraged this expedition. It seemed to be a blind man's stroke, aimless, vacant. For twenty days the army was at sea ; Charles of Anjou advised his brother to land in Tunis. Eight days after, the plague fell on the defenceless host ; the marshals died ; the King's youngest son died ; it was the end. Louis, calm as ever, had himself laid out on ashes ; he blessed his followers ; and sighing forth his lifelong aspiration, "Jerusalem, ah Jerusalem !" passed away (August, 1270).

The last Crusade ! Glance for a moment at Edward of England drawing his sword, in those sacred fields, against the infidel ; then look westward again. Never any more will the chivalry of the Franks mount the walls of Zion, to the cry of *Dieu le veult*. Christians, Saracens, are doomed to flee before an enemy from the salt Asiatic steppes, fiercer than the Arab, impregnable to civilisation ; the Turk is coming who will seize Egypt with one hand, Byzantium with the other. He will advance to Belgrade, plunder Otranto, besiege Vienna ; he will last on, century after century, till Holy Russia has gained strength to grapple with him. Islam survived the Crusades. By an undreamt-of revolution, the Moslem world, which two hundred years' hard fighting left everywhere except in Spain as it had been, was to be subdued or ringed round about with fire, by England, after it had thrown off its allegiance to Rome, and by the Orientalised Muscovites who revere the Church of Constantinople. What the Crusades did for Europe ; how they opened larger horizons, broke feudalism, gave an entrance to Eastern art, philosophy, science, and superstition ; how they first exalted the Pope, and then tempted to the multiplication of Holy Wars which were but civil butcheries, the reader has doubtless been considering, and there is no space to tell. With St. Louis they ended, once for all. The conquests of England or Russia in the East have drawn their motives from commerce, policy, and adventure but never from religion.

XXIV

PHILIP THE FAIR AND POPE BONIFACE

(1287–1300)

THAT new world, which was so unlike the old, is painted by Michelet in forbidding colours—" attorney, usurer, Gascon, Lombard, Jew "; such are the epithets under which he presents it to modern students for whom the Middle Age possesses a complex charm derived from its poetry, art, romance, knight-errantry, and a religion the most picturesque, naïve, and heroic. Feudalism travestied with purple patches of the grand old Roman Law; Kings, in make and descent barbarian, styling themselves Cæsars; litigious Gauls, professing the eloquence of Cicero, and outdoing in hypocrisy the augurs whose technique they imitated; we cannot admire all this, even if it brought mankind a stage further on its way. The lawyer-King is Philip the Fair, that mere " handsome image," said Bernard de Saisset; and his task may be summed up as the establishment on a free secular basis of the Civil Order. What

Frederick II. meant to do, but could not succeed in, Philip the Fair did. In 1287 he ordained that all those who had temporal jurisdiction in France, from Dukes, Counts, and Archbishops down to simple gentlemen, should institute laics for their bailies, provosts, and officers of justice; that they should by no means appoint clerics, who in case of delinquency would have pleaded their "clergy"; and that no Churchman should act as procurator in the royal or baronial courts. At one stroke the Parliament, the tribunals, were taken out of sanctuary. It is the Roman Law come to life again, not in the Pope but in the King.

Let us keep firm hold of this clue; without it we shall never understand why Philip and Boniface quarrelled. But to sketch the ground on which they fought their battle, we must take up the story of the Popes where we left it on the death of Honorius IV. (April, 1287). The conclave was long and stormy; broken up in the hot months, it lasted till February, 1288, when the Bishop of Palestrina was elected. Nicholas IV. had been General of the Grey Friars; poverty mounted the Papal Chair with him; but his short reign was a chapter of misfortunes. He abrogated to no purpose the treaty of Campo Franco, by which Charles II., the lame King of Naples, gave up Sicily to Arragon. Though raised to the purple by Nicholas, the Orsini Pope, he greatly advanced the Colonnas, by this time more powerful than any other Roman house. In 1291 Acre fell, and no Crusade avenged the shame of Christians. The Powers made war and peace without regard to the

Holy See. But Nicholas, like earlier Pontiffs, was said to have died of a broken heart on hearing the disastrous news from Palestine.

Another Conclave, April, 1292; twelve Cardinals debating in Rome till summer chases them away; two rival Senators, with their ruffians set in array and blood flowing,—a year of interregnum. The Electors meet again at Perugia; Charles the Neapolitan comes to overawe them, and is himself overawed by Benedict Gaetani; but no decision follows. Then, with dramatic suddenness—the character of this time—a hermit-saint and visionary is dragged from his cave and acclaimed Pope. Peter Morone had lived the austerest life, hidden in the Apennines above Sulmona, revered by the people and the spiritual Franciscans, in whose eyes he practised the poverty and was absorbed in the contemplation dear to their dead master. It was a scene worthy of the pre-Raphaelite canvas when Cardinals in their purple came, with wild crowds about them, to the barred window of this white-bearded anchorite, bringing him the Papal crown. He looked up from his ecstasy, wept, submitted; he suffered the crimson mantle to be thrown over his sackcloth, and rode on an ass into Aquila where he was hailed with joy by enormous crowds. Then he was taken by King Charles, virtually a prisoner, to Naples.

Extraordinary scenes followed; touching, yet grotesque. Cœlestine V. could converse with angels; among men he was lost. Like a child he gave whatever they asked to friends at hand; he knew only faces from the Abruzzi; the regular officials, broken in to Canon Law, were aghast, angry, dexterous in undoing what he had done, as the witty Jacobus a Voragine said, "in the fulness of his simplicity." Charles II. compelled or persuaded (it was much the same) this good Pope to create thirteen Cardinals, of whom seven where French. But he longed for his cave in the mountains ; and rumour, it is probable, lied when it asserted that Gaetani, who had come to Naples, terrified the hermit with nightly warnings, feigned of Heaven, and brought him to abdicate. "From cowardice he made the grand refusal," sings Dante in undying scorn. He resolved on laying down the tiara. This was without parallel. Could it be lawfully done ? Cœlestine, in a solemn pronouncement, said yes, it could ; he would do it ; and in his old sackcloth he went back rejoicing to the barred cell. Who should be Pope in his stead ?

In that lofty place the Franciscan ideal had shone for a moment, only to be eclipsed. Now the Canon Law, personified in Gaetani, was to have its turn. By what sleight of hand Boniface VIII. outdid his competitors we know not. He was chosen, despite the King, at Naples ; or was it after a bargain with the King, as Villani affirms ? Chosen, however (December 23, 1294), he "came in like a fox, ruled like a lion, died like a dog." How much of his legend can we believe ? "Of all the Roman Pontiffs," says Milman, "Boniface VIII. has left the darkest name for craft, ambition, even for avarice and cruelty." But names prove nothing. Who are the witnesses against Boniface ? Unhappy man, it was his misfortune to find himself at war with all the Catholic

Kings ; with the Religious Orders, with the Roman nobility, with Florence, and the Italian Democrats. In the popular songs and lampoons of Jacopone da Todi he was held up to satire ; his good fame was blasted by sworn accusations in French Parliaments ; Philip the Fair would not let him rest in a dishonoured grave, but pursued his memory as if it had been a living thing, to be transfixed with arrows ; and, beyond all this, he awakened the sad and terrible spirit of Dante, sublime but pitiless, to hate him with an everlasting hatred, amid the flames of which Boniface looks upon us, in the deep gloom of the Inferno. Most miserable of Popes ; not therefore most guilty ! His remembrance will never fade ; long, long he will be banned, and scarcely at all find apologists, in the debate which his pretensions, even more than his acts, cannot cease to provoke. But in the great arena he fell vanquished—he and his Canon Law ; some pity is due to the dying gladiator ; some pathos stirs at the passing of a sovereignty which, contested or triumphant, had lasted down from Charlemagne five hundred years.

Benedict Gaetani was a native and noble of the little mountain-city, Anagni, to which our history alludes so often. An old man now, but vigorous and even violent, he had gone through every stage of Roman training. With Ottobuoni in England he saw, but surely did not see into, the revolution led by Simon de Montfort which, by Charter and Parliament, was to create an English Constitution. He was sent to adjust the quarrel over Provence which divided Charles of Anjou and the Emperor Rudolph,

on which occasion he took the Cardinal's hat.   He
had dealt with the affairs of Portugal.   Lately, in
Paris where as a youth he studied law, he had gone
on a message to Philip the Fair ; had offered, in the
name of Pope Nicholas, to arbitrate between him and
Edward I. ; and at Tarascon had determined articles
of peace between Naples and Arragon.   There is no
reason to cast a shadow on his morals, or to charge
him with impiety.   Such accusations, made afterwards by his deadliest foes, and never proved, were
the disgraceful weapons with which Italian factions
did not scruple to assail adversaries.   Boniface
showed neither the meekness of a saint nor the self-
control of a statesman on the Papal throne ; but that
he was a profligate has never been asserted on
grounds worthy of consideration.

His vigour was at once apparent.   In majestic
terms he granted Naples once more to King Charles
as vassal of the Holy See.   Returning to Rome, he
had himself crowned magnificently.   He consigned
the Abbot of Monte Cassino to a dungeon beneath
the waters of Lago di Bolsena.   He acted as liege
Lord of Hungary on the death of its young prince.
By an official declaration he made sure that Cœlestine's claim should not be revived.   That poor
solitary, fleeing across the Adriatic, was brought
back, lay prostrate before his successor, and was
kept in the Castle of Fumone till he died (May, 1296).
That he underwent harsh treatment does not seem
likely ; the Fraticelli noised abroad his virtues,
miracles, and sufferings ; but only their efforts could
have made him formidable, and Boniface condemned

them as heretics, who aimed at suppressing the
Papacy itself. Their "reign of the Holy Ghost,"
foreshadowed in commentaries on the Abbot
Joachim, would, it is certain, have been a reign of
the Spiritual Friars, the end of Canon Law, the
abolition of the clergy. But in these wild schemes
Cœlestine had neither lot nor part; he was a saint
of the Eastern type, to be canonised for his simple
goodness; none of these Fifth Monarchy visions, we
may be sure, ever haunted his lonely cell.

Boniface dreamt his dream, too; and that scarcely
a sober one. Europe had need of peace; he would
restore the truce of God, outraged by Edward and
Philip at war over Guienne; by the Arragonese in
Sicily; by Albert of Austria, who would not
recognise the penniless Adolphus of Nassau as
German Emperor. In Sicily, as we do not require
to learn, he failed. Adolphus, the soldier of fortune,
having won his crown by large and shameful "capitu-
lations," which surrendered Imperial rights in all
quarters, especially on the Rhine, was to be killed
not far from Worms by Albert in 1298; so that here,
in like manner, Boniface suffered defeat. His argument with Edward I. demands more notice; it led
up to the decisive hour when Philip of France,
staking his kingdom on the issue, met and overthrew
the medieval system, under which no monarch could
be absolute, and Rome was the ultimate Court of
Appeal between the nations and their rulers.

That Edward I. proved himself ablest of the
English Kings is now universally admitted.
Religious, brave, hard, resolute, he meant to leave at

his death a united Kingdom in these islands ; but without war and some chicanery it could not be done. He subdued Wales ; what havoc he wrought in Scotland needs no recalling.   For his wars he required personal service from the barons, subsidies from the clergy, hateful to both.   Edward annulled his people's debts to the Jews and banished them. But still he wanted money.   Against the Friars chiefly, as it is said—they had grown exceedingly rich —he passed the celebrated Statute of Mortmain, which was to hinder the absorption of real estate into hands that yielded little to the Crown, and that only as a gift.   But he went further still.   He asserted the right of taxing the clergy ; obtained from Nicholas IV. a tenth of their income (1291) ; and three years afterwards demanded one-half. They attempted to excuse themselves ; the Dean of St. Paul's, who was to speak for them, fell dead at the King's feet.   It was a principle of Magna Charta that the Crown could not raise taxes without the consent of Parliament ; the clergy had, in addition, their own privilege ; but they were forced to submit.   Soon afterwards, the troubles which had long been threatening in France came to a head ; Boniface, without an ally, wedded to his Canon Law, found the two mightiest Kings in Christendom setting at naught clerical immunities, laying what he deemed sacrilegious hands on spiritual rights. It did not occur to him to yield.   He fought.

Among the strong sayings of Gregory VII. is this, "Kings and dukes are descended from men who, with pride, robbery, and perfidy, usurped a tyrant's

KING EDWARD THE I.ˢᵗ

EDWARD I., KING OF ENGLAND.

399

power." But the Church had gained her vast
dominions by the bequest of her grateful children.
On those riches monarchs and nobles had ever
looked with a covetous eye. No sooner did a
bishopric or an abbey fall vacant than its lands and
goods were seized, to be rendered in worse condition
when the new appointment was made. Much of the
usage known as the "regale" in various European
countries resembled the Highland custom of black-
mail. In the Middle Ages, that wonderful machine
of taxation with which we are familiar did not exist.
But dues, charges, impositions grew with the growth
of a complex society ; and general causes contributed
to make the King a universal, but for many years an
odious, tax-gatherer. Nobles, clergy, free towns alike
resisted the movement. In Papal Bulls, no less than
in English Charters, the claim of a monarch to lay
on fresh taxes, was condemned under the same
anathema which struck at piracy or at those who
furnished arms to Saracens. But especially was it a
crime to invade the patrimony of the poor, with which
Church property was identified. Not that the clergy
refused their gifts when the country was in danger,
or the Crown in distress. They gave largely ; but as
a benevolence, as constrained by charity, on the
higher ground of freedom not of legal necessity.
Above all, they did not wish to be confounded in one
assessment with lay folk, and thus abandoned to the
mercy of a power which, in pursuing its own designs,
would show them scant indulgence. The history of
Europe proves that they were not mistaken. Church
property has been confiscated, again and again,

during the last five hundred years, to secular purposes, and on the plea of State necessity. That it should be surrendered without a protest would be too much to expect from human nature, and among those who have defended it as *Divini juris* are not the least noble of Christians.

Undoubtedly Boniface had law on his side—law, and custom, and admitted privilege. Philip did not love war; but he had retained Guienne by an attorney's trick; he saw an alliance formed against him by Edward between the Empire, Flanders, Burgundy, and Bretagne; money he must procure, and his ministers were apt in devices. All sprang from the middle class. The brothers Marigny were Normans; Nogaret was of Languedoc, Paterine by descent, ferociously antipapal. Pierre Flotte and Plasian were plebeians; the bankers Francesi had migrated from Florence. These were the men that imagined and collected the "maltôte," the evil excise, with every circumstance of harshness and cruelty, from an afflicted people. They clipped the currency which had been struck from silver-plate seized all over his kingdom by Philip, and deposited "for security" in the Louvre, now little else than a coiner's den. Their bailiffs were in every house, making a spoil of industry. The "maltôte," says Michelet, sucked out the marrow of the nation. But at first it spared the Estates of the Church. In 1296 it struck them in the general assault. Then Boniface VIII. published his defiance to Philip, the Bull "Clericis Laicos," thrice unhappy in name and fortunes.

27

Imprudent, headlong, but in its main contention
founded on history, this extraordinary State-paper
declared that the laity had always been hostile to the
clergy, and were so now as much as ever. But they
possessed no jurisdiction over the persons, no claims
on the property of the Church, though they had dared
to exact a tenth, nay, even a half, of its income for
secular objects, and time-serving prelates had not
resisted. Now, on no title whatsoever from henceforth
should such taxes be levied without permission of the
Holy See. Every layman, though King or Emperor,
receiving these moneys, fell by that very act under
anathema; every churchman paying them was
deposed from his office; Universities, guilty of the
like offence, were struck with interdict.

Robert of Winchelsea, Langton's successor as
Primate, shared Langton's views. He was at this
moment in Rome, and had doubtless urged Boniface
to come to the rescue of a frightened downtrodden
clergy, whom Edward I. would not otherwise regard.
In the Parliament at Bury, this very year, the clerics
refused to make a grant. Edward sealed up their
barns. The Archbishop ordered that in every
cathedral the Pope's interdiction should be read.
Hereupon the Chief Justice declared the whole
clergy outlawed; they might be robbed or murdered
without redress. Naturally, not a few gave way; a
fifth, and then a fourth, of their revenue was yielded
up. But Archbishop Robert, alone, with all the
prelates except Lincoln against him, and the Dominicans preaching at Paul's Cross on behalf of the
King, stood out, lost his lands, was banished to a

country parsonage. War broke out in Flanders. It was the saving of the Archbishop. At Westminster Edward relented and apologized. He confirmed the two great Charters; he did away with illegal judgments that infringed them. Next year the Primate excommunicated those royal officers who had seized goods or persons belonging to the clergy and all who had violated Magna Charta. The Church came out of this conflict exempt, or, more truly, a self-governing Estate of the Realm. It must be considered as having greatly concurred towards the establishment of that fundamental law, invoked long after by the thirteen American Colonies, " No taxation without representation," which is the corner-stone of British freedom.

In France the issue was different. There arose no Robert of Winchelsea to stay the King's proceedings : Magna Charta did not exist. By a double Ordinance Philip forbade his subjects to leave the kingdom or send specie abroad without licence from the Crown, and foreigners to enter or carry on trade. This was equivalent to cutting off appeals, supplies, petitions for graces, to Rome, which in no small measure lived on such benevolences or juridical fees. Boniface could not draw back. His policy, the old Guelf tradition, leaned on France ; he would still be looking to Charles of Valois, Philip's brother, inviting him to settle the dissensions of Italy, to carve out for himself a new Eastern Empire. But the Canonist proved not unequal to the occasion. In a second, devout and politic letter addressed to the King, he asserted the Church's freedom, the subjection of all persons under the moral law to his Pontifical judgment; he rebuked the royal Council; he swept away as insane prohibitions which would affect the clergy in their relations with himself; he charged on Philip the war now raging; yet, in fact, he was open to a reconciliation. Philip replied with no less subtlety, with some flashes of sarcasm, a glance towards the Roman Emperors who had granted their privileges to the Roman Bishops, and the strong assertion of his own right to subsidies from the clergy whom he was protecting. At that point the quarrel was interrupted by events nearer home, which cost Boniface a bitter payment in the sequel.

Perhaps he had tricked the Colonna Cardinals into electing him Pope. At any rate, they were Ghibellines, masters of strong castles down in the Campagna, plotters, or like to be such, with the Imperial, Arragonese faction in Sicily. Two brothers were in the Sacred College. It was always possible that they would challenge the validity of an election which had taken place while an undoubted Pontiff was alive. For these and other reasons now debatable, the rash Pope determined on ending the Colonnas root and branch. It was a desperate move. Pretexts, good or bad, were never yet wanting to Italian diplomacy; and these princes, like their neighbours, played at brigandage, not sparing even Boniface. He asked them to surrender their strongholds. They refused. Thereupon he issued a Bull, depriving the two Cardinals as rebels, and marking their partisans with the brand of heresy and schism. In reply they denied his right to the Papal Chair; accused him of circumventing his saintly predecessor; and appealed to a General Council.

But they had no forces in Rome at that time. Boniface answered by excommunicating the prelates in unmeasured language, and—a thing unheard of—by confiscating the estates and interdicting the persons of the whole family, sons, brothers, kinsfolk, to the last generation. They were to be delivered up to his vengeance, wherever found; a crusade, yea, in sight of the Lateran, cries Dante, was proclaimed against the late Cardinals. Their fortresses were taken; Palestrina was got by absolute treachery, by " long promises and short performance," as Guy of Monte Feltro counselled. In these events we seem to be flung back from the close of the thirteenth century to the days when Popes and prelates strangled one another. To explain, or even understand, this horrible business would be impossible to us. Whatever the Cardinals had done, their kindred were not wolves or tigers to be exterminated; yet every step which Boniface took proves that he thought them his deadly foes. No wonder that people asked whether he had not coerced Cœlestine after all?

He demolished Palestrina, and talked of sowing its place with salt. The wretched Cardinals knelt humbly before him at Rieti; they were given some kind of absolution; after which they hid themselves till better times. Their relatives fled. Stephen appeared at the French Court. Sciarra was taken by pirates, ransomed by King Philip, and reserved for a dreadful fame. Others, fleeing to Sicily, strengthened the suspicion against them.   This catastrophe it was which had delayed the rupture with France, and now led to the suspension of " Clericis Laicos."   Philip had paused in his attack on the clergy.   Boniface, " interpreting " his own law, declared that even Church fiefs were bound to suit and service ; the King might not exact, but he was free to request benevolences, and if the State were in danger, he might lay equal taxes on all. By way of splendid peace-offering the Pope now canonised St. Louis (1297).

Like many impetuous statesmen, Boniface had entered into a quarrel without seeing his way out. Allies he had none.   But Philip, or his lieutenant, Charles of Valois, was carrying all before him in Flanders ; the wealthy citizens revolted to him from their Count ; and Edward I., deserted by his barons, had lost Bruges, nor was in a position to attempt a fresh campaign.   Scotland in arms called him to the North.   Under these circumstances the two Kings were willing to accept truce and arbitration ; but the French lawyers would not allow Boniface as Pope to exercise a sort of masterdom over France, which by and by might be called suzerainty.   The peacemaker was to be Gaetani, the man, not the Pontiff.   An agreement was signed in Rome (June, 1297) equitable in its provisions, with restitution on both sides.   Guienne was to be English ; Edward was to marry Philip's sister, and his son Philip's daughter Isabel, the " she-wolf of France," well known to our history.   Until all differences were settled, Papal officers would adminster the debated territories.   In such terms, and amid his Cardinals at Rome, did Boniface pronounce

POPE BONIFACE VIII.

(A Satirical Portrait from Joachims' " Pope Book.")

the final award. He was acting on the best traditions of the Holy See; but he published the judgment as Pope in the form of a Bull, and thus broke his solemn pledge to arbitrate as a private person. This man never could forget that he had been a lawyer.

With Edward I. his disputes, carried on in the haughtiest language, had been successful, although from Edward's accession the feudal tribute of a thousand marks to Rome was no longer paid. The Scots, in extremity, appealed to him now, maintaining that Scotland was a fief of Rome and therefore could not be subject to the Crown of England—which proves for the last time that the suzerainty of the Pope, a juridical fiction in this case, implied real independence and was far from dishonourable when countries at a distance, like Scotland or Denmark, gloried in it. The Pope accepted their view; laid his imperious commands on Edward to release certain Scottish prelates; denied the feudal claims of England; and summoned the King by his ambassadors to appear in the Curia. Robert of Winchelsea did not deliver this challenging document till some time after it reached him; the great Jubilee came between; and Edward held Scotland in his eagle's claws.

XXV

DANTE'S VISION—ANAGNI—END OF THE MIDDLE AGE

(1300–1303)

THIS Jubilee, first of its kind, to mark the passing, to welcome the new century, was very splendid, famous, and triumphant, but it need not detain us. Dante saw it, among the thousands of pilgrims who passed to the Apostle's shrine over the bridge of St. Angelo; it is the date which he assigns to his journey through the Kingdoms of the Invisible World; and that perhaps gives its true significance. The great Jubilee was a vision and a farewell. The whole Middle Ages were passing. Princes and poets, friars, canonists, lawyers, the Pope himself, bore witness to a change from sacerdotal to secular supremacy, from the hieratic to the modern or absolute State. One moment suspended, the contest with Philip was speedily resumed, and went on to its fatal issue.

Edward and his Parliament at Lincoln cast aside the Pope's claim to interfere with Scotland. Charles

of Valois, descending upon Italy as an avowed
champion of the Holy See, permitted the Neri
faction to rage in Florence, made Dante a Ghibelline,
and roused the country to strong detestation of himself
and the Pontiff who had called him across the Alps.
With the Fraticelli Boniface had always been at war.
He now, by an inconceivable oversight, took from the
Franciscans for his own use forty thousand ducats
which they had left in his hands, thereby alienating
his most devoted followers, of whom he would soon
be in need as never before.   He abandoned the
Scots ; but he did not secure the assistance of King
Edward.   In earlier days, if the Pope was at enmity
with one sovereign he could rely upon another to
take up his quarrel.   Not so now ; by a succession of
arrogant, though not always ill-meant practices, Boniface had lost every friend who might have come
beween him and the least scrupulous monarch that
ever sat on the throne of France.

We shall never know the whole story ; it is obscure
and half-drowned in picturesque falsehoods, told at the
time or invented not long after.   During the Jubilee,
as rumour went, Boniface appeared on one day in the
Papal vestments, on the next in those of the Emperor.
Before him were carried two swords and the golden
orb ; he called himself successor of Peter and Charlemagne, the universal monarch.   Again, he sent into
France his Bull of Arbitration, sealed in the Pope's
name ; Robert of Artois flung it into the fire while
Philip looked on.   These are incredible fictions.
But there were unpleasant facts.   Robert, in spite of
censures, held half the city of Cambrai against its

Archbishop. The King sequestrated Laon, because its Bishop had gone to Rome. He would not give back its full estates to the Church of Rheims. He had opened his palace to the Colonna exiles. On the other hand, at Narbonne, conquered long ago from the Albigenses, Viscount and Archbishop were disputing over the feudal homage. Saisset, Bishop of Pamiers, despatched by the Pope on a mission to King Philip, acquitted himself so insolently that on returning to his diocese he was arrested by the royal order, brought to Senlis and put in custody of his Metropolitan. To imprison a Papal Legate was the height of audacity. If it be true that Peter Flotte, arriving in Rome, defended the step in such language as we find attributed to him, we cannot feel surprise at the Pope's indignation. On one single day he put forth, in rapid succession, letter upon letter, demanding that Saisset should be sent immediately to Rome; enacting again the Bull "Clericis Laicos"; citing Bishops, Archbishops, and the leading French clergy to appear in Curia on next All Saints' Day, then and there " to take counsel touching the excesses, crimes, and acts of violence committed by the King of France and his officers," on the Church of God. These four documents appeared in December, 1301. Never, in any previous controversy, had the like of them been published on French soil. What else could they be aiming at, men argued, than to stir up civil war and depose the King?

But Nogaret, Flotte, and the lawyers, did not wait until Boniface had struck the blow. They scattered far and wide an insolent brief paper in which the

Pope was brought in saying to Philip, "We do you to wit that you are subject to us in temporals as in spirituals. Your collations to benefices are null and void. All who disbelieve us are heretics." Philip, in a genuine counterblast, replied immediately "To

PHILIP THE FAIR, KING OF FRANCE.

Boniface, who calls himself Pope, little or no greeting. We do your Fatuity to wit that in temporals we are subject to no man. We will uphold the collations we have made. Those who think otherwise are out of their minds." Such were the amenities which ushered in that authentic and sufficiently dignified letter, the

"Ausculta Fili." "Let no one persuade you," said the Pope, "that you are not subject to the chief of the heavenly Hierarchy." What did this mean? Spiritual jurisdiction, acting with spiritual weapons? Or a feudal supremacy, backed up by the arms of this world? There lay the point of antagonism. Boniface went on to tell Philip of his injustice and oppressions, which had lost him the people's love ; he repeated, in set terms, that no layman had any power over an ecclesiastic ; and he still summoned the French clergy to his presence. Philip's answer was emphatic. On January 26, 1302, he had this solemn document publicly burnt before his eyes, all Paris crowding to see the thing done, and its execution announced by sound of trumpet. In April he called the States-General, nobles, clergy, burgesses. They met in Notre Dame. The King was appealing from the Pope to the nation.

In a skilful address Peter Flotte charged Boniface with maintaining that the King held France, not from God but from the Holy See. It was a question of feudal sovereignty. So the nobles understood ; so the Third Estate, which seems to have cherished anti-papal sentiments. The clergy knew better but held their peace. Remonstrances were drawn up in French and Latin, signed, and sent to the Cardinals, to the Pope himself, all on the King's side, though in varying tones. Boniface rebuked the clergy for their cowardice, reviled Peter Flotte and branded his doctrine as Manichæan ; for such offences he might depose Philip as if he were a groom—had not his predecessors taken their crowns from three French

Kings?   The prelates must appear at his bidding or
they would be deprived.   Thus he spoke in Consistory.

The States-General had met in April, 1302.
Almost immediately after, Flanders was up in arms
against Philip, the most intolerable of oppressors ; and
on July 11th a company of "weavers and fullers," as
Villani exclaims, beat and scattered the choicest
French chivalry at Courtrai.   Artois was killed, with
Chatillon, Brabant, a crowd of knights whose golden
spurs became a spoil.   Peter Flotte was left dead on
the field.   This severe blow compelled Philip to make
peace with England ; but it did not bring him to his
knees before the Pope.   All Saints' Day arrived.
Forty-five French bishops and abbots attended the
meeting in Rome.   On November 18th, Boniface,
who had all along denied the interpretation put on
his words by the lawyers, published the Bull "Unam
Sanctam," in which he insisted that there were two
swords at the Church's disposal ; that the clergy
wielded the sword of the spirit ; but that kings and
soldiers must wield the sword of the flesh at their
bidding ; that the temporal order must be judged by
the spiritual ; and that every human creature was
subject to the Roman Pontiff.   This language was
not new ; it had been taken from Innocent III.   But
Philip's counsellors, dominated by Nogaret, and with
the Colonnas to urge them on, had resolved on a
definite and perhaps irrevocable break with the
Papacy.

Both sides prepared for the last struggle.   Philip
made peace with England ; endeavoured to conciliate
his own people by concessions and fair speeches ;

confiscated the goods of those Bishops who had gone
to Rome; and drew the nation together in a common
bond. The Pope, reluctant but compelled, was
making terms with Albert of Austria, whom, in
May, 1303, he recognised as German Emperor. He
consented to the separation of Sicily from Naples.
To Philip himself he sent fourteen articles, fierce and
peremptory, by Cardinal Lemoinne, which the King
answered, not without evasion. In May he was excommunicated, three months' grace being allowed for
submission. Again the States-General were convoked
in the Louvre, June 13, 1303, "to take counsel on the
crimes and disabilities of Benedict Gaetani, calling himself Pope Boniface VIII." In that assembly, Plasian,
the royal Attorney-General, produced his charges; he
swore on the Gospels that Gaetani was a heretic,
infidel, notorious evil-liver, who had a familiar spirit,
and had committed every possible crime. His
repeated attacks on the King of France showed an
implacable hatred towards their realm and nation.
All which could and would be proved by this same
William of Plasian at a General Council. Philip
assented to the requisitions made; he appealed on his
own behalf to a Council and the next lawful Pope.
The clergy sat silent. But they were compelled to
do more. After the King had signed the document,
five Archbishops, twenty-one Bishops, eleven of the
greater Abbots, among them Cluny, Prémontré,
Citeaux, St. Victor, and the Visitors of the Temple
and the Hospital Knights, subscribed to these
monstrous fictions, in which it is safe to say that
not a man there believed.

Still the lawyers were not satisfied. King, nobles, clergy, had all agreed not only to promote the holding of a Council, but to suffer no interdict within the bounds of France, and to disregard every mandate from Rome. The appeal was sent out to every chapter, convent, and religious house, to be signed by clerics and friars. Seven hundred acts of adhesion were thus obtained. Franciscans, Dominicans, military Orders,—including one of the doomed Templars,—all said ay at the King's behest. The University of Paris did not hold out ; it was earnest and loud in the same cause. " The unanimous voice of the national conscience," says a German historian, had " grown strong against Papal arrogance." But it is not easy to believe that the clergy, taxed and galled by their opponents, Nogaret, Plasian, and the other lawyers, signed at the bidding of conscience. They may not have loved Boniface ; they had every reason to fear King Philip. Their unbroken silence in the States-General is the best explanation of what they felt but dared not say. In a like dilemma the Convocation of Canterbury, challenged by Henry VIII., took refuge in the same silence and allowed the title of Supreme Head of the Church to pass. We cannot describe such cowardly surrenders as acts of the national conscience.

Boniface had gone out to Anagni. It was told him what had been done at the Louvre. He called his Cardinals about him ; brushed aside with infinite scorn the accusation of heresy,—" We were sound Catholics as long as we favoured King Philip," he said with a grim smile—and fixed on Stephen Colonna as the man

who had raised this tempest. He suspended throughout France the right of election to benefices; he
deprived the Universities of their teaching privileges.
Then, from the exalted throne of St. Peter, he struck
Philip with his two-edged sword. He was excommunicate; his people were forbidden to obey him;
the clergy must take no preferment from his hand;
all oaths sworn to him were abrogated, and leagues in
which he had a share were dissolved. On September
8th next ensuing, he would cease to be King of
France.

In this lightning-like manner did the spiritual sword
glance and gleam round Philip's head. But where
was the sword of flesh? Boniface, without even a
household guard, was weak and defenceless. He
might have been aware that Philip's messengers, citing him to the General Council, were on the way to
Anagni. We cannot tell. All we know is that the
Paterine, Nogaret, with Sciarra Colonna and one of
the Francesi bankers, had arrived near Siena; that
they were buying up cut-throat barons in Romagna;
and that much intrigue was rife, close to the Pope's
person. The French envoys bought their cut-throats
and came on. Nogaret had received from Philip a
sign-manual which gave him unlimited powers. What
to do? Evidently to prevent the execution of a
Bull which would leave Philip at the mercy of his
enemies. September 7th had arrived; not a moment
was to be lost.

On that black and memorable day, Boniface was
seated with his Cardinals, feeling how near the crisis
had drawn, when they heard the narrow streets of

28

Anagni resounding with shouts, hoofs clattering, and three hundred horse rushing on as to an assault. "Death to the Pope! life to the King!"   That was the battle cry which told them what had happened. Sciarra was there, the banner of the fleur de lys over him ; and in his train the kinsfolk of men whom Boniface had banished or cast into prison.   The city bell rang ; the people assembled ; they found themselves under command of Arnulf, a Ghibelline, and were led against the Pope.   His palace was assaulted ; likewise that of his nephew and the Cardinals loyal to him.   But all the Cardinals fled through subterranean passages, and only Boniface held out.   He demanded a truce.   Eight hours were given.   On what terms must he surrender?   "Restore the Colonnas to their rank and possessions ; abdicate ; and yield yourself to Sciarra."   He refused with sobs.   The assault began once more ; Sciarra set the neighbouring Church gates on fire ; the Pope's nephew surrendered, making terms for himself and his family, and left Boniface to make his own.

In this hour the sense of his sacred office did not desert him.   Arraying himself in stole and crown, bearing the cross keys, he sat in the Papal Chair to await these French ambassadors.   They approached and did no homage.   With insult they told him he must abdicate.   "Here is my neck," said the dauntless old man.   Nogaret threatened him with the Council ; Boniface cast in his teeth the name of Paterine.   But Sciarra, like the ruffian he was, would have killed the Pope with his own hands, had not the less brutal Frenchman interposed.   It is said that he

struck Boniface on the cheek with his iron gauntlet.
Then they set him on a restive horse, paraded him
about the streets, and plundered his treasures. At
length, after a passion which lasted three days, the
people of Anagni came to his relief, when the
soldiers were gone. "Good people," he said, "give
me a morsel of bread and a cup of wine; I am
dying of hunger." He had yielded nothing; but in
his desolate palace, which was stripped bare of all it
contained—infinite riches, as the tale went—he found
no one except the crowd of peasants on whom to
bestow absolution.

He was now taken by the Orsini with a mounted
squadron back to Rome. But he remained a prisoner.
The Colonnas he would not restore to the Sacred
College. His spirit was yet, perhaps, unbroken.
Calumny has pursued him to the end, telling how he
died of rage or poison, or beat out his brains against
the wall. His last day in this world was October 11,
1303. When his body was exhumed at the beginning
of the seventeenth century, in 1605, it was still entire,
and no marks of violence could be seen upon it. We
may conclude that his death was more tranquil than
his life, and that his breath failed before his reason.
Nor can we trust the furious invectives of Dante, who
calls this unwise, but energetic and apparently sincere
spirit, "the prince of the new Pharisees," and makes
St. Peter himself pronounce his doom in heaven.

But this was true, which the poet sings in tones of
pity and horror, that Philip, King of France, had
inflicted a second time the Passion of Christ on His
Vicar. France, which once gave its Charlemagne as

a guardian to the Apostolic See, and took the Imperial Roman crown for its reward, was now transformed to a secular power, which in the Papacy beheld no more the Father and Judge of Christendom. Europe cried out at the sacrilege—the crucifixion between two thieves—the second Pilate. But one era had closed ; another was opening. With Philip of France the layman began to rule over the clergy ; Roman Law had conquered in temporals the Roman Pontiff ; our eyes are henceforth set towards the Renaissance, though it tarries in its coming ; we have bidden farewell to the Middle Age.

ANAGNI.

EPILOGUE

FOR that shameful outrage at Anagni, as the sequel informs us, no one was ever brought to account. Philip, who had pulled down the living Boniface from his seat, pursued him though dead with redoubled animosity. Still he would insist that a General Council should try, convict, and degrade the new Formosus. He was master now. Benedict XI., a mild Dominican, who had been consenting neither to the violence of the Pope nor to the treachery of his enemies, did indeed release from censure the King as well as the French people. He explained away the infelicitous words of " Clericis Laicos " from which all subsequent troubles might seem to have arisen. But he would assemble no Council to try a dead Pope. In self-defence he excommunicated Nogaret and some chief culprits along with him. Yet he restored the Colonna Cardinals to their rank as before. All would not suffice. Within the year he was himself a corpse, poisoned, said the common talk, by Philip, the Ghibellines, or Napoleon Orsini.

An interregnum of nine months followed. It came to an end after Philip, in the Forest of St. Jean d'Angely, had entered into a secret compact with Bertrand de Goth, Archbishop of Bordeaux. The terms were known afterwards, all but one, which is conjectured to have been the destruction of the Templars. If he were chosen as Pope, the Gascon Archbishop undertook to reconcile the King and his partisans with the Church in the fullest manner ; to condemn Boniface ; to give the Colonnas their castles and lands again. One farther condition, not exacted but fulfilled, of more consequence than all the rest, was that Clement V. should never set foot in Rome. He was elected ; crowned at Lyons ; and surrounded himself with a Court of French Cardinals. In 1306 he abrogated the Bull "Clericis Laicos" altogether. He interpreted the Bull, "Unam Sanctam," in a spiritual and non-feudal sense. He released Edward I. from his oaths to keep the Charters. He excommunicated Robert Bruce. He consented to hold a Council at Vienne, where he would take all the charges made by Nogaret against his deceased predecessor. He saw the Templars perish. This was the Pope who in 1309 took up his abode at Avignon, on the left bank of the Rhone, and began the seventy years of Babylonish captivity. With his accession the Papacy had fallen a prisoner into the hands of France.

At Vienne, nevertheless, Philip was, so to speak, nonsuited ; Boniface escaped condemnation. Within the term of a natural life, the house of Capet had lost its male heirs, struck by some mysterious disaster. The long war of a hundred years between France and England broke out. And a schism, which lasted down to the Council of Constance in 1415, set up French against Italian Popes, scandalised all Christians, led to Wycliffite heresies, to Lollard risings, to the deposition of three reigning Pontiffs. From Avignon to Constance, from Constance to Basle, from Basle to Luther at the Diet of Worms, we trace an ever-widening path, at the end of which appears the Reformation.

It is wonderful how many large movements and long-standing institutions came to an end in the second half of the thirteenth century. With Frederick II., as we have seen, the Holy Roman Empire ceased to be either Holy or Roman ; it was henceforth a name attached to some German Prince, bold and edifying like Rudolph of Hapsburg, degraded and despised like Louis of Bavaria. Rome itself becomes a blank in the world's history—except during Rienzi's brief masquerade—for a hundred and twenty years. With Conradin on the scaffold at Naples the Pope's deposing power may be said to have expired. Never again did the Holy See, in effect, transfer crowns or take them away, though until the seventeenth century forms implying this supreme act of jurisdiction lingered in the Roman Courts, or were gravely set down by canonists and theologians. The enthusiasm, purity, and charm which had shed their lustre on St. Francis, faded or were transmuted into less delightful visions long before the century closed. His brethren, as the Cluniacs, Cistercians, Templars, and many more, gave point to the terrible saying of Lord Falkland, " Religion brought forth riches, and the daughter slew the mother." Those among them who conquered this temptation went often to the other extreme ; they became wild mystics with the Fraticelli, schismatics with Michael da Cesena, and by a singular course of events, Erastian or Cæsarean with their English philosopher, William of Occam.

And the Crusades were done ; Palestine was abandoned to the Turks, while Spain was wrested from the Moors. Other signs of an approaching consummation of all things might be observed. The Schoolmen drew out a perfect theory of medieval life, thought, government. The architects enshrined it in cathedrals erected and adorned by the people. Dante immortalised it in his superhuman Epic, or Pilgrim's Progress from this world to the world to come. This was the swan song of that astonishing age, without example before or since, when the priesthood ruled over Europe with crozier and sceptre, sword and pen, with Bible, Canon Law, and prophetic oracles, sanctioned by penalties from which neither individual nor nation could escape. It was beyond question a Theocracy. The Pontifex Maximus, King of Kings and Lord of Lords, judged all men and was judged of none.

His temporal power, in this magnificent application of the word, has passed away. But not until it had fulfilled the task allotted to it. The Barbarians, free men but destitute of culture, had been brought under the creative influence of a humane religion ; they had been taught the elements of Greek and Latin civilisation; and equality before the law, which was a principle at once Christian and Roman, had begun to be

established as the foundation of modern liberty. To
the monks who made the wilderness blossom like the
rose, had succeeded industrial and republican cities—
the League of Lombardy, the Hansa towns, Venice,
Florence, Amalfi, Genoa, Bruges, Ghent, Antwerp,
London. All over Europe learning was held in
honour ; the Universities were centres of intellectual
freedom. Slaves had become serfs ; serfs had been
largely emancipated. War itself put on the graces
of chivalry. There was a Christendom, the ideals
at least of which were peace, brotherhood, holiness.
From Councils provincial or Œcumenical emerged
a sense of the nation's unity, and in due time
a Law of Nations. Every church gave shelter to
innocence, if sometimes also to guilt. Hospitals,
almshouses, cloisters opened their gates to the sick,
the aged, the outcast. Talent, without regard to
birth, might aspire, and not seldom attain, to the
highest seats in a spiritual order which held the
temporal in check and thus made for independence.
Looked at from above, the Church was a Theocracy ;
seen from below, it was a Democracy. While it
leaned on the people, its triumph was assured ; when
it submitted to the feudal system, it courted disaster.
Then the royal authority took away its rod of
dominion ; the King became Pope ; the Pontifex
Maximus retired into the holy place before him.

Crimes, abuses, usurpations, scandals, and a secret
change about religion in the thoughts of men, will
account for this latter-day revolution. But it is
difficult to imagine how Europe could have survived
from the Fall of the Empire to modern times, had

THE PAPAL PALACE AND BROKEN BRIDGE OF AVIGNON.

427

there been no central, supreme, and acknowledged power like the Papacy, guardian at once of faith, learning, law, civilisation. That it always rose to the height of that great enterprise will not be maintained by the historian; but its benefits outnumbered by far its abuses; and the glory is not dim which hangs round its memory, when we call to mind that it consecrated the beginnings of a peaceful, Christian Europe, and watched beside the springs of art, science, industry, order, and freedom. These are its claims to our admiration and our gratitude. Rome is the meeting-place of all history; the Papal succession, oldest and newest in Europe, filling the space from Cæsar and Constantine to this democratic world of the twentieth century, binds all ages into one and looks out towards a distant future in many Continents. Its chronicle has been a tragedy and a romance; or, as the millions of its faithful believe, a prophecy and a fulfilment. In whatever light we regard it, one stage is marked, and a turning-point fixed, when we stand on the broken bridge of Avignon to contemplate that vast Palace of the Popes, now converted into French barracks, which was for well-nigh seventy years their gilded prison.

LIST OF THE ROMAN PONTIFFS.

(As in the Registers of the Roman Church.)

ST. PETER, PRINCE OF THE APOSTLES, 41–65–67.

———

	A.D.		A.D.		A.D.
Linus.	67	Anastasius I.	398	Vitalian.	657
Cletus.	79	Innocent I.	402	Deusdedit II.	672
Clement I.	91	Zosimus.	417	Donus I.	676
Evaristus.	100	Boniface I.	418	Agatho.	678
Alexander I.	109	Cœlestine I.	422	Leo II.	682
Sixtus I.	119	Sixtus III.	432	Benedict II.	684
Telesphorus.	128	Leo I. (the Gt.)	440	John V.	685
Hyginus.	138	Hilary.	461	Conon.	686
Pius I.	142	Simplicius.	468	Sergius I.	687
Anicetus.	157	Felix III.	483	John VI.	701
Soter.	168	Gelasius I.	492	John VII.	705
Eleutherius.	177	Anastasius II.	496	Sisinnius.	708
Victor I.	190	Symmachus.	498	Constantine I.	708
Zephyrinus.	202	Hormisdas.	514	Gregory II.	715
Callistus I.	218	John I.	523	Gregory III.	731
Urban I.	222	Felix IV.	526	Zachary.	741
Pontian.	230	Boniface II.	530	Stephen III.†	752
Anterus.	235	John II.	532	Paul I.	757
Fabian.	236	Agapitus.	535	Constantine II.	767
Cornelius.	251	Silverius.	536	Stephen IV.	768
Lucius I.	253	Vigilius.	537	Hadrian I.	771
Stephen I.	254	Pelagius I.	555	Leo III.	795
Sixtus II.	257	John III.	560	Stephen V.	816
Dionysius.	259	Benedict I.	574	Paschal I.	817
Felix I.	269	Pelagius II.	578	Eugene II.	824
Eutychian.	275	Gregory I. (the		Valentine.	827
Caius.	283	Great).	590	Gregory IV.	827
Marcellinus.	296	Sabinian.	604	Sergius II.	844
Marcellus I.	307	Boniface III.	607	Leo IV.	847
Eusebius	309	Boniface IV.	608	Benedict III.	855
Melchiades.	310	Deusdedit I.	615	Nicholas I. (the	858
Silvester I.	314	Boniface V.	619	Hadrian II. [Gt.]	867
Mark.	336	Honorius I.	625	John VIII.	872
Julius I.	337	Severinus.	640	Marinus I.	882
Liberius.	352	John IV.	640	Hadrian III.	884
Felix II.*	355	Theodore I.	642	Stephen VI.	885
Damasus I.	366	Martin I.	649	Formosus.	891
Siricius.	384	Eugene I.	655	Boniface VI.	896

* Pope during exile of Liberius.   † Steph. II. (752) died before consecr.

Stephen VII. A.D.	896	Coelestine II. A.D.	1143	Nicholas V. A.D.	1447
Romanus.	897	Lucius II.	1144	Callistus III.	1455
Theodore II.	897	Eugene III.	1145	Pius II.	1458
John IX.	898	Anastasius IV.	1153	Paul II.	1464
Benedict IV.	900	Hadrian IV.	1154	Sixtus IV.	1471
Leo V.	903	Alexander III.	1159	Innocent VIII.	1484
Christopher.	903	Lucius III.	1181	Alexander VI.	1492
Sergius III.	904	Urban III.	1185	Pius III.	1503
Anastasius III.	911	Gregory VIII.	1187	Julius II.	1503
Lando.	913	Clement III.	1187	Leo X.	1513
John X.	914	Coelestine III.	1191	Hadrian VI.	1522
Leo VI.	928	Innocent III.	1198	Clement VII.	1523
Stephen VIII.	929	Honorius III.	1216	Paul III.	1534
John XI.	931	Gregory IX.	1227	Julius III.	1550
Leo VII.	936	Coelestine IV.	1241	Marcellus II.	1555
Stephen IX.	939	Innocent IV.	1243	Paul IV.	1555
Marinus II.*	943	Alexander IV.	1254	Pius IV.	1559
Agapitus II.	946	Urban IV.	1261	Pius V.	1566
John XII.	955	Clement IV.	1265	Gregory XIII.	1572
Leo VIII.	963	Gregory X.	1271	Sixtus V.	1585
Benedict V.	964	Innocent V.	1276	Urban VII.	1590
John XIII.	965	Hadrian V.	1276	Gregory XIV.	1590
Benedict VI.	973	John XX.(XXI.)	1276	Innocent IX.	1591
Benedict VII.	974	Nicholas III.	1277	Clement VIII.	1592
John XIV.	983	Martin IV.*	1281	Leo XI.	1605
John XV.	985	Honorius IV.	1285	Paul V.	1605
Gregory V.	996	Nicholas IV.	1288	Gregory XV.	1621
Silvester II.	999	Coelestine V.	1294	Urban VIII.	1623
John XVII.†	1003	Boniface VIII.¶	1294	Innocent X.	1644
John XVIII.	1003	Benedict XI.	1303	Alexander VII.	1655
Sergius IV.	1009	Clement V.	1305	Clement IX.	1667
Benedict VIII.	1012	John XXII.	1316	Clement X.	1670
John XIX.	1024	Benedict XII.	1334	Innocent XI.	1676
Benedict IX.	1033	Clement VI.	1342	Alexander VIII.	1689
Gregory VI.	1045	Innocent VI.	1352	Innocent XII.	1691
Clement II.	1046	Urban V.	1362	Clement XI.	1700
Damasus II.	1048	Gregory XI.	1370	Innocent XIII.	1721
Leo IX.	1049	Urban VI.	1378	Benedict XIII.	1724
Victor II.	1055	Clement VII.		Clement XII.	1730
Stephen X.	1057	(Avignon).	1378	Benedict XIV.	1740
Nicholas II.‡	1059	Benedict XIII.		Clement XIII.	1758
Alexander II.	1061	(Avignon).	1394	Clement XIV.	1769
Gregory VII.	1073	Boniface IX.	1389	Pius VI.	1775
Victor III.	1086	Innocent VII.	1404	Pius VII.	1800
Urban II.	1088	Gregory XII.	1406	Leo XII.	1823
Paschal II.	1099	Alexander V.	1409	Pius VIII.	1829
Gelasius II.	1118	John XXIII.	1410	Gregory XVI.	1831
Callistus II.	1119	Martin V.	1417	Pius IX.	1846
Honorius II.	1124	Eugene IV.	1431	Leo XIII.	1878
Innocent II.	1130				

* Marinus I., II., were also called (Martinus) Martin II., III.
† John XVI. (997) Antipope.   ‡ Benedict X. (1058), Antipope.
¶ Boniface VII. (974), Antipope.

INDEX

A Selection from the
Catalogue of

G. P. PUTNAM'S SONS

Complete Catalogue sent
on application

The Story of the Nations

IN the story form the current of each National life is distinctly indicated, and its picturesque and note-worthy periods and episodes are presented for the reader in their philosophical relation to each other as well as to universal history.

It is the plan of the writers of the different volumes to enter into the real life of the peoples, and to bring them before the reader as they actually lived, labored, and struggled—as they studied and wrote, and as they amused themselves. In carrying out this plan, the myths, with which the history of all lands begins, will not be overlooked, though these will be carefully distinguished from the actual history, so far as the labors of the accepted historical authorities have resulted in definite conclusions.

The subjects of the different volumes have been planned to cover connecting and, as far as possible, consecutive epochs or periods, so that the set when completed will present in a comprehensive narrative the chief events in the great STORY OF THE NATIONS; but it is, of course, not always practicable to issue the several volumes in their chronological order.

For list of volumes see next page.

THE STORY OF THE NATIONS

GREECE. Prof. Jas. A. Harrison.

ROME. Arthur Gilman.

THE JEWS. Prof. James K. Hosmer.

CHALDEA. Z. A. Ragozin.

GERMANY. S. Baring-Gould.

NORWAY. Hjalmar H. Boyesen.

SPAIN. Rev. E. E. and Susan Hale.

HUNGARY. Prof. A. Vámbéry.

CARTHAGE. Prof. Alfred J. Church.

THE SARACENS. Arthur Gilman.

THE MOORS IN SPAIN. Stanley Lane-Poole.

THE NORMANS. Sarah Orne Jewett.

PERSIA. S. G. W. Benjamin.

ANCIENT EGYPT. Prof. Geo. Rawlinson.

ALEXANDER'S EMPIRE. Prof. J. P. Mahaffy.

ASSYRIA. Z. A. Ragozin.

THE GOTHS. Henry Bradley.

IRELAND. Hon. Emily Lawless.

TURKEY. Stanley Lane-Poole.

MEDIA, BABYLON, AND PERSIA. Z. A. Ragozin.

MEDIÆVAL FRANCE. Prof. Gustave Masson.

HOLLAND. Prof. J. Thorold Rogers.

MEXICO. Susan Hale.

PHŒNICIA. George Rawlinson.

THE HANSA TOWNS. Helen Zimmern.

EARLY BRITAIN. Prof. Alfred J. Church.

THE BARBARY CORSAIRS. Stanley Lane-Poole.

RUSSIA. W. R. Morfill.

THE JEWS UNDER ROME. W. D. Morrison.

SCOTLAND. John Mackintosh.

SWITZERLAND. R. Stead and Mrs. A. Hug.

PORTUGAL. H. Morse-Stephens.

THE BYZANTINE EMPIRE. C. W. C. Oman.

SICILY. E. A. Freeman.

THE TUSCAN REPUBLICS. Bella Duffy.

POLAND. W. R. Morfill.

PARTHIA. Geo. Rawlinson.

JAPAN. David Murray.

THE CHRISTIAN RECOVERY OF SPAIN. H. E. Watts.

AUSTRALASIA. Greville Tregarthen.

SOUTHERN AFRICA. Geo. M Theal.

VENICE. Alethea Weil.

THE CRUSADES. T. S. Archer and C. L. Kingsford.

VEDIC INDIA. Z. A. Ragozin.

BOHEMIA. C. E. Maurice.

CANADA. J. G. Bourinot.

THE BALKAN STATES. William Miller.

THE STORY OF THE NATIONS

Heroes of the Nations

A SERIES of biographical studies of the lives and work of a number of representative historical characters about whom have gathered the great traditions of the Nations to which they belonged, and who have been accepted, in many instances, as types of the several National ideals. With the life of each typical character will be presented a picture of the National conditions surrounding him during his career.

The narratives are the work of writers who are recognized authorities on their several subjects, and, while thoroughly trustworthy as history, will present picturesque and dramatic "stories" of the Men and of the events connected with them.

To the Life of each "Hero" will be given one duodecimo volume, handsomely printed in large type, provided with maps and adequately illustrated according to the special requirements of the several subjects.

For full list of volumes see next page.

HEROES OF THE NATIONS

HEROES OF THE NATIONS

FREDERICK THE GREAT. By W. F. Reddaway.

WELLINGTON. By W. O'Connor Morris.

CONSTANTINE THE GREAT. By J. B. Smith.

MOHAMMED. By D.S.Margoliouth.

CHARLES THE BOLD. By Ruth Putnam.

WASHINGTON. By J. A. Harrison.

WILLIAM THE CONQUEROR. By F. M. Stenton.

FERNANDO CORTÈS. By F. A. MacNutt.

WILLIAM THE SILENT. By Ruth Putnam.

Other volumes in preparation are :

BLÜCHER. By Ernest F. Henderson.

MARLBOROUGH. By C. T. Atkinson.

MOLTKE. By James Wardell.

ALFRED THE GREAT. By Bertha Lees.

GREGORY VII. By F. Urquhart.

JUDAS MACCABÆUS. By Israel Abrahams.

FREDERICK II. By A. L. Smith.

New York—G. P. PUTNAM'S SONS, Publishers—London

CPSIA information can be obtained at www.ICGtesting.com
Printed in the USA
BVOW06s1035240314

348580BV00006B/233/P